# Archery

## THE ART OF REPETITION

# Archery

## THE ART OF REPETITION

**Simon S. Needham**

THE CROWOOD PRESS

First published in 2006 by
The Crowood Press Ltd
Ramsbury, Marlborough
Wiltshire SN8 2HR

**www.crowood.com**

This impression 2014

**British Library Cataloguing-in-Publication Data**
A catalogue record for this book is available from the British Library.

ISBN 978 1 86126 869 3

**Acknowledgements**
In order to succeed at anything one needs to be determined and also to have the
support of others. Reaching the Olympics in Sydney 2000 necessitated a huge
personal effort but it also required the support and encouragement of family
members, friends and work colleagues. It should also be noted that when obstacles
emerged this only hardened my resolve to succeed.

So that the knowledge acquired while reaching for the top in archery should not
be lost, I was encouraged to write it down. This again required the support of
family and friends, but with their help I was able to bring all the information
together in a coherent, illustrated form so that others would be able to benefit from
my experiences and succeed more easily in archery. Of all the people that have
helped with this endeavour, I would especially like to thank: Karen Henderson and
Bob Provan, who helped to edit my manuscript, made grammatical changes and
provided advice on content; Barry Eley, Lana Needham and Andrew Calloway for
contributing additional photographs; the British team archers for posing for
photographs; Lana for putting up with photographs and drawings being strewn all
over the living room floor; the many archers who illustrated their skills; and others
too numerous to mention who helped in countless ways.

Unless otherwise credited, photographs are by the author.

Throughout this book, 'he', 'him' and 'his' are used as neutral pronouns and as such
refer to both males and females.

Designed and typeset by Focus Publishing, Sevenoaks, Kent

Printed and bound in India by Replika Press Pvt. Ltd.

# Contents

# Introduction

The aim of this book is to provide a comprehensive guide for anyone interested in archery, whether they are new to the sport, have shot a little, or are of a reasonable standard. Whatever your skill level, this volume will be an invaluable aid to improving both your shooting and your understanding of archery.

I wish that, twenty years ago when I began my archery career, I had known what I know now. I have therefore aimed to put all of my accumulated knowledge into this volume, so as to provide a bank of ideas and knowledge upon which archers of all levels and abilities can draw. If you are a newcomer, starting your archery career with a good method will mean that your progression through the sport will be much easier.

Archery, like many other experiences in life, is easier to learn if it is broken down into the various parts which make the whole, such as style, equipment, fitness, psychology, tuning and so on. However, once compartmentalized for ease of reference, these parts should such not remain separated, or even, perhaps as in the case of fitness, ignored. You must always remember that ultimately each of the component parts is integral to the whole. While you may get by in your shooting by ignoring some parts of the whole, inevitably this will hold you back from attaining your true potential.

Reaching your potential in archery is like completing a personal jigsaw; each of us will have our own jigsaw of excellence. The key to success is in finding all the individual pieces to it. All archers have the same ultimate focal point – 'the centre of the picture'. It is the differences in body build and make-up of the neural pathways, in the main, that will determine the pieces that form your own personal 'archery jigsaw'.

The simplest way of explaining archery is that you need to be able to carry out the same actions and thoughts repeatedly, to hit the centre of the target every time – 'the art of repetition'. In theory, you can hold the bow however you want, stand on one foot, stick your finger in your ear when you pull the string back, and if when you let go the arrow hits the middle of the target, you will score a 'ten'. But the chances of being able to achieve a ten every time from this method are negligible. Ask yourself: 'Am I able to repeat the movement easily, and is there any way to make what I am doing easier to repeat time and time again?' You need to consider that the body and mind work in a specific way. Biomechanics refers to how the body works mechanically and psychology to how the mind works – utilizing these two underlying mechanisms is vital to your eventual success in archery.

This book will enable you to put together the main part of your jigsaw, quickly and easily. You will be able to shoot well from the very start. Archery should be a learning progression which begins the moment you first start shooting and which enables you to maximize your potential. The photographs here all show archers who have reached international level and have shot over a score of 1300 for a FITA (maximum 1440), or are international medal winners.

*Glasgow's shooting ground – all ages practising together.*

# Chapter 1

# Starting Out

Archery is a sport for all. Whether you are six or sixty-nine years old, are fully fit or have physical challenges, you can have a go at archery. I know of one-armed archers and even blind archers. They all shoot in the same competitions. The age at which you can take up archery varies between clubs. Due to the shorter attention span of younger children, some clubs may require the parents to stay and supervise their offspring, thus providing an opportunity for the whole family to participate in the activity.

Generally, archery is taken up in the first place as a hobby or recreational sport, with most people content to shoot at their local club and enjoy the social side of archery. Some people then 'get the bug' and start entering local competitions, eventually moving on to national competitions. A few of the most determined may even reach the Olympics. However, archers of all ability levels need to be able to learn to focus on the control of their minds and bodies. Accordingly, many professional people find that archery is an excellent distraction from the rigours of a high-pressure working environment.

## Costs

*Club*
Inevitably, one of the first questions to be asked is: 'How much will it cost?' How much will the initial outlay be and how much additional equipment will be required if the sport is taken to competition level?

All archery clubs run induction courses for beginners; these are usually one-hour sessions run over six weeks to allow for individual work routines. There will be a minimal payment (for example, my club, Links Archers, currently charges £15 for the induction course). During

a beginner's course all the equipment will be supplied free of charge and instruction is provided on safety and shooting technique. At the end of the course individuals then decide whether or not they wish to join the club. Those deciding to join will need to pay both the club and Grand National Archery Society (GNAS) fees. Although the safety rules are always strictly enforced, anyone shooting at a club has to be insured and this is included in the club fees.

On joining a club, you will be given a card containing your individual GNAS number, which will provide proof that you are insured to shoot at any club or venue. As might be expected, each club has slightly different fees depending upon its facilities and running costs.

*Equipment*
Most clubs have a store of equipment that new archers can use without charge for a period of time. Therefore there is no need to buy any equipment in the first instance. As in most sports, at the top end equipment can be very expensive and I would urge new archers not to rush out and buy lots of new equipment.

## Finding a Club

There are strict rules governing safety in archery, meaning that shooting venues tend to be located in areas that have restricted access to the public, in order to avoid the possibility of passers-by being injured. As a result, archery clubs tend to be tucked away and so the easiest way to find a local club is to access the GNAS website (www.gnas.org), or send an email to enquiries@gnas.org and ask GNAS to assist you. Libraries and sports centres may also be useful sources of information.

## The Importance of Good Technique

It is vital from the start that you shoot with a good style and technique. Whether you have competition in mind, or initially view archery as a diversion from your working life, you will want to get the arrow in the middle of the target as frequently as possible. To achieve this, archery needs to be a progressive improvement of your style and technique that will realize your potential. If you start with a poor style and stance it can take a long time to correct later on.

Another reason to have a good style is that, if you use your body correctly, you will be able to shoot without causing injury to yourself. When at a later stage you shoot at 'higher' poundage (the force required to pull the string back), if you do not use your body structure and position correctly (biomechanics), then undue strain may result. When you start, you will use a bow with a low poundage, but generally your natural strength will soon exceed that required for a beginner's bow. However, if you have started with the correct techniques, you will be able to hold the bow and shoot it without incurring any injury problems.

## Stages of Learning

In archery, as with most things in life, a number of learning stages are involved. If you are aware at the outset what these stages are, it will be easier to assess how you are progressing. We can identify these stages as follows:

- **Unconscious incompetence** You have experienced something new. You do not know what to do or what to expect, therefore you are relaxed because you have no expectation of the outcome.
- **Conscious incompetence** You now know what you want to do and are trying to master it, but are not achieving it on a regular basis.
- **Conscious competence** You know what you want to do, are trying to do it and for the most part get it right (teaching the subconscious).
- **Unconscious competence** The subconscious governs the operation of the given task and so the task is carried out automatically.

(For further reading on this subject, see 'Neuro-linguistic Programming' in Chapter 9.)

*Best Practices of Learning*

In anything you do, if you follow the styles and routines of the best practitioners in the world you will maximize your chances of reaching your potential. For example, let us take two people who have never shot a bow before and put them in separate rooms. They are both furnished with identical archery equipment. However, one of the rooms is supplied with a television, a video player and a collection of videotapes featuring top archers shooting. The person with the additional information will not only be able to fit the bow together more quickly, but will also learn to shoot it more quickly and will improve at a much faster rate. Bows have been shot for thousands of years, so it is preferable to watch and learn from the best, rather than try to reinvent the method all over again.

## Basic Range Layout

You will find that all archery ranges are set out in the same way: targets at one end, with a shooting line, waiting line and equipment line at the other end. The shooting line is where you stand to shoot the bow. The waiting line is set back from the shooting line; this line should not be crossed until the signal is given that it is safe to shoot. The equipment line is behind the waiting line; all the equipment is kept behind this line when not being used.

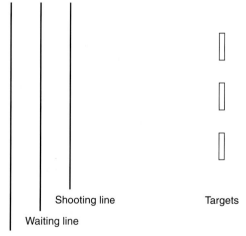

Shooting line

Targets

Waiting line

Equipment line

*The shooting line ensures that all archers can shoot safely.*

*The shooting line, showing all archers standing astride the line for safety.*

## Basic Safety Rules and Procedures

To ensure that shooting is carried out in a safe manner there are set rules and procedures that must be rigorously followed:

- Only approach the shooting line once a signal of one whistle blast has been given.
- The bow should only be pulled back (drawn) when an archer is standing with one foot either side of the shooting line. The bow should be drawn so that the arrow does not rise above a level that is parallel to the ground. This ensures that if the archer should accidentally 'let go', the arrow would stay within the shooting range.
- The arrow should only be put into the bow when the archer is standing on the shooting line and then it must, at all times, be kept pointing down the range (towards the target). Arrows must be carried in a quiver or facing point down at the side of the body when walking back from the target or moving around behind the shooting line.
- Stay behind the shooting line until the signal has been given to indicate that no more arrows can be shot (two whistle blasts); it is then safe to move forward to the target. The word 'Fast!' can be called by anyone who's spotted a potentially dangerous situation, for example someone stepping over the shooting line while others are preparing to shoot. If 'Fast!' is shouted, all archers must stop shooting immediately and remove the arrow from the bow. Shooting may only recommence when one whistle blast has been given to indicate that it is now safe to shoot.
- If the instructor asks you to 'come down' this means that he or she wants you to lower the bow without shooting the arrow and to relax the pressure on the string.
- Always *walk* to and from the targets; the nock end (back) of the arrow can be as sharp as the point. Walking into the arrows embedded in the target can cause serious injury.
- Walk to the side of (between) the targets as it is easier to see the arrows; also look on the ground

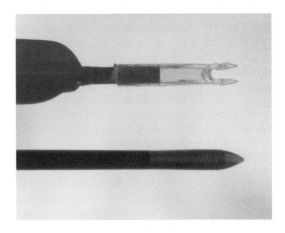

*X10 arrows: the nock is sharper than the point.*

*The drawing-hand thumb points down the arrow, keeping the shaft straight.*

in front of the target, as some arrows may have fallen short. When pulling out arrows, both hands must be used: one to hold the arrow, the other to press against the boss (target) adjacent to the arrow. Make sure that no one is behind the arrow; it can then be pulled. Pull the arrow with the thumb pointing down the shaft towards the target (this ensures that the arrow shaft remains straight). At the same time, press against the boss with the other hand, using the same pressure as being employed in the pulling action (this ensures that the boss is not pulled over).

## Right- or Left-Handed?

Why is determining whether a person should shoot right- or left-handed so important in archery? The brain is made up of two hemispheres, left and right, but is linked together by the *corpus callosum* (bridge), which allows the exchange of information between the two halves (women tend to have a larger *corpus callosum*, but more about that below). In nearly all functions, the left hemisphere controls the right side of the body, while the right hemisphere controls the left. However, these two sides are not equally balanced. One side will be dominant – generally the left side for right-handed people and vice versa for left-handed people. Thus, the eye dominance and reflex tests carried out by a new archer will establish which is his or her dominant brain hemisphere, ensuring that the most effective tie between hand and eye is utilized.

### Determining Handedness

From the outset, it needs to be ascertained whether a new archer should shoot with the right or left hand. This is established first by asking questions, then by carrying out simple tests, such as catching or kicking a ball in a warming-up exercise. Prior to any sporting activity, the body should be warmed-up by gentle exercise and stretching in order to reduce the chance of strains and injury, and one such exercise is the one-handed throwing of a ball to each other, or kicking it. With the prospective archers placed in a circle performing these exercises, the instructor can establish whether the beginners tend towards the right or the left hand/foot.

### Eye Dominance

However, the most widely used method for deciding which side of the brain is dominant is an eye-dominance test. If the right eye is dominant, this means that the left side of the brain is dominant and the beginner will start with the bow held in the left hand. If the left eye is dominant, the right side of the brain is dominant and so the beginner will start with the bow held in the right hand.

The two simple and similar methods of conducting this test are:

- The individual is asked to place his hands on top of each other, with the index fingers and thumbs forming a hole. He then holds his arms out in front of him and looks through the hole into the instructor's *right* eye. The instructor will be able

*The right eye is dominant.*

*The left eye is dominant.*

to see which eye the beginner uses and this will help him to ascertain the beginner's eye dominance.

- The beginner will be asked to point with his index finger to his instructor's right eye. Again, the instructor will be able to see which is the beginner's dominant eye as his finger will appear to be in line with it. Moreover, the finger that the beginner uses to point with will help to confirm brain dominance.

### Eye Health Challenges

When ascertaining eye dominance, special care needs to be taken over the health of the prospective archers' eyes, especially when working with juniors. For example, some youngsters may have a 'lazy' eye, so just using eye-dominance tests to determine left or right brain dominance can be misleading. It also needs to be taken into account that some people do not wear their glasses when they should. If prospective archers do wear glasses,

*Right hand – right eye, start the archer right-handed.*

*Left hand – left eye, start the archer left-handed.*

*Ensure that the frame of the glasses is clear of the line of focus.*

ensure that the rim of the frame does not block their view. This can be carried out by asking them to point their left index finger in a similar position to when shooting.

In short, it is essential that instructors are made aware of any sight/eye problems that their beginners might have. If, after conducting these simple tests, the instructor is still unsure whether the beginner is left or right brain dominant he should start him off with the bow in the left hand as for a right-eye dominant archer and see how the beginner progresses.

## Starting to Shoot

(N.B. The information provided throughout this book is for right-handed archers; left-handed archers should therefore carry out a mirror image of these instructions)

### Clothing and Equipment

It is essential to wear suitable upper-body clothing. It should be close-fitting, because loose-fitting clothing will interfere with your shooting. It also needs to be long enough to cover your midriff when raising your arms to shoulder height.

When you start a beginner's course, all the equipment should already have been laid out ready by the club instructor; usually the club will have 'simple' archery kits for beginners. The instructor will first ensure that you have fitted a bracer to your bow arm. A bracer is a small flat 'shield' that is fit-

*Shooting stance at full draw; Anna Karaseova (Belarus).*

ted to the inside of the arm holding the bow to protect it from the string as the bow is shot. The instructor will then give to you the rest of the equipment you will use for the session.

### Standing on the Line

Adopting a good body position on the shooting line is vital. It is the first thing you need to master when you begin shooting. Any type of shooting depends upon natural alignment of the body; this is achieved in archery by aligning your body with the target. Your feet should be placed astride the line, approximately your own shoulder width apart.

If a line were to be drawn from your right toe to your left toe and then extended towards the target, that line should bisect the centre of the target. Lines drawn from right to left hip and right to left

*Shooting stance from behind, note the line of the elbow and body; Wietse van Alten (The Netherlands).*

*Ready to shoot. Margarita Galinovskaya (Russia).*

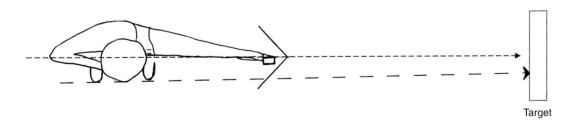

*Feet, hips and torso aligned with the target.*

*Starting the draw; draw shoulder is slightly forward to reach the string.*

*Draw shoulder is brought into line as the string comes back.*

*At full draw with the string touching the centre of the face.*

*Full draw from behind, showing alignment of body and elbow.*

shoulder should also line up with the target when the bow is held up. The front arm and the forearm of the drawing arm should point towards the target. To give you an idea of how to get to the correct upper body position for full draw, follow the sequence of photographs on the opposite page.

### Picking up the Bow

Take the bow in the left hand; it is best if you can start your shooting using a bow sling. The bow sling 'ties' the left hand holding the bow to the bow, allowing you to keep the bow hand relaxed during the shot. The bow needs to be held lightly in the left hand with the wrist behind the bow. Remember that the only place you are allowed to draw the bow (pull it back) is when you are on the shooting line and facing towards the target.

When the bow is being held it should never be rested on the ground, although the bottom limb of the bow may be rested on the toe of your shoe. This ensures that the bow is never used as a 'leaning post' and prevents damage to the lower limb tip.

### Fitting the Arrow onto the String

Each arrow has three fletchings (feathers), two of which are the same colour. The third is a different colour and is known as the 'cock fletching'.

The string will have a 'nocking point' that indicates the place where the arrow is to be fitted onto

*The different-coloured fletching faces out from the bow to give maximum clearance of the fletchings against the bow. (Karen Henderson)*

the string. The arrow has a nock (groove) in the end of it that will fit onto the string. The arrow needs to be fitted to the nocking point so that the 'cock fletching' is set 90 degrees to the line of the string facing out from the bow. This ensures that when you shoot, the arrow will leave the bow without hitting it. The nock is designed so that it 'clips' onto

*Ensure that the hand is behind the bow and relaxed on the grip.*

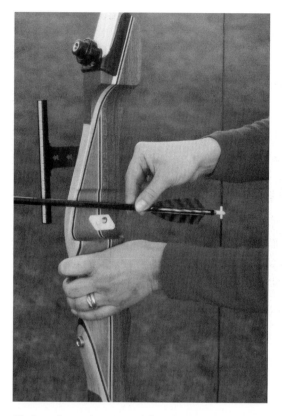

Fit the nock onto the string and then place the arrow onto the rest. *(Karen Henderson)*

the string. As a result, when the bow is drawn the arrow will stay attached to the string.

The best way of fitting the arrow into the bow is to fit the nock onto the string, then lay the arrow onto the rest. While you are fitting the arrow to the string with your right hand, the left hand should remain on the grip of the bow. This is important because new archers have a tendency to hold the arrow onto the rest with the index finger of the left hand. This causes damage to the rest, which is not designed to have the weight of the finger pulling on it and, in addition, holding onto the front of the arrow in this way tends to pull the nock off the string.

### Placing the Fingers on the String

You will start shooting by using a bow that will be easy to pull (light poundage). It is therefore preferable not to use a 'tab' (leather finger protector). This will enable you to get a good sense of how the fingers should feel on the string. The fingers that are used in drawing the bow are the first three (index, middle and ring); the index finger is placed above the arrow and the other two below.

The key finger of the drawing hand is the middle finger, which should be placed so that you can feel the string lying in the first joint of that finger. The other fingers should then be placed in a similar manner. Your middle finger is the strongest (the tendons of this finger run straight up the arm) and it should therefore take 70 per cent of the weight

The fingers are placed on the string in the first joint, with the back of the hand relaxed.

*The second woman on the left is preparing to shoot; as she draws the bow she will align her body with the target, as archers one and three have done.*

of the bow. If too much of the bow's weight is taken on the other fingers, there will be an increased chance of injury as you progress to a higher poundage of bow.

### Preparing to Shoot the Arrow

Once the arrow is loaded into the bow, you need to align your body as you draw the bow, as noted above. The loading of the muscles as you draw the bow is directly related to how the muscles operate when you let go of the string. Stand astride the shooting line (as in the drawing on page 15), align

your hips and torso, then turn your head towards the target.

### Drawing the Bow

In order to draw the bow, raise the arm holding the bow upwards until it is aligned with the target, then draw the hand holding the string directly back to the face. To do this effectively, you need to think of your fingers as 'hooks' that are attached to your elbow by a 'chain' (your wrist and forearm).

Once your fingers are hooked onto the string, draw the hand back by rotating the upper arm in a flat arc.

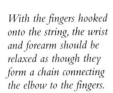

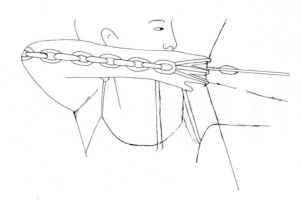

*With the fingers hooked onto the string, the wrist and forearm should be relaxed as though they form a chain connecting the elbow to the fingers.*

*The hand runs along the jaw line and the string is drawn to the centre of the face; Vic Wunderle (USA). (Andrew Callaway)*

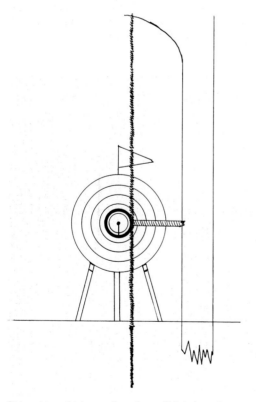

*String picture. Lining up these three will help keep the arrows centralized on the target.*

Bring the string back so that it touches the centre of your nose and centre/side of your chin, with your fingers running along your jawline. The forearm of the drawing arm should be kept parallel to the ground.

*Lining up the Bow to Shoot*
As you look at the target, the string will be in front of your right eye. Looking past the left side of the string, the string, the sight and the target should form a single line. The string will appear blurred, as it is so close to the eye. This is known as the 'string picture'.

*Releasing the String*
Once the bow is lined up with the target, relax the fingers of the drawing hand and shoot the arrow.

## Summary

When starting out on a new endeavour it is essential to adopt the correct methods and techniques from the very outset. This will enable you to develop and continually improve. Should you pick up poor habits from the start, you will constantly have to retrain in order to master particular aspects of your craft and this will considerably slow your progress. So, 'Start as you mean to go on.'

# Chapter 2

# Choosing and Using Equipment

Whatever stage of shooting you may be at, it is always best to take both time and care when selecting your equipment. Choosing the wrong equipment may not only be expensive, but may also adversely affect your shooting and result in avoidable injuries. You do not need to buy all your equipment – some items you can make for yourself, such as the bow sling, bow stand, quiver and box. This will help to keep the cost down if you are working to a budget. I feel that it is advantageous to buy your equipment in stages, rather than all at once. The equipment needs to be 'built' around the bow and your physique; in doing this, you will be able to develop the right combination of equipment as your style and technique evolve.

Do not start buying your equipment until after you have finished the beginner's course and joined the archery club. By the end of the course you will have a better understanding of the sport and how you feel you want to progress within it. Major items, and particularly the bow, should be left, if possible, for about two months after the end of the beginner's course, although the timing of purchases will naturally depend on the amount of equipment available at a particular club. To give yourself an idea of what archery equipment is available you could order a catalogue from one of the main archery retailers, or go on-line. The sling, tab, bracer and quiver can be bought soon after you start shooting.

In most cases, there are two phases in the acquisition of equipment: the first phase we can call 'getting used to it' and the second, 'wanting a bow'. On taking up archery, you will discover that you use muscles that are not normally used. Therefore, in the early stages of learning, you should use a bow of low poundage (power). As you get used to shooting and progress, you will want to increase the power of the bow; with most modern bows you are now able to increase the poundage to some extent. This will involve buying stiffer limbs, which can

cost from £150 upwards. The limbs are the part of the bow that flexes to impart power to the arrow. Accordingly, by using the club equipment for an extended period, you will be able to strengthen your shooting muscles, and so when you purchase your first bow you will be able to buy one more compatible with your strength.

Buying a bow too early, or getting one with poundage that is too high on the grounds that you will 'grow into it', will cause your shooting style to suffer. Of course, you may well get used to it, but it could take months or even years of hard work to get back to a good style of shooting.

*The string is attached to the ends of the limbs; Tserempilov (Russia).*

## Phase One Equipment: 'Getting Used to It'

Some clubs offer finger/wrist/bow slings and tabs as part of the beginner's course, which is a very useful start to your archery equipment and may well get you off to a better start with your shooting. However, both need to be adapted to the individual.

The finger/wrist/bow sling is fitted to the hand that holds the bow. It allows you to keep the bow hand relaxed during the shot and the bow is then 'caught' by it. The purpose of the sling is to allow you to have the bow hand relaxed during the draw and the subsequent shot. The adjustment requirements for all three are similar – they must be fitted so that they feel secure but are slightly loose around the bow, so that as you shoot the bow, it can leave the hand and is then caught by the sling. If the sling is too loose, there will be a tendency to try to catch the bow with the bow hand. If the sling is set too tightly, it will induce a torque (twisting motion) into the bow. The bow hand needs to remain

relaxed during the shot, so that the bow is not affected by changing tensions in the hand. Relaxing the hand during every shot, combined with the correct adjustment of the sling, is part of the 'art of repetition' that leads towards consistent shooting.

### The Finger Sling

This tends to be a good sling to start using at the outset, as it is simple in construction and easy to use. Finger slings are available from retailers, but in most cases you will need to adjust them to fit your hand and bow correctly. It is generally better to make your own using either thin nylon cord or a flat shoelace. To make the cord type, use 3–4mm thick nylon cord cut to a length of approximately 200mm (8in). Carefully set light to each end; when the material has melted a little blow it out and join the ends together. Next, slip three small lengths of polyurethane tubing, which can be bought from hardware stores or pet shops, over the loop. The sling may well need further adjustment; to do this,

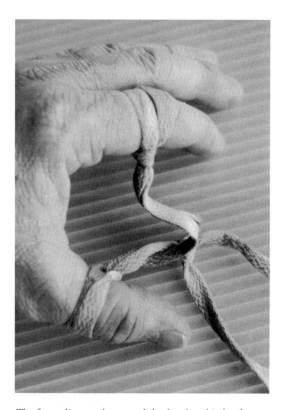

*The finger sling attaches around the thumb and index finger.*

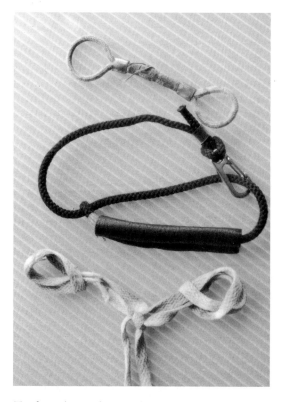

*Two finger slings and a wrist sling.*

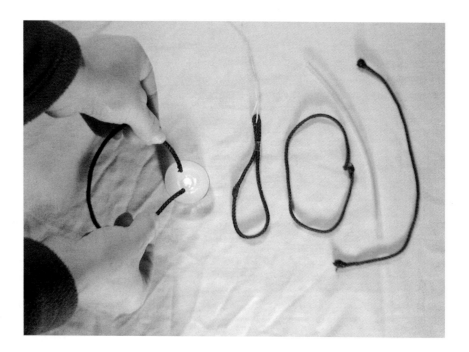

*Heating the ends of the cord to make the loops for the finger slings.*

cut either side of the melted joint, make the cord shorter and then re-melt the ends to form a smaller loop. The correct length is when you are at full draw the sling grips the index finger and thumb but has a slight gap around the front of the bow.

To make the flat shoelace type, knot the lace into a large loop. Two loops are then formed in the ends of the large single loop, and these then fit over the thumb and index finger joint of the bow hand. This again needs to be adjusted properly.

Being able to use a finger sling tends to depend on the shape of your fingers – if you have tapering fingers, you may find that the sling will slip off as you shoot, and so a wrist sling may be preferable.

*The layout of the flat shoelace in order to tie a finger sling.*

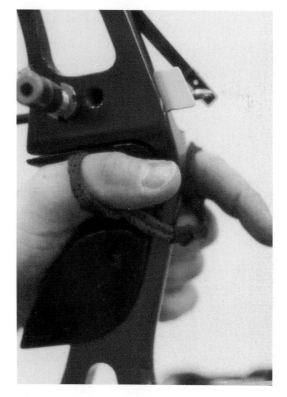

*The sling is slightly loose around the front of the bow.*

*Wrist slings usually tie onto themselves; the string type (far left) attaches to your thumb.*

*The string lies between the index and middle finger.*

### The Wrist Sling

This type of sling usually fits around the wrist of the bow hand. It has an adjustable cord that goes over the back of the hand, between the index and middle finger, then around the bow and clips back to itself on the inside of the wrist. It usually has a dual adjustment system – one for the wrist fitting and the other to adjust the length around the bow.

### The Bow Sling

This is made of a loop of cord or leather that is fitted to the bow. The bow hand goes through the loop, so that when the bow is shot the weight is transferred onto the wrist. This type of sling can work well and some clubs fit them to their club bows. It is also a useful training device to keep the hand relaxed throughout the shot.

### Tabs

Tabs have two main functions: to protect the fingers as the bow is drawn and shot, and to help align the hand with the jawbone at full draw. There are many types of tabs on the market, but they all fall into two categories. One type is aligned to the hand and is adjusted to become part of the hand. The other type is aligned with the bowstring and

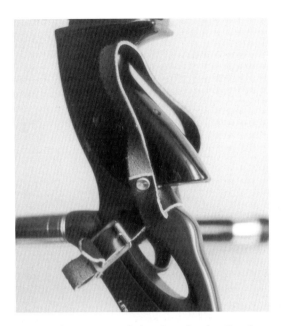

*The bow sling remains on the bow. It needs to be adjusted so that it is loose over the back of the hand at full draw.*

*On the A & F tab the bottom screw needs to be in place to hold the tab face in position.*

becomes part of the bow. The two most popular are the A and F Dutch tab and the Cavalier Elite tab. Both of these can be aligned with the hand, but the Cavalier Elite can also be adjusted so that it becomes part of the bow.

The key point with both types is that the string must be placed in the first joint of the middle finger. Tabs generally come in three sizes. When choosing a tab, you need to ensure that it is wide enough so that your fingers are fully on the leather backing, but not so big that there is spare facing around the edge of the fingers.

*The Cavalier Elite tab has a front plate draw string to hold it on the finger and the tab faces.*

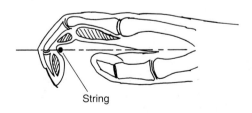

String

*ABOVE AND RIGHT: The string should sit in the first joints of the fingers.*

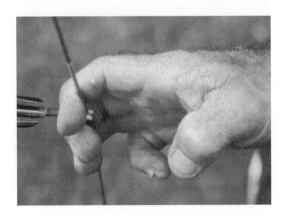

*The elastic needs to be firm around the finger and the index finger slightly squeezed between the spacer and the top anchor plate.*

### Aligned with the Hand

If a finger spacer is fitted to the tab, it is of the type that is fitted to the hand. The A and F is a good example of this. You need to adjust it so that the index finger just fits between the spacer and the platform. This should be a snug fit, but not so that it restricts circulation. The elastic loop fits around the middle finger and is adjusted so that again it is a snug fit. The elastic can be replaced with a cord or leather strap, if you prefer. The face of the tab must be attached at the bottom of the plate with the bolt and insert supplied; this will ensure that the tab face remains fixed to the back plate and aids consistency.

The tab may need some work on it to make it fit your hand and fingers satisfactorily. This may involve extending the slots in the leather and back plate; you can use a small file to cut the faces accordingly. Once the tab is adjusted properly it should be stable in the hand and not easily twisted away from the line of the fingers. When you use this type of tab, the spacer needs to be pushed back towards the knuckles and the first three fingers placed on the string, with the string in the first joint of the middle finger. Once the bow is being drawn back, the spacer should be clamped firmly between the fingers, helping to keep the alignment with the hand. As you draw the string back, ensure that the fingers stay in place, curled on the string.

At full draw, the platform of the tab is placed under the jaw, ensuring that the distance between the nock and the eye is consistent. The angle of the spacer can be adjusted so that the platform can be better fitted to the jawline.

*The spacer keeps the tab aligned with the hand and the platform ensures the distance between the nock and eye is consistent. Wietse van Alten (The Netherlands). (Andrew Callaway)*

*The tab is placed with the fingers in the first joint and aligned with the string; Jim Buchanan (GB European gold medallist).*

*Aligned to the Bow*

The Cavalier Elite tab is a dual tab, as it can be used with or without the finger spacer. When using it without the finger spacer, it is adjusted so that the cord loop fits snugly over the middle finger. The front of the tab plate is placed up against the string; your first three fingers then need to be placed so that the string is in the first joint of the middle finger. With this type of tab, compared to the A and F tab, you will find that the tab and loop sit further towards the tips of the fingers. Once the fingers are placed on the string, they should remain curled around the string, until the arrow is released. At full draw, the platform must, as with the A and F, make contact under the jawline. On this tab, the angle of

the platform can be adjusted so that it will fit your jawline better.

*Bracers*

A bracer protects the inner part of the bow arm from the bowstring, which can come in contact with the arm as the arrow is shot from the bow. It also holds your clothing out of the way. Not wearing one can be quite painful and so bracers should be provided on a beginner's course. There are many different types on the market. Some even cover the upper arm – although this is a little excessive it is useful to have at least one of these in the club's equipment box as some beginners are scared of the

*The bracer protects the arm from the string on release; A. Karaseova (Belarus). (Lana Needham)*

*A bracer can be made from thin flexible plastic to suit the archer. (Lana Needham)*

string contact and wearing one of these will allow them to concentrate on learning how to shoot. When you come to buy a bracer, choose one that will cover a larger part of your inner forearm, as some are short and so may not protect your arm fully. Also, make sure that it has a smooth finish and that it is not too thick, otherwise it will bulk out your arm and interfere with the string's trajectory.

In good old 'Blue Peter' fashion, you can make a bracer out of a plastic washing-up bottle and elastic.

### Quivers

Quivers are used to hold your arrows. If there is not a quiver available on a beginner's course, you can put your arrows in your jeans' back pocket. This will allow you to reach your arrows without bending over and possibly moving your feet, and so will assist in keeping your line and flow of shooting. As with most equipment, there is a huge choice of types and materials, and prices to go with them. It is worth getting one that has a pocket, so that you can keep your tab in it, and enough room so that you can carry more than six arrows. When you shoot outside, in most competitions you will have to shoot six arrows. In case one of your arrows becomes damaged, it is prudent to have at least one spare in your quiver.

A simple quiver can be made from a piece of 3in plastic pipe blocked at the bottom end. Attach two strings at either end to hold it to your belt. Some clubs use these for the beginner's courses. They are simple to make, or you can make a copy similar to commercial ones.

## Phase Two: 'Wanting a Bow' (and the Rest of Your Equipment)

As already noted, it is best to leave buying your first bow until you have settled in your archery a little and the muscles needed to shoot the bow have been developed. The following equipment will be needed:

- bow – ask around for a second-hand bow and always acquire a bow before you purchase any arrows; arrows are matched to the bow and not the other way around!
- bowstrings
- arrows
- sights
- stabilizers
- clickers
- buttons/rests
- tackle box.

### Buying a Bow

The limiting factor on buying a bow or any equipment is how much you can afford and want to spend on it. It is a good idea to try to purchase a second-hand bow as your first

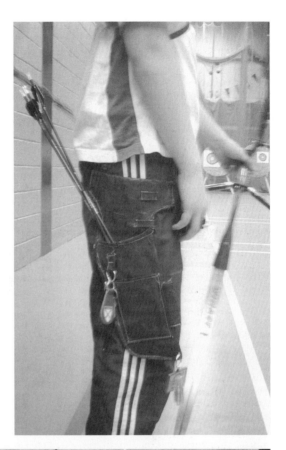

*ABOVE LEFT: A quiver holds the arrows and tab when not shooting and can hold a small amount of equipment; Tim Cuddihy (Australia). (Lana Needham)*

*ABOVE RIGHT: A simple homemade quiver ensures that limited funding can be spent on the necessities.*

*RIGHT: Bows can come in many colours and types. (Lana Needham)*

bow. A good second-hand bow (£100 to £150) will shoot better than a new bow of a similar price. Not only do you need to think about how much you want to pay for a bow, you must also consider the cost of the other items that will be needed to complete your equipment. The bow you normally use on a beginner's course will be a 'training bow'; this bow is designed as an introductory level bow for learning to shoot. I therefore suggest that you purchase a better standard of bow than a training bow, otherwise you will find it necessary to upgrade quite quickly.

When you are looking to buy your second bow, this may well be the time to buy 'new'. You can then sell on your first bow; in most cases, second-hand bows hold their price quite well. The important point to remember when buying any bow is that it needs to be suitable for you; it does not matter if it is a good price or a nice colour, it needs to be the correct length and poundage for you.

## Understanding the Bow

Bows are measured by their length, how tall they are and how much effort it will take to pull them (this is measured in pounds [lb] and is directly proportional to how far you draw the bow back). Standard bow lengths are manufactured in increments of 2in; 64in, 66in, 68in and 70in being the most common sizes. Bows for juniors are generally shorter than these and the length may be made up of different combinations of riser and limb.

Risers (centre of the bow) usually come in two lengths: 23in and 25in (short and long).

The limbs commonly come in 'short', 'medium' and 'long' and will be marked with the weight of the limb for a given length of bow. This will be shown as, for example: 'Medium 68" 30lb @ 28"' or 'Medium 66" 32lb @ 28"'.

This would indicate that these are medium limbs, which can be fitted to a short or long riser. In a short riser, they would make a 66in bow and in a long riser a 68in bow. If these medium limbs were fitted to a short riser, and the string were to be drawn back so that the distance from the string to the pivot point + 1.75in (1¾in), (the pivot point and the button position is in the same vertical alignment so it can be easier to measure 1.75in in front of the button) of the bow would measure 28in. The poundage on the fingers (to hold the string) would be 32lb, although it is best to use a set of bow scales to ensure that the marked indication on the limbs is accurate.

### Bow Lengths

| Limbs | Short | Medium | Long |
|---|---|---|---|
| Short riser 23in | 64in | 66in | 68in |
| Long riser 24in | 66in | 68in | 70in |

Now you need to calculate your draw length to determine the length of arrow you will need. If you use a 28in arrow and, when you draw the bow

*Limbs made by Hoyt and Win & Win; both sets are the same poundage and length.*

| Weight marked on limbs → | 20 | 21 | 22 | 23 | 24 | 25 | 26 | 27 | 28 | 29 | 30 | 31 | 32 | 33 | 34 | 35 | 36 | 37 | 38 | 39 | 40 | 41 | 42 | 43 | 44 | 45 | 46 |
|---|---|---|---|---|---|---|---|---|---|---|---|---|---|---|---|---|---|---|---|---|---|---|---|---|---|---|---|
| Draw length ↓ | | | | | | | 8 | 9 | 10 | 11 | 12 | 13 | 14 | 15 | 16 | 17 | 18 | 19 | 20 | 21 | 22 | 23 | 24 | 25 | 26 | 27 | 28 |
| 20 | | | | | 8 | 9 | 10 | 11 | 12 | 13 | 14 | 15 | 16 | 17 | 18 | 19 | 20 | 21 | 22 | 23 | 24 | 25 | 26 | 27 | 28 | 29 | 30 |
| 21 | | | 8 | 9 | 10 | 11 | 12 | 13 | 14 | 15 | 16 | 17 | 18 | 19 | 20 | 21 | 22 | 23 | 24 | 25 | 26 | 27 | 28 | 29 | 30 | 31 | 32 |
| 22 | 8 | 9 | 10 | 11 | 12 | 13 | 14 | 15 | 16 | 17 | 18 | 19 | 20 | 21 | 22 | 23 | 24 | 25 | 26 | 27 | 28 | 29 | 30 | 31 | 32 | 33 | 34 |
| 23 | 10 | 11 | 12 | 13 | 14 | 15 | 16 | 17 | 18 | 19 | 20 | 21 | 22 | 23 | 24 | 25 | 26 | 27 | 28 | 29 | 30 | 31 | 32 | 33 | 34 | 35 | 36 |
| 24 | 12 | 13 | 14 | 15 | 16 | 17 | 18 | 19 | 20 | 21 | 22 | 23 | 24 | 25 | 26 | 27 | 28 | 29 | 30 | 31 | 32 | 33 | 34 | 35 | 36 | 37 | 38 |
| 25 | 14 | 15 | 16 | 17 | 18 | 19 | 20 | 21 | 22 | 23 | 24 | 25 | 26 | 27 | 28 | 29 | 30 | 31 | 32 | 33 | 34 | 35 | 36 | 37 | 38 | 39 | 40 |
| 26 | 16 | 17 | 18 | 19 | 20 | 21 | 22 | 23 | 24 | 25 | 26 | 27 | 28 | 29 | 30 | 31 | 32 | 33 | 34 | 35 | 36 | 37 | 38 | 39 | 40 | 41 | 42 |
| 27 | 18 | 19 | 20 | 21 | 22 | 23 | 24 | 25 | 26 | 27 | 28 | 29 | 30 | 31 | 32 | 33 | 34 | 35 | 36 | 37 | 38 | 39 | 40 | 41 | 42 | 43 | 44 |
| 28 | **20** | **21** | **22** | **23** | **24** | **25** | **26** | **27** | **28** | **29** | **30** | **31** | **32** | **33** | **34** | **35** | **36** | **37** | **38** | **39** | **40** | **41** | **42** | **43** | **44** | **45** | **46** |
| 29 | 22 | 23 | 24 | 25 | 26 | 27 | 28 | 29 | 30 | 31 | 32 | 33 | 34 | 35 | 36 | 37 | 38 | 39 | 40 | 41 | 42 | 43 | 44 | 45 | 46 | 47 | 48 |
| 30 | 24 | 25 | 26 | 27 | 28 | 29 | 30 | 31 | 32 | 33 | 34 | 35 | 36 | 37 | 38 | 39 | 40 | 41 | 42 | 43 | 44 | 45 | 46 | 47 | 48 | 49 | 50 |
| 31 | 26 | 27 | 28 | 29 | 30 | 31 | 32 | 33 | 34 | 35 | 36 | 37 | 38 | 39 | 40 | 41 | 42 | 43 | 44 | 45 | 46 | 47 | 48 | 49 | 50 | 51 | 52 |
| 32 | 28 | 29 | 30 | 31 | 32 | 33 | 34 | 35 | 36 | 37 | 38 | 39 | 40 | 41 | 42 | 43 | 44 | 45 | 46 | 47 | 48 | 49 | 50 | 51 | 52 | 53 | 54 |
| 33 | | | | | | | 36 | 37 | 38 | 39 | 40 | 41 | 42 | 43 | 44 | 45 | 46 | 47 | 48 | 49 | 50 | 51 | 52 | 53 | 54 | 55 | 56 |

*Limb weight selection. Find your draw length on the left-hand side, then work across the columns until the desired weight in the fingers is located. Move to the top of the chart to find the marked weight on the limb that you require for that bow weight.*

back, the point of the arrow is level with a point that is 1.75in in front of the button, you will have on your fingers whatever poundage the limbs are marked at. However, it is likely that your arrows will not be 28in long. As a rule of thumb, the poundage will differ from the marked weight by 2lb per inch of the actual draw length, whether it is shorter or longer than the 28in datum. The more you pull the bow back, the heavier the poundage. Therefore, if you draw a medium–limb 66in bow, marked at 32lb, and the measurement of the arrow is 26in to a point 1.75in in front of the button, this is 2in shorter than the limbs are marked; consequently you will need to take 4lb (2lb per inch) from the 32lb. This should give you a weight on the fingers of 28lb. It is always better to confirm the actual weight by using bow scales, because with second-hand limbs the weight indicated on the limbs may have changed slightly.

I have included a chart will help you to select the limbs for your draw length. To use the chart you need to calculate the distance from the string to the pivot point + 1.75in. This is your 'draw length'. Draw length is always calculated using this method; it is not calculated on the length of your arrow.

Finally, be aware that most bows now have adjustable poundage. Usually this will mean that for the marked poundage on the limbs you will be able to increase/decrease the weight up to 10 per cent, depending on the bow manufacturer. Generally, a bow will work better if you have higher poundage limbs set light, rather than light poundage limbs set at the highest poundage setting. This is covered in more detail in Chapter 4 ('Limb Geometry').

The following factors should be considered when buying a bow:

- Is the person still growing?
- What length of bow will you require?
- What weight (poundage) of limbs and mass of bow will you require?
- How often are you intending to practise?
- Are you considering entering competitions?
- How much do you want to spend?

**Is the person still growing?** Juniors have annoying habit of growing and never at the rate you think they will. Therefore, consider getting a slightly longer bow, so that as the junior grows the bow will last a little longer. But also bear in mind that, as they grow, they will use a longer arrow and the draw length will increase, therefore the poundage will increase. Consequently, make sure that as the junior grows the poundage of the bow does not increase to above what they can handle and control.

**What length of bow will you require?** The length of the bow is determined by your draw length. You may have noticed on the bow length chart that there is an overlap between the long and

*Limbs of this type are made to the same standard so are interchangeable between different manufacturers of limbs and risers.*

short riser lengths – as a result, you can have, for example, a 68in bow that is made up of a short riser and long limbs, or a long riser and medium limbs. For an established poundage, the long riser will have a better 'cast' (throw of the arrow). The chart gives you an idea of the bow-to-arrow length to help you select the correct length of bow.

### Bow-to-Arrow Length

| Length of bow | 64in | 66in | 68in | 70in |
|---|---|---|---|---|
| Length of arrow | <26in | 25–28in | 27–29in | 29–32in |

There is also an overlap of arrow sizes to the length of the bow. Consideration should be given to the length of the bow versus the requirements of the shoot. With a longer bow, the cast of the arrow will be slower, meaning that it will be in the air for longer and so may be affected by the weather. With a shorter bow of the same poundage, the arrow will travel faster. In most aspects of archery, there are positives and negatives to consider when determining your equipment and achieving the correct balance.

**What weight (poundage) of limbs and mass of bow will you require?** When starting out in archery, it is best to use the club's bows for the first few months while your muscles become conditioned to their new exercise. If you buy a bow too soon, you will most likely find that you outgrow its poundage in a matter of months and will soon have to upgrade, thereby incurring unnecessary expense.

Juniors will tend to use a lighter poundage for longer, as their muscles are still developing and are not as strong as an adult's.

In selecting the bow weight, you need to go for a draw weight that you can hold reasonably well without too much strain. Try to borrow a bow from the club that is of a draw weight that you think you can handle. If you can shoot it for a two-hour session without too much difficulty, this will be a good indication of a weight that will suit you. Remember that most bows have a weight adjustment.

It is better to have a slightly lighter poundage than too heavy. If the weight is more than you can manage your style will suffer and may cause you injuries, resulting in you stopping shooting. You must work up to the final poundage, which will take some months. The final thing to consider is the distances that you feel that want to shoot. Some people only like shooting indoors, whereas others will want to shoot the full distances – 90m for men and 70m for women. Even as an established archer, care needs to be taken in selecting the weight of the limbs. If it is too high, you will loose the control you need for an accurate shot.

**How often are you intending to practise?** Think about what you want from your archery. For many it is a hobby that they enjoy pursuing once or twice a week. For others, it may turn into a competitive sport to which they want to give their full commitment. However, everyone will be trying to do well and hit the middle more often, so ensure that the bow you buy will assist your aspirations. Your club and its facilities will determine how often you are able to practise, although of course your job may also be a limiting factor. But the more you are able to practise, the faster you will come on with your shooting.

**Are you considering entering competitions?** If this is the case, find out what distances you will need to shoot. In your first year you are considered a novice and so do not need to shoot the full distances for your age and gender. I feel it is better to buy a bow from the outset that will help you to progress in competitions; chopping and changing bows will only slow your development.

**How much do you want to spend?** Look to your pocket, buy what you can afford and try to get the best for your money. As I have already noted, you will get more for your money when buying a good second-hand bow than a new one of lesser quality for the same price. Remember that there is other equipment you will need to buy to go with the bow.

Once you have considered the factors above, it is time to select your bow. I suggest you look at what is being shot in the club and at local competitions. A bow that is popular implies reliability and consistency. I would suggest buying a good quality riser that will take international limb fittings (a standard fit of limbs to the riser used by most of the major companies). With a good riser you can upgrade your limbs as you develop, maintaining the feeling of the shot from the riser.

*Bowstrings*
A bowstring is likely to come with your first bow, but separate bowstrings can be ordered from retailers. The cheaper bowstrings are machine-made, although the retailer may also have a stock of custom-made strings that will be of a better quality; however, either will suffice to get you started. Making your own bowstrings is best and if you want to get the most out of your shooting, this will be part of your progression. Producing quality strings for yourself is dealt with in Chapter 11.

*Selecting Arrows*
You must match your arrows to your bow, not the other way around; although arrows can be expensive, the bow will cost you more. You must first match the bow to your strength and reach, and then match the arrows to that set-up – otherwise it would be the same as buying some wheels, then finding a car to fit them to.

When you shoot the arrow out of the bow, the arrow must bend the correct amount. If the arrow is too thick (stiff), it will not bend enough. If it is too thin (weak), it will bend too much. The amount the arrow will bend is called 'spine'. This is calculated by resting the ends of the arrow on two 'v' blocks and hanging a weight on the centre of the

---

**Buying a Bow**

Look on the Internet to compare the prices from different companies as bows may be on 'special offer'. However, if possible it is best to buy new equipment from a reputable company with a showroom – if you are able to visit the showroom, the staff will be able to advise you on a final choice. Most of these companies have a good after-sales reputation so if you do have problems with the equipment you will be better supported than if you buy from abroad just to save a couple of pounds. In going to the showroom, you will be given the opportunity to try out the bow first as most have shooting ranges as part of the shop.

---

arrow, then measuring the deflection of the shaft (the AMO standard is the amount of bend in thousands of an inch when the arrow is placed on two points 28in apart with a weight of 880g hung in the centre of the arrow).

Therefore, you will need to select the arrow that is correct for you and your bow. First, you will need to work out the *total length* of the arrow, *not* your draw length. How many pounds on your fingers at full draw? You well have already calculated when this buying the bow, but it is important to check again before buying the arrows. Easton arrows produces a selection chart that will give you a good idea of which arrow spine will suit you; this is published in various retail magazines and can be found on the Easton website: www.eastonarchery.com If you are buying arrows from a retailer, the staff will advise you on the correct spine of arrow to match your bow.

Due to the amount of information on arrows and arrow selection, and matching them to your bow, I have devoted a whole chapter to this topic (*see* Chapter 10).

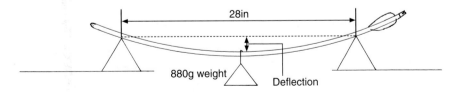

*The weight hung on the centre of the arrow bends the shaft. The amount of bend is measured, determining the spine of the arrow.*

*Sights*

In its most simple terms, the sight is a device that holds a pin (the bit you aim at the target with) to the bow and allows the pin to be moved to the appropriate position, both in height and windage (side to side), to allow for distance and wind.

Sights come in two main types, one with the vertical adjustment on the bow and the other with the vertical adjustment away from the bow. There are many different variations of these two types, but I would suggest one that has a gearing of some sort on the vertical adjustment; this means that if the thumb lock comes a bit loose, which it may well do, it will not slide down on its own and spoil your aim.

You pay for what you get with most equipment. In a good sight you are paying for the engineering and the total weight/mass. A good sight will always be able to be moved to the same place every time you shoot that distance and should not be too heavy; some even have carbon parts to keep the weight down.

Most sights will come with a sight pin; most are interchangeable, so you can choose a sight then fit the pin that you like shooting with.

Personally, I like a sight that 'clicks' as you adjust it, both vertically and horizontally, and with as few thumbscrews as necessary to keep the pin in place. I have used the Sure-Loc for the past few years and found it to be very reliable.

The main consideration when setting the sight on the bow is: 'How far out from the bow should the sight pin be?' It is always a trade-off – if you put the sight out a long way, thereby increasing the distance from the eye (back sight) to the pin, the more accurate it will be, but the more it will seem to move around. The closer to the bow, the closer to the eye, but it will be less accurate; however, the pin will seem to move around less.

Some archers advocate going to your longest distance and setting the sight so that you can hit the target but still have a comfortable distance between the arrow and the sight pin. The further away the target is, the lower the sight needs to be (you may have to bring the sight in towards the bow to be able to sight on the gold and achieve the distance). You can then leave the sight at this setting for all distances so that the pin is always the same distance from the eye. However, I like to make use of the accuracy and keep the sight at full extension, which is about 9in on the Sure-Loc. Fortunately, with the poundage I shoot at, 45lb at full draw, I can keep the sight at full extension for all distances. (This does not mean that you should raise the poundage just to get all distances at full sight extension.)

*Sight Pins*

There are many types of sight pins available. You can shoot either with an open sight (sight ring), or use one with a pin/pointer, which are available with many different sizes of aperture. When you are starting out, try to keep it simple, as you will have enough to think about without fiddling with different pins. When you do get to the stage of testing sight apertures, Beiter manufactures a good sight

*Roy Nash sighting on the target at 70m, Cyprus. (Barry Eley)*

*The height adjustment and windage is out from the bow.*

*The height adjustment is on the bow, but the windage is still out from the bow. The main weight of the sight remains on the bow.*

pin that comes with interchangeable apertures, which allows you to test to find the right one.

If selecting an open sight ring, consider the following factors: the edge of the ring should not be so thick that it obscures the gold at different distances, nor so thin that it is not clear as you are looking through the sight. The pin, if you are using that type, should not hide the gold as you aim. Many archers try to use a pin type where the pin is too thick; this means that when they aim at a large target face at a close distance, there is no problem, as the gold is visible at all times, but as they progress, they find that at some distances the pin obscures the gold, leading to hesitation when shooting. What actually happens is that as you look at the gold through the sight pin, the gold disappears; the mind is set to look for the gold and makes the arm move the pin aside, which means that though you can now see the gold you will actually shoot to the side of it. Once you are aware of this condition, either find a pin that does not cover the gold or use the method of sighting so that the sight covers the gold and then you shoot.

### Using the Open Sight

I use an open sight; this means that it is basically an open hole. I use an Arten sight ring with the pin cut out of it. Using this sight, I do not think of 'aiming' but of 'looking' through a round window. If you look at something through a window, you will tend to look through the centre of it. Shooting with an open sight is similar – the brain is very good at centring the object at which you are looking, especially if it is also round. This means that all you need to do is look at the 'point of aim'. On a calm day, this will be the centre of the gold, but on a windy day it may well be to the side of the gold. The point

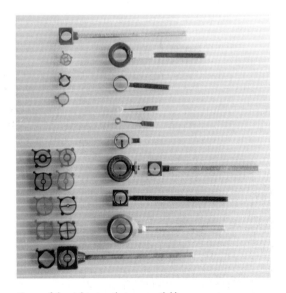

*Some of the sight pins that are available.*

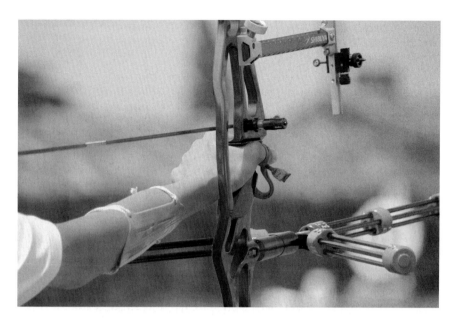

*A Shibuya sight and pin.
(Andrew Callaway)*

of aim is the point you pick on the target that will allow the arrow to hit the centre, taking into consideration the wind and light conditions (*see* Chapter 12 for more about 'aiming off').

### Principles of Aiming a Bow

When shooting a rifle or a compound bow you have both a front sight and a rear sight (peep sight for a compound), so all you need to do to aim is to align the rear sight and the front sight and shoot. If the rifle/bow is held steady you will hit your target.

If you had a rifle without a rear sight, but you could rest your cheek in exactly the same place on its stock every time, you would not need the rear sight, as your eye would be in the same spatial alignment with the front sight. Shotguns only have front sights and rely on the back of the gun to come to the same relationship with the face every time for a successful shot. Shooting with a recurve Olympic bow is similar to this as there is no rear sight. Therefore, the key to aiming is ensuring that the nock is in the same relative position to the eye every time. This is why the string placement on the chin and the hand alignment at full draw is so important, as this will give the vertical alignment. The rules do not allow recurve bows to have a rear sight, but in lining the string up with the sight ring the string then acts as a vertical rear sight, ensuring that the arrows are kept central to the bows axis.

You can make your own sight apertures, but be aware of the rules. The main ones are that the length of the sight tunnel cannot be longer than the diameter of the aperture. In addition, for recurves it may not contain a lens.

### Stabilizers

As the name suggests, these help to control the bow's movements so that the bow sits more

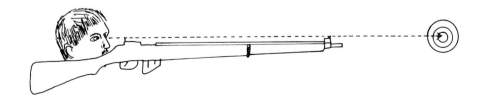

*After lining the rear and front sight on the target, when you pull the trigger you will hit what you are aiming at.*

*The position of the butt against the cheek must be the same every time; Iain Stewart, Scottish international, Olympic Skeet. (Iain Stuart)*

*The nock is directly underneath the eye; its distance is maintained by the hand position. (Barry Eley)*

steadily in the hand while at full draw and during the shot. The long rod helps to steady lateral and vertical movement. The twins or top/bottom rods help to steady against rotational movement of the hand, but both allow the bow to move backwards and forwards easily.

### Long Rods

There are two main types of rods – those that are made of a light, stiff tube, normally of parallel construction with the weight on the end, and those that have the weight distributed along the length (for example, the Beiter Multirod is usually made up of a number of thin rods). The difference in price tends to reflect in the performance; the more expensive stabilizers do tend to work better.

The design of the parallel type of rod is to have a weight 'out' from the bow to control the bow's

ABOVE: *26in-long rod with Doinker 4in extension, V bar and 8in twins; Olena Sadovnycha, Ukraine. (Olena Sadovnycha)*

RIGHT: *Parallel type rods; Anna Karaseova (Belarus).*

BELOW: *Beiter stabilizers; Katya Muliuk (Belarus). (Lana Needham)*

movement, but with the rod being as light and stiff as possible. When considering the length of your long rod, as a rule of thumb for this type of long rod try to find one the length of your arrow plus about 4in.

The Beiter Multirod has the weight distributed along its length, but with the rods connecting the weights being as light as possible (thin carbon tubes in this case). The Beiter Multirod is longer than the parallel type: 32in for recurves and 40in plus for compounds are the suggested lengths from the designer, Mr Werner Beiter. If in doubt buy a longer one and cut if down as required. The tuner/weight distances are set so that the rod is stiffer closer to the bow (to achieve this, the gaps between the tuners get progressively closer the nearer to the bow).

There are pros and cons to using either type of long rod, although I find my groups tend to be more consistent with the parallel type of rod. Try them out at your club first to establish which suits you best.

*Twins and Short Rods*
These can be made from two types of construction, but generally they work in a similar fashion, putting weight out from the bow to help stabilize rotational movement. A good starting set-up is a 4in extension, a flat 'V' bar, 8in to10in twins and a long rod.

Juniors normally start with just a long rod as the bow needs to be kept light. The long rod can even be used without weights if required, as it will still take some of the torque out of the riser when it is shot.

The setting-up of stabilization is covered in Chapter 3.

*Clickers*
The clicker blade enables the archer to come to his correct (natural) draw length every time. This ensures that there is the same poundage behind the arrow on every shot and therefore the same trajectory. Remember that 1in difference in draw length, whether shorter or longer, will give you a difference of 2lb draw weight. However, the clicker should not be introduced to the new archer at an early stage – it is important to develop a consistent draw length first.

There are many different makes of clicker, but most of them consist of a short strip of spring steel that is placed over the arrow. Once an archer's draw length has been reached, the blade slides off the end of the point and 'clicks' onto the body of the riser, signalling the release of the fingers from the string.

Magnetic clickers are also available and do a similar job, although you will need to check that there

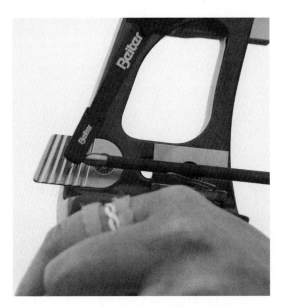

*At full draw, the clicker needs to be 2mm away from the end of the arrow. (Barry Eley)*

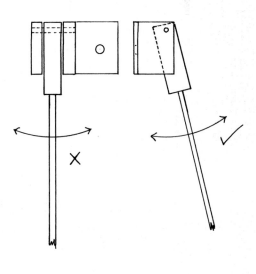

*Check that there is no lateral movement in the clicker rod.*

is no side movement in the pivot of this type of clicker. If there is too much side movement, as the arm of the clicker gets to the point of the arrow it will jump down the point, leading to inconsistency in the flow of the shot.

A good clicker is made of quality spring steel that retains its form over use. When the clicker slides from the point of the arrow, it needs to make a good, clear 'click' on the riser or clicker extension. This will ensure that the shot is executed well, if the clicker is soft or not adjusted correctly you will not get the positive shot that you need.

*Setting the Clicker*
Once a new archer is shooting with reasonable form and consistency, a clicker may be fitted. Either an observer or a video camera is needed when setting the clicker position. The archer needs to shoot a few dozen arrows without the clicker, with the observer watching where the point of the arrow comes to against the bow on average (or use a video recorder). The clicker should then be set to this average point. From this position, it should not be

necessary to move the clicker position more than 2–3mm (0.78–0.12in) in either direction to complete the set-up.

One of the major faults when placing a clicker is moving it too far back towards the archer, which leads to overdrawing (pulling the bow back too far); underdrawing (when the clicker is too far forward) seems to be less problematical, although both should be avoided.

*Shooting with the Clicker*
Once the clicker is in place, practise shooting the arrow as soon as the clicker 'clicks'. It will take a little practice, but after a few weeks you will find that when the clicker 'clicks' you will naturally shoot the arrow (so ensure that you are always pointing the bow towards the target).

*Buttons/Rests*
The button and the rest hold the arrow in the correct position on the bow. Adjusting the button and rest to get the arrow in the correct position is an

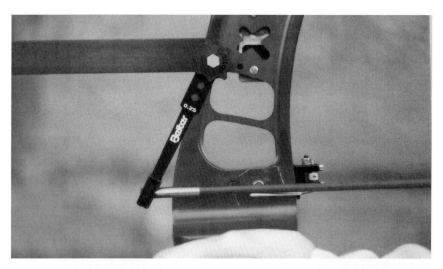

*Shooting without a clicker to find the clicker position.*

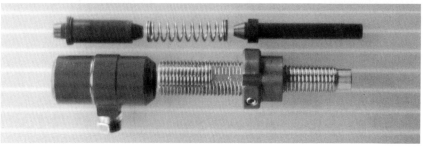

*The Beiter button with the internal parts laid out in their relative positions.*

*Tackle boxes come in different sizes, but ensure that it is big enough for your requirements while still fitting in your car. (Karen Henderson)*

integral part of tuning the bow, which is dealt with in greater detail in Chapter 4.

The button is made up of a body to fit the bow and hold the parts, a tip that contacts with the arrow, a spring and adjustment to change the pressure of the spring, and a securing nut to lock the button to the bow and set its position.

Look for a button that has a smooth movement when you press it with your thumb. The DX button is a good one to start with. The best is the Beiter button, which has micrometre adjustment that allows it to be reset perfectly and has tips that do not wear. This means that the button, once set, will stay at that setting until you decide to adjust it. If a button has a tip that wears, it will allow the arrow to move closer to the riser, so affecting your settings and arrow flight.

### Tackle Box

Your tackle box needs to be big enough to hold all your equipment and keep it protected. Many archers have arrived at competitions to find that the arrow tube or stabilizer is still at home because they do not fit into their tackle box. Both hard and soft cases are available. I prefer a hard case as it protects the equipment better, although it does tend to be bulkier and heavier than a soft case. Once you have started shooting you will see many variations in design, many of them homemade.

## Summary

With archery, it tends to be the case that you get what you pay for, although having the best equipment will not make up for a poor shooting style, and, in some areas (such as arrows), the best is less forgiving and requires more consistency in style to achieve good results. When buying equipment, if possible try other people's first and do not rush in. Decide your budget and see what you can get for your money, bearing in mind that most of the time you can buy better quality second-hand equipment than new for the same price.

# Chapter 3

# Setting Up Your Equipment

The bow is just a machine; it needs to be set up to optimize its performance. Although the equipment set-up is only 10 per cent of shooting the arrow into the gold, if you take care in the set-up, your bow will perform well from the first time that you shoot it.

When I get a new bow, or set up a new combination of bow and limbs for myself, it can take up to four hours before I shoot a single arrow. Most archers are too eager to shoot their new bow; they literally get it out of the box and shoot it without making any adjustments. This invariably means that the bow will perform poorly from the start and will not have the right feel, so psychologically doubt is induced in the bow's performance, making the archer take longer to gain full confidence in the new bow. From my experience, when the bow is set up properly, my current performance level is maintained and, with minor tuning, it actually increases.

I use a standard routine for setting up bows, whether they are new or used. This routine is the same one for checking existing set-ups. Prior to any tuning of a bow a set-up check should always be carried out, as good tuning is dependent upon a good set-up. The set-up order listed below needs to be followed exactly, as this will give an excellent initial set-up that will enable the bow to shoot well from the very first arrow.

## Set-Up Schedule

1. Examine the bow, checking for defects.
2. Fit the limbs to the riser.
3. Fit the stabilizers to the riser.
4. Find the true centre of the bow.
5. Align the limbs to the true centre.
6. Set the tiller.
7. Fit and adjust the rest and button.
8. Fit and adjust the sight.
9. Set the nocking point.
10. Adjust the arrow alignment.
11. Set the clicker.
12. Adjust the stabilizer/bow balance.

## 1. Examine the Bow, Checking for Defects

When you first get a bow, take a good look at the riser to make sure it has not been damaged in transit and that all the parts are accounted for. Make sure that all the screws have been fitted. Check the limbs carefully. Most limbs come in matched pairs, so ensure that the serial numbers on both limbs match. Take a close look at the edges of the limbs and the string grooves for signs of any damage to the lacquer coat that covers the limbs. Check that the string grooves are evenly cut and at the same height. If the bow is second-hand you may well see indentations in the lacquer left by the string. This is quite normal and is not a concern.

Familiarizing yourself with the riser and limbs at this stage will help you to get to know the bow and the attachment points that are for fitting weights and stabilizers and so on.

## 2. Fit the Limbs to the Riser

The limbs need to fit accurately to the riser. Some may be a little tight initially, which can be alleviated by putting a thin smear of vaseline in the 'U' cut-outs at the base of each limb. There should be no lateral movement of the limb in the riser, as this will cause the bow to shoot inconsistently, It must therefore be remedied before proceeding with the set-up, either by replacing the defective parts or if possible by adjustment.

Lateral movement in the limbs can be caused by the 'U' cut-out in the limbs being oversized, the

*The 'U' cut-out and dovetail with a sprung locator in the centre.*

*The fit of the limb around the locating pin needs to be snug.*

locating pins that the 'U' cut-out fits into being undersized, or the groove in the riser that the dove-tail fits into being too wide. This can be checked before stringing the bow. Keeping pressure on the limb (both into the limb pocket and down onto the seating), try to rock the limb left and right in the pocket; if the limb fit is good there will be no movement.

Once the bow has been strung, the limbs need to be settled in by 'flicking' the string – pulling it back about 2in, then letting go. This will help to snap the limbs fully into place. Once you have done this, you can test for lateral movement by placing the side of the pocket against your knee and gently pulling the riser and limb, first from one side then the other. There should be no side movement of the limbs in the pockets. If there is, a check needs to be made to see where the movement is coming from. If you try to shoot a bow that has movement between the riser and the limb, it will not shoot consistently as the alignment of the limb in the riser will be changing with every shot.

*With the limbs fitted into the riser try to move the limb from left to right; there should be no lateral movement. (Karen Henderson)*

*Once the string has been fitted, the limb can be pulled against the knee, turned around and pulled in the opposite direction; no movement should be felt. (Karen Henderson)*

Once you are happy with the limb fit, the bracing height can be set. The bracing height is the distance between the string and the pivot point in the grip; this is the same measurement to the centre of the button as these two points are in line with each other. Your bow will come with manufacturer's rec-

ommendations for bracing heights. Initially, set the bow at the mid-range of this recommendation.

I usually set it so that the string sits fully in the string groove in the bottom limb and a little out of the groove on the top limb. This ensures that you get good vertical stability of the string. If, however,

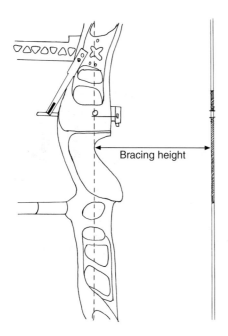

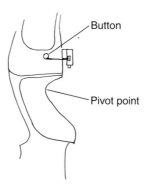

Button

Pivot point

*The bracing height is the measurement from the string to the pivot point; the button is directly above the pivot point, so can also be used to determine the bracing height.*

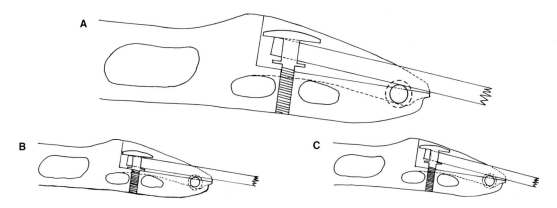

*The further the adjuster is wound into the bow, the higher the poundage: C = low; A = medium; B = highest poundage.*

you have the string sitting too far out of the groove, a high bracing height, you will find that it is easier to move the string vertically, which will give you taller groups, which is not desirable.

At this point, you need to check that the limbs are set to an appropriate poundage for what you want to shoot; this is carried out by moving the poundage adjusters. In most cases the domed bolt that the end of the limb fits into can be moved in and out of the riser. If you screw it into the bow the poundage of the bow will increase; winding it out will decrease the poundage. The manufacturer will set a limit to how far this bolt can be wound out, and if you exceed that you may seriously damage the bow. Initially, set both the top and bottom limb adjusters by the same amount to obtain the desired poundage – fine adjustments to them will be needed later as you set the tiller.

## 3. Fit the Stabilizers to the Riser

Fit the stabilizers at this point. I usually use a 4in extension, 8in twins and a long rod – once they are fitted it makes it easier to rest the riser on the back of a chair. But, more importantly, a long rod is required to ascertain the true centre of the bow in the next step, so borrow one from your club if you do not yet have one.

## 4. Find the True Centre of the Bow

You need to find the true centre of the bow so that, in the next stage, the limbs can be aligned to ensure that the power stroke of the limbs, moving forward,

is directly through the centre of the bow. I was fortunate enough to be invited to a competition in Wonju, South Korea, in 2001. Before the event the Korean coaches ran a seminar on setting up the bow for shooting. The speaker, Mr Kyung-Rae Park, declared: 'To set the true bow centre is the most important thing; this is the basis for setting up the rest of the equipment.'

To ascertain the true centre of the bow I use the long rod as a visual guide; at home, I use a new uncut aluminium arrow. Any parallel shaft arrow

*With the stabilizers fitted, the bow balances well on the back of a chair. (Karen Henderson)*

45

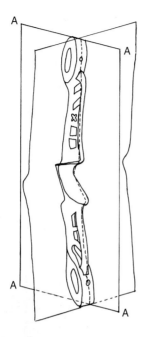

*A–A = true centre line.*

*Place a straight parallel arrow in the sight window. (Karen Henderson)*

can be used (the ACE and X10 arrows are tapered in design and so are unsuitable, although if this is the only arrow you have available you can use the front part of the shaft as this is parallel). Rest the riser over the back of a chair, ensuring that the limbs do not rest or touch anything while you are carrying out adjustments to the alignment, as this

will deflect the limbs, causing an error in the set-up. Place the arrow in a part of the sight window that appears to be cut in line with the bow.

With the arrow running parallel to the long rod when looked at from the side, look down on the arrow from the top and see how it lines up with the long rod. If the long rod and bushings are straight,

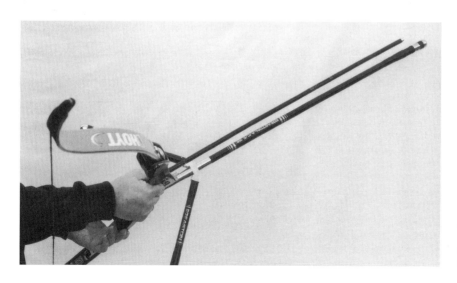

*Look down on the arrow to see if the long rod is aligned with the true centre. (Karen Henderson)*

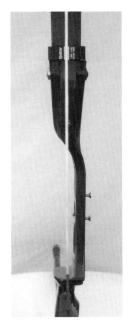

*The string should fall through the centre of the limb and the centre of the long rod. (Karen Henderson)*

*Once the string is aligned with the centre of the limb, look to see if it is also through the true centre of the long rod; if not, it will need adjusting. (Karen Henderson)*

*A card can be attached on the end of the long rod to help with the alignment. (Karen Henderson)*

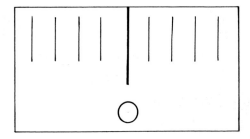

*The hole in the card can be tailored to fit the thread on the long rod weights.*

the arrow will run parallel with the long rod. I put the arrow against the riser in a number of positions, on the riser both in the sight window and on the outside of the bow. Putting the arrow against the sight block is usually a good indicator.

With some bows it can be quite easy to find out how the long rod lies. If the long rod and the arrow run parallel, then the centre of the rod will lie in the true centre of the riser. If they are not parallel, you can determine where the true centre lies in relation to the long rod by lining one edge of the arrow with the centre of the long rod where it joins the riser. Then run your eye forward, following the same edge of the arrow, to the end of the long rod to see where the long rod lies in relation to the edge of the arrow.

If need be, a card with a hole cut in it can be attached to the long rod by means of the weights.

The card can then be marked to indicate the centre line (true centre) of the riser. This can aid you when setting the limbs to the true centre.

You may find that the long rod will appear to be

off to one side. This could be because the long rod bush is not straight in the riser, or the stabilizer bushing is out of line. The first point to look at is the stabilizers. Try borrowing different ones, or try fitting the long rod without an extension to see if that makes a difference. If this does not change the angle, then it is likely that the bushing is slightly out.

If the centre line is not within the width of the long rod, you may wish to modify the bushing. Only do this if you are certain that the long rod does not lie on the centre line and you are confident with a file, as you will need to chamfer the bush to straighten how the long rod lies. It is best to take a little off at a time, as a small amount can make a significant difference. The riser needs to be held firmly; I put it in an adjustable workbench, with the ends of the riser wrapped in a towel for protection.

## 5. Align the Limbs to the True Centre

Most modern risers incorporate a system for the lateral (side to side) alignment of the limbs in the bow. This is to allow for discrepancies in manufacture. The distance between the base of the limb and the location pin is one-tenth of the length of the limb, so a discrepancy of 0.1mm between the location pin and the base of the limb will give an error

of 1mm at the tip of the limb. However, were the risers to be manufactured to these very fine tolerances, the cost would be prohibitive, so a trade-off is reached between accuracy and cost by fitting a system for final fine-tuning to be done by the archer.

There are four main types of limb fittings:

• fixed – no lateral adjustment
• pivoted on the location pin
• pivoted on the base of the limb
• fully adjustable pockets.

*Fixed*
These types of risers can be found at both the cheaper and the top ends of the market. At the cheaper end, they tend to be made with limited fittings and adjustments, and may not have a mechanism for adjusting the poundage of the limbs. At the top end, the price will reflect the fact that a lengthy manufacturing process has gone into making a straighter finished product. Although the riser can be machined straight, the alignment of the limbs relies on the accuracy of the finished limbs. At the top end of the market the limbs will have been produced within close tolerances. If at all possible it is worth going to a retailer in order to select the limbs to fit the riser, as there may be differences among the limbs in stock and some will match your riser better than others.

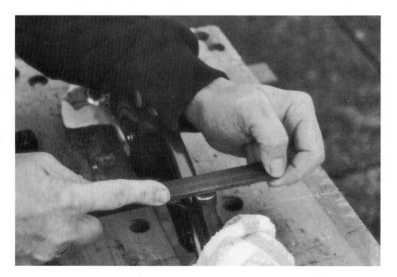

*If the bushing is not quite straight it can be filed to the centre of the long rod. Note that very little needs to be removed to change the alignment. (Karen Henderson)*

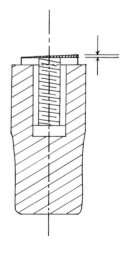

*A cross-section of the long rod bush showing the area to be removed.*

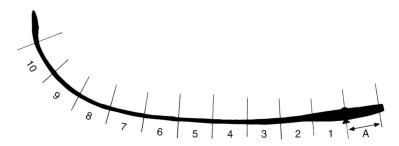

*The distance 'A' between the dovetail and the 'U' cut-out is one-tenth of the length of the limb.*

### Pivoted on the Location Pin

In this type of limb, the limb location pin is fixed in the riser and becomes the pivot; lateral adjustment is made by moving the base of the limb. This type of adjustment is usually achieved by utilizing an eccentric cam in the design.

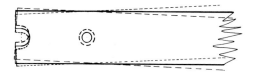

*Lateral adjustment is achieved by pivoting around the dovetail pin.*

### Pivoted on the Base of the Limb

The lateral adjustment of this type of riser is made by using the base of the limb as a pivot and moving the location pin to make the adjustment.

*Lateral adjustment achieved by pivoting through the 'U' cut-out.*

**Note:** With the two previous methods of adjustment, successful alignment relies on the pivot point being accurately placed on the centre line of the riser and the location pin and 'U' cut-out being in the centre of the limb.

### Fully Adjustable Pockets

With this type of riser, the whole of the pocket is adjustable with no fixed pivot. Although in theory it ensures that the bow can be fully aligned to take into account any inaccuracies in manufacture, it can be a lot harder to set up than the other two adjustable types, as the whole pocket can float over the centre line of the riser. In addition, due to the increased amount of parts required, there are more parts to work loose when in use.

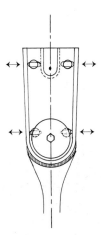

*The whole of the limb pocket is laterally adjustable.*

---

**Always Read the Instructions**

With all types of risers, it is important to read the instructions that come with the bow, as they will detail how to achieve any adjustment required. This will prevent damage occurring by making an incorrect adjustment to the bow.

---

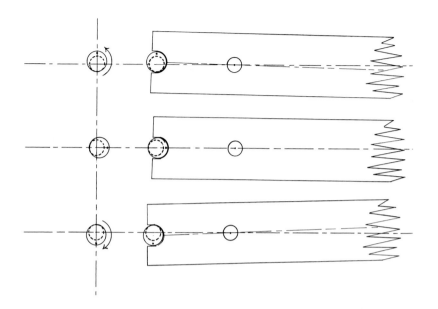

*An eccentric cam is used to adjust the position of the 'U' cut-out, achieving limb alignment.*

## Adjusting the Eccentric Cam Type

The eccentric cam adjustment is usually part of the poundage adjustment pin that the end slot of the limb fits into. An eccentric cam on a bow is made by machining a cylinder, then creating the pivot-centre offset, which means that, as the cylinder is rotated, it will move it from side to side and move the limb to the desired position. The main benefit of the eccentric cam is that the limb can be adjusted to any position by turning the cam on the pivot.

*The eccentric cam is offset and will usually have a datum marked on it.*

Take a good look at the mechanism of the cam without the limbs in place to acquaint yourself with how it works and to ensure that it moves freely. On most bows, the adjustment can be made with the limbs and string in place. You will also find that most of the cams are marked with a datum line/point, to show when the cam is central. This is very useful when making the adjustments. On cam systems that do not have any datum mark, a small spot of paint can be put on the cam so that the relative position of the cam can be seen when adjusting. It does not matter if the mark is not on the centre line of the cam as you are only using it as a reference point.

Once you have set this type of system, it is best to note where the datum mark is relative to the riser. If need be, an adjacent point on the riser can be marked, because if the lock bolts come loose and the cam moves, the bow will need resetting. During a shoot, putting the points adjacent again to the marked points will allow you to complete the shoot with the bow close to your correct set-up.

## Adjusting the Hoyt Shim System

The Hoyt shim system that is used on the Matrix, AeroTec and Axis bows is an excellent system that adjusts the lateral position of the limbs using shims (very thin washers), which pivot the limb at the base with the shims adjusting the position of the location pin in the riser. The bow comes with four shims fitted on both the top and bottom

*The riser comes shipped from Hoyt with two shims either side.*

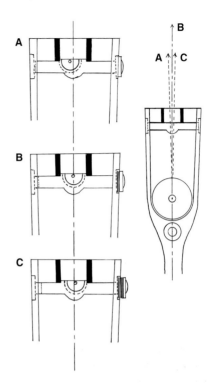

A: With no shims fitted the limb dovetail locator is adjusting the limbs to the left.
B: Two shims locate the locator to the central position; the risers are usually shipped with two shims on the adjustment side.
C: Four shims move the locator fully to the right, adjusting the limbs to the right.

adjustment pins. The shims only have an effect when they are fitted between the side of the pin (head) that has the fixed flange and the riser. When no shims are fitted between the pin's head and the riser, the centre of the pin will be to the right side of the riser.

As the shims are placed on the pin between the pin's head and the riser, the pin's placement in the riser is moved across the centre. Once the best limb position is found, the extra shims are then fitted under the removable end of the pin. When the shims are fitted in this position they do not affect the pin's position in the riser, but are kept 'safe' for if further adjustments are required.

The downside of this system is that the limb position is limited by the thickness of the shim. Therefore, you may find that with two shims on the adjustment side, the limb is not far enough across, but with three working shims, it moves too far across-centre. However, this is acceptable as you are trying to get the limbs to the best available position to allow the power stroke of the limbs on the shot to be as central as possible.

Further fine adjustments can be made to this shimming system. To do this, you must adjust the bow so that the limbs are brought too far across-centre by one shim. One shim can then be removed from the pin and made thinner by carefully rubbing it on very fine emery paper (800). Using the end of your finger, work a little at a time and continually refit the shim so that you do not take too much off. However, this fine adjustment should not be carried out until the bow has shot about 1,000 arrows in order to allow it to settle. If the pins come loose on this system after adjustment, you just need to tighten them up again and the adjustment will be as you previously set it.

*Adjusting Other Systems*
Most of the other systems use a threaded arrangement to move the lateral position of the limb, but

be aware that most of these systems utilize an adjustment screw and a locking screw/nut. This locking device will have to be loosened in the case of a nut, or removed in the case of a screw, before any adjustment can be made. This is carried out in two stages: the first is to align both limbs so that the string runs parallel with the centre of the riser; the second is to align the string with the true centre of the bow, keeping the string parallel with the centre of the riser.

**Stage One** You will need to 'pluck' the string three or four times. This involves pulling back the string approximately 3in, then letting go. This is required so that the limbs fully settle into position. This needs to be done every time the limbs are taken out and replaced during the set-up process.

With the bow resting on the back of a chair,

stand behind it and see how the string aligns with the riser. This can be facilitated by using the Beiter Limb Alignment Gauges, which should be placed on the limbs close to the riser; if, however they are not available, look to the centre line of the riser. The bolt holes for the limb attachment should be in the centre of the riser and these can be used to help align the string to the centre. If possible, rest your head against a door jamb, wall, or even on the end of a broomstick, so as to keep your head steady while looking up and down the riser and limbs. If the string does not line up with the centre line of the riser top and bottom, it will need adjustment.

If I am setting up a bow from scratch, I will initially ensure that the adjustment system, whether cams or shims, is set to the central position. Once you have read the instructions that come with your bow, pick any direction to move the limbs. Either it will be the correct way, or it will not – if it is the correct direction, carry on; if it is not, move it in the other direction! In the first stage, you will have to move the top and bottom adjusters in opposite directions to align the string up with the riser. Once you have adjusted the limbs so that the string runs though the centre of the riser you can move on to the second stage.

**Stage Two** Although the limbs are now aligned with the centre line of the riser, they will now need to be adjusted so that not only does the string pass through the centre of the riser, but it is also aligned with the 'true centre' of the bow. To keep the string running parallel to the riser, the limb adjusters need to be moved in the same direction. Pick a direction and move them. If it moves away from the true centre move the adjustment of both limbs the other way.

Once you have finished, the string should not only cut through the centre of the riser, but it should also run through the true centre of the bow, which was ascertained in the previous step.

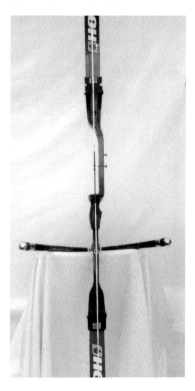

*If the top and bottom limbs are out of alignment, adjustments will need to be made. (Karen Henderson)*

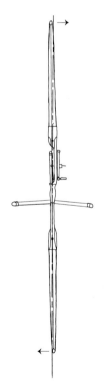

*The first step is to align the string with the centre line of the bow.*

*Once the string is aligned with the centre line the limbs must be moved in the same direction so as to align the string with the true centre.*

*With the bow fully aligned, the string will run through the true centre of the riser and the sight will be set slightly left of centre. (Karen Henderson)*

**Recording the Adjustments**

When you are new to adjusting the bow, use a sheet of paper to help you to keep a note of the changes you are making as you carry out the adjustment. Simply draw a line across the centre of the paper and mark on the top half any adjustment made on the top limb, and on the bottom half any adjustments made to the bottom limb.

that the limbs are set in the riser, when viewed from the side. If the measurement at the top and the bottom are the same, this is 'zero' tiller. In most cases the tiller is set as a 'positive', which means that the gap between the top limb and the string is bigger than the gap between the bottom limb and the string. Most bows seem to shoot well between 4–6mm (0.16–0.23in) positive (top gap bigger than the bottom), so a good initial setting is 5mm (0.2in) positive.

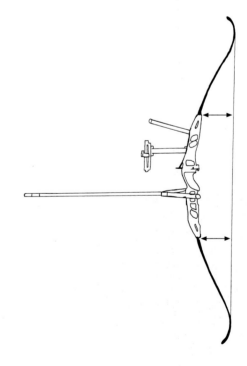

*The distance is measured between the string and the point that the limb fits into the riser.*

## 6. Set the Tiller

Tiller is the term used to describe the distance that the string is from the top and bottom limb at the point they both join the riser and the difference between these two measurements. Changing the difference between these two measurements adjusts the power of each limb in the riser, so as to take into account the fact that the bowstring is not pulled from its centre. When the tiller is set correctly, it allows the top and bottom limb to work in unison, so that once the string is released, both limbs finish the power stroke at the same time. In the old one-piece bows, the tiller was adjusted by the bowyer, who made the bottom limb stronger than the top limb. It is set in modern bows by adjusting the angle

When adjusting the tiller, refer to the manufacturer's instructions for the individual bow type. Most bow types utilize the poundage adjustment bolts to adjust the tiller. Adjusting the tiller can therefore alter the poundage of the bow by a small amount. Remember to take care when doing this adjustment, as there is usually a limit to how light the poundage adjustment bolts can be set. Therefore, if the bow is on the lightest setting, you will only be able to increase the adjustment/poundage on the lower limb. So increasing the poundage of the lower limb will decrease the gap between the bottom limb and the string.

## 7. Fit and Adjust the Rest and Button

Fitting the rest and button is reasonably simple, depending on the type of rest you are using. The rest needs to be fitted so that it takes into account the size of the arrow. The button will be one of two types: it will either be a one-piece 'plunger' (the point which comes in contact with the arrow), or have interchangeable tips.

I use a Beiter button and fit the rest so that the arrow shaft contacts the plunger on the centre. This means that at any time while I am shooting I can check the arrow position on the rest and as long as the arrow is central on the plunger I know that the rest set-up has not moved. If it has moved, it can be easily reset so that it once again sits on centre. The benefit of the Beiter button is that the plunger material does not wear; for example, the one I am

shooting at present is over five years old and still shows no sign of wear.

Other buttons tend to wear a little, so with these it is best to set the arrow against the plunger below centre. Set this way, the friction of the arrow passing against the plunger as it is shot will cause the plunger tip to rotate a little at a time, leading the button to wear evenly. This can be a double-edged sword – if you set the arrow centrally on the plunger you will see the wear occurring but it will make a groove, which is not desirable. Therefore you will have to flatten it off with a small file and then move the button out to compensate for the arrow moving closer to the riser and affecting your tuning. If you set it lower than centre the plunger will wear evenly, but you will be less aware of it, so you will need to keep a watchful eye on the alignment of the arrow.

Some buttons have changeable plunger tips and these screw on to the shaft of the plunger. With this type, right-handed archers need to ensure that the arrow rests against the bottom, lower than centre, and left-handed archers that it is above the centre line of the plunger. This is because, if you have set it as I have suggested, as you shoot, the arrow passing the button will keep the tip tightened on its thread. If you have it set the other way, the friction of the arrow passing the button will rotate it, undoing the tip and changing the arrow alignment. Eventually, the tip will fall off.

Once the arrow position against the plunger has been decided, the rest can be adjusted. Many of the wire type rests have a raised end to, apparently, keep the arrow on the rest. Before I fit the rest to the bow

*The arrow is placed on the rest with the shaft resting against the centre line of the button.*

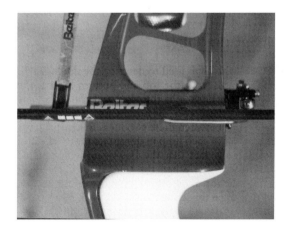

*With the hook left on the rest the arrow will have to 'jump' over it as the arrow leaves the bow.*

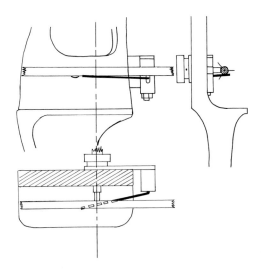

*The rest should be adjusted so that it has a slight up angle when viewed from the side and should not be seen extending out from the arrow when viewed from the top.*

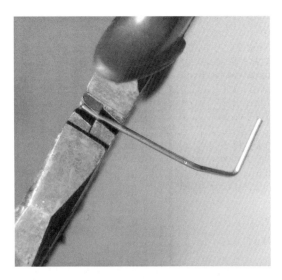

*A good strong pair of pliers will be needed to cut the spring steel of the rest. It should be covered when being cut to ensure that the end does not injure anyone.*

I straighten the wire using two pairs of pliers; once straightened; it will give a better clearance to the arrow as it exits the bow. Once the rest is fitted, there should be a slight up angle on the rest in relation to the arrow, looking from the side. This needs to be adjusted so that the arrow touches the rest under the plunger. If the rest is too flat, the arrow may move away from the button just prior to the shot, giving erratic groups.

Looking down from the top onto the rest and

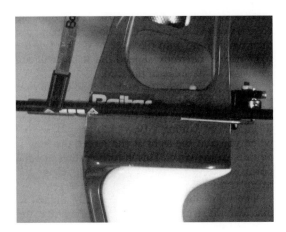

*With the cut rest fitted, the arrow is clear to leave the bow. The arrow touches the rest in-line with the plunger.*

button, the adjustment needs to be made so that you can only just see the end of the rest sticking out from the arrow. You may need to cut the end off the rest wire to shorten it, otherwise the rest can interfere with the arrow when it leaves the bow. Remember that you have to tune the bow first, so do not be too hasty cutting the end off. Once these two parameters have been set you need to make sure that the rest arm stays just below the plunger. If the rest catches on the underside of the plunger as it moves in towards the riser, as the arrow leaves the bow it will change the operation of the plunger action, making the groups larger.

## 8. Fit and Adjust the Sight

There are many types of sights, but in all cases they are there to hold the sight pin, with an adjuster mechanism so that it can be moved for the different distances and be adjustable from side to side. Sights come with assorted thicknesses of blocks to fit them to the riser, so when you fit the sight block to the bow, ensure that the screws you use are the correct thread and length for your riser. The depth of the sight bushings in the riser can be checked by putting the end of a match into the hole and marking the depth against the shaft of the match.

The screws need to be slightly shorter than the depth of the hole, so that they will not 'bottom

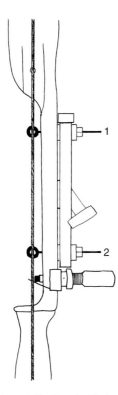

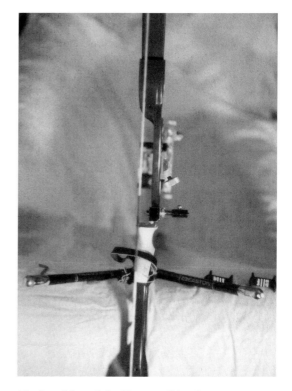

*When the sight is vertically aligned with the string, it will appear to be in the same position relative to the string when the sight is at the top or bottom of the track (positions 1 and 2).*

*The line of the card should run parallel to the string.*

out', which would cause the sight block to come loose and potentially damage the threads. The screws also need to have at least five threads protruding from the back of the sight block, or else they will strip the threads out of the riser. It is better to get longer screws and cut them down with a junior hacksaw, then smooth off the end with a fine file. Test the thread in a nut of the correct thread to check the finish before screwing it into the riser.

Once the sight has been fitted onto the bow it will need to be aligned vertically with the bow's true centre, so that as you move the sight block up and down the track for the different distances the sight pin will remain parallel to the centre line. There are two methods of doing this. One method is to move the sight to the top of the sight track and line the string up with the centre of the riser, adjust the pin so that the string cuts through its centre, then move the sight to the bottom of the track. If the track is parallel to the string the pin will remain centred on the string. If the pin does not remain

centred, the track's lateral position will need to be adjusted.

The other method is to attach a rectangle of card to the sight track so that the edge of the card runs parallel to the sight track and the card's opposite edge is situated in the sight window; the string can then be lined up with the edge of the card. If the sight track is correctly aligned the string will run parallel with the edge of the card.

Now that the sight has been aligned to the riser the sight ring can be set. The sight ring needs to be set in conjunction with the 'string picture' (*see* 'Principles of Aiming a Bow', Chapter 2), so that when you aim the sight at the target, the bow is pointing at the target. This in turn ensures that the power stroke of the limbs, when you release the string, is working directly towards the target.

The sight ring needs to be initially aligned so that, with the string running down the centre of the riser and the long rod, it appears to the left of the string. Everything should now be aligned with the centre of the target when you are aiming the bow.

*The sight should be aligned so that the bow is pointing directly to the target when the archer is looking at the target.*

*The sight should be aligned to keep the bow pointing at the target.*

## 9. Set the Nocking Point

The vertical placement of the nocking point is not critical at this time, as its placement will be adjusted during the initial tuning. Using a bracing height gauge, fit the nocking point approximately 5mm (0.2in) above the centre line of the rest and button. If you have had your own bow before, you can set it to the same height as the nocking point of your old bow.

Initially, a temporary nocking point can be made using insulation tape. Cut a 25mm (1in) length of tape, then cut it down the centre; this can be put on the string as top and bottom nocking points. However, even with a temporary nocking point the fit on the string needs to be correct. If it is too tight or too loose, 'initial tuning' will be less reliable. Too loose and the arrow will leave the string too early, too tight and the arrow will stay on the string too long, affecting the arrow's flight. This is more critical the lower the poundage, as with a tight fit you will find that the arrow will release from the string

*The bracing height gauge is clipped onto the string. When the height is being checked the limbs must not rest on anything; Roy Nash, GB. (Andrew Callaway)*

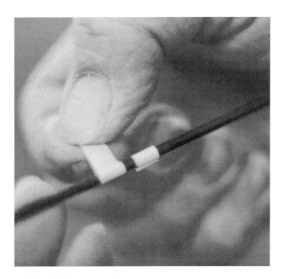

*Insulation tape can be used as a temporary nocking point. (Karen Henderson)*

*The nocks are shaped so that they clip onto the string.*

*When the string is tapped with two fingers the arrow should release from the string. (Karen Henderson)*

inconsistently, making the groups bigger than expected.

To test the nock fit on the string, place the arrow on the bowstring and on the arrow rest, against the plunger. Point the arrow at the ground just in front of you. Lightly tap the string with the side of your index finger. The arrow should stay on the string. Then tap the string firmly from about 3in distance; the arrow should now disconnect from the string. As this is a subjective test as to what is firm, you can double-check by looking closely at how the nock fits on the string at the nocking point.

The nock is designed so that the throat of the nock 'groove' is narrower than the base of the nock 'groove'. Therefore when the nock is fitted onto the nocking point and the nock is fully located on the string, you should be able to rotate the nock on the string a very small amount. (If you are using the Beiter nocking system, you will get the correct nock fit every time.)

## 10. Adjust the Arrow Alignment

The bow will now be set up so that everything is aligned along a centre line. You now need to set the arrow so that it shoots correctly from the bow.

As the fingers release the string, the string and the nock end of the arrow move out to the left, inducing the first bend into the arrow. As the string moves towards the bow and the arrow moves out of the bow, the arrow is still attached to the string.

As the arrow reflexes from the initial bend and the string crosses the centre line, the arrow flexes the opposite way to the initial bend.

To allow the arrow to exit the bow in-line with the centre line of the riser, the front of the arrow needs to be set in relation to the riser. This will be dynamically set during tuning and is only set statically at this time. To achieve this, initially the arrow needs to be set so that the arrow points left of the centre line (right of centre for left-hand archers).

To set the arrow, taking into account the length of the arrow that you are using, you will need to envisage the point of the arrow divided into three segments from the centre to the edge of the point. The centre of the point to the right-hand edge is divided into three. For arrows up to a length of 26½in the centre third is used for alignment; for arrows longer than 26½in the outer third is used. This means that for the different arrow lengths the arrow will be set in the bow at the same angle.

With the bow resting on the back of the chair, place your arrow into the bow. With the string running down the centre of the limbs, look down onto the arrow. The button now needs to be moved in or out so that the arrow sits out to the left of the string/centre line of the bow. (I find it helps if I keep my head steady by resting it against a

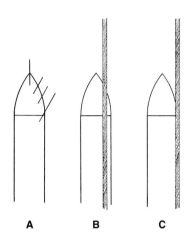

'A' – the point is divided into three parts; 'B' – aligning the arrow (up to 26.5in); 'C' – aligning the arrow (over 26.5in).

doorpost or on a broomstick with the bow in front of me; this makes it easier to see the alignment.) Setting the arrow at this angle will give it a good placement in the bow; although not crucial, if the arrow is placed close to the final setting, this will speed up the latter stages of tuning the bow.

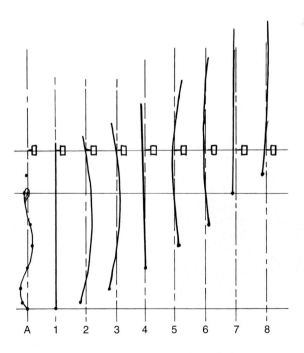

'A' shows the string's path on release. 1–8 show how the arrow bends as it leaves the bow.

*Point of release. (All photographs Werner Beiter)*

*As the fingers start to release the string, the nock end of the arrow moves to the left, initializing the first bend in the arrow.*

*As the release of the string continues, so the nock moves further out to the left.*

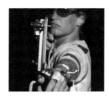

*Now that the string is fully released from the fingers, it starts moving towards the bow.*

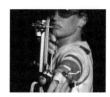

*As the arrow moves faster, so it tries to straighten out; at this point it is working against the button pressure.*

*As the arrow straightens out the string is pulled back to the centre line and the arrow starts to move away from the button.*

*The arrow comes fully away from the button and rest, and starts the second bend.*

*Both ends of the arrow move onto the centre line.*

*The back of the arrow crosses the centre line; the centre of the arrow is the maximum distance away from the riser.*

*The string moves back to the centre line as the arrow tries to straighten again.*

*The nock detaches from the string as the string and nock travel in the same direction.*

*The arrow continues to flex horizontally; the back of the arrow moves back in towards the riser.*

*The arrow has not yet started to spin and has just cleared the riser.*

*The riser and string remain in position.*

*The arrow just starts to spin.*

*The string is still moving slightly from left to right.*

*The arrow is just leaving the bottom of the picture and the hand has only just started to move back away from the bow.*

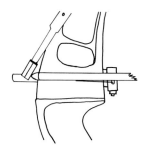 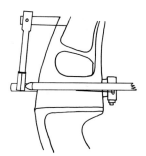

*The clicker should be set up as vertically as possible; a clicker extension may be required to enable you to do this.*

## 11. Set the Clicker

If you are using a clicker it can be fitted to the riser. If you have used one before you can set it to approximately the same distance as the clicker setting on your old bow. You need to set the clicker so that the clicker blade covers the shaft of the arrow and is as perpendicular to the arrow as possible. If the clicker is set at too much of an angle to the shaft, when the point of the arrow gets to the clicker blade the pressure of the clicker exerts a downward force on the arrow, causing the arrow to 'jump' as the clicker operates. With the clicker perpendicular to the arrow shaft, this down pressure is eliminated.

The final position of the clicker can only be determined when the bow is being shot.

## 12. Adjust the Stabilizers/Bow Balance

The stabilizers have a dual role on the bow. One is to counteract the torque induced into the bow through shooting, both from the mechanics of the bow itself and through the movement of the archer's body and interaction with the bow on the shot. The other it to set both the neutral balance and the dynamic (moving) balance of the bow.

*Neutral Balance*
Ideally, there should be a neutral balance with the centre of gravity at the pivot point (throat of the grip) at full draw. This means that when you are at

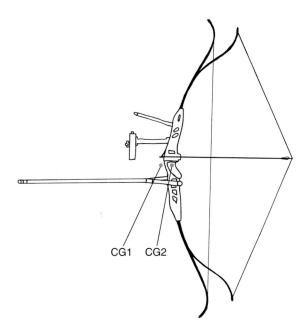

CG1  CG2

*As the bow is drawn back the centre of gravity (CG) moves from CG1 to CG2.*

*The bow is held upside-down and should be balanced on the long rod approximately 1in (25mm) in front of the riser; Elena Sadovnycha (Ukraine).*

full draw the stabilizers should not make the bow front or back heavy.

If the stabilizer settings make the bow front heavy, the bow will have to be 'held up' at full draw. As the grip is not held when you are shooting, the pressure that is holding the bow up tends to induce a raising motion to the bow when the string is released. As the long rod appears to 'flick up' on the shot from the upward force, the tendency is to put more weight on the long rod to 'hold it down'. What this achieves is that more 'holding up' force is required to compensate for the heavy front weight of the stabilization. Conversely, if stabilizer settings make the bow's back heavy, the bow will have to be 'held down', which will lead to the opposite effect.

The neutral balance point can be found by balancing the bow on the long rod, approximately 25mm (1in) in front of the riser. This is easier if the bow is held upside-down. Setting it at 1in in front of the riser takes into account that as the bow is drawn, the centre of gravity is moved back into the riser as the weight of the limbs is moved backwards.

### Dynamic Balance

Dynamic balance is concerned with the turning forces on the riser as the bow is shot. If the dynamic balance is correct, the turning forces above and below the pivot point, are equal. As the bow is shot, the riser will stay in the same vertical position. The dynamic balance and tiller are mutually influenced by each other, due to the fact that the turning forces on the riser about the pivot point are affected by the tiller setting. If the tiller is set correctly, the limbs will work in unison and make a balanced stroke. If, however, there is an imbalance in the

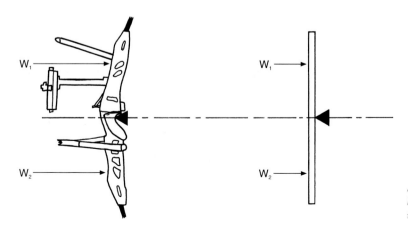

*When the mass of the bow above and below the pivot point is balanced (W1 and W2), the riser will remain stable as it is shot.*

*The bow should balance opposite the pivot point.*

power of the limbs it will cause one limb to work harder than the other, imparting a turning force into the riser. The mass of the riser either side of its pivot point also needs to be balanced. If the top of the riser is heavier than the bottom half, the disparity in mass will cause the top limb to work harder, causing a dynamic imbalance of the limbs' power stroke.

Therefore the riser must be balanced prior to tuning, otherwise the tiller will have to be re-adjusted to compensate for the dynamic imbalance causing the bow to be less efficient and more critical on the shot, because one force is compensating for the other.

The dynamic balance is easy to find – balance the bow on your finger opposite the pivot point (throat of the grip); the bow should balance evenly at this point. If this occurs, the mass above and below the pivot point is equal and neutral balance has been achieved.

You may need to adjust the stabilizer weights and extensions to realize both these points. There are many combinations of stabilizer set-up that will achieve the desired combined balance. Ideally, try to adjust the balance by putting the weight on the end of the stabilizers and not on the bow. For

anyone requiring a lighter set-up, there are combinations that will achieve neutral balance without a weight penalty.

Once you have adjusted the stabilizers so that you achieve both these balance points you will have a good starting point. Once you are shooting the bow, you will be able to make small adjustments to the stabilization. (For further details about neutral and dynamic balance, *see* Chapter 13, 'Tiller Tuning'.)

## Summary

If you are trying to tune your own bow or are helping someone else to tune theirs you should always carry out the above steps before shooting, otherwise you will be wasting your valuable shooting time by trying to tune a bow that is not properly set-up. Any time spent tuning will be wasted as you have to readjust the bow. Although it seems a lot to get through prior to shooting, once you have been through the procedure a few times you will soon be able to complete these settings quickly, with only a few minor adjustments.

The bow is now ready to shoot.

# Chapter 4

# Initial Tuning

Tuning is the term used in archery to describe the adjusting of the settings of the bow, the string and the arrows to allow them to perform efficiently in conjunction with each other and the archer. Initial tuning, the setting-up of the bow, must be carried out before more advanced dynamic tuning is undertaken. Initial tuning will bring the match between the bow, the arrow and the archer closer to the ideal.

If an untuned bow were to be put into a 'shooting machine' and set to shoot the bow, the machine would shoot every arrow in the same spot every time. This is because the set-up of the bow and the release will be exactly the same every time. Because the bow is working in combination with a human being, it needs to be adjusted to make it as 'forgiving' as possible. 'Forgiving' means that any shooting errors and erroneous movements by the archer will not be amplified by a poor set-up, enabling the bow to shoot the arrows into more consistent groups.

On a specific shot, if the bow is not well tuned, the arrow may hit the six ring. If, however, the bow is well tuned on a similar shot, the arrow may hit the nine or eight ring. For that reason, a tuned bow will shoot smaller groups than an untuned bow.

I have taken part in a number of archery workshops and coaching weekends over the years; my first step in evaluating an archer's shooting is to check his equipment set-up and tuning. I have found that many archers are let down by not having their bows set up correctly. This chapter will show you how to perform the initial tuning of your equipment to enable you to start shooting better groups. As with most steps in archery, it is quicker and easier if a routine is followed. In today's society, where leisure time is at a premium and for most archers their practice time is limited, the less time spent adjusting equipment, the more time spent shooting.

It is therefore important, before you carry out initial tuning, that your equipment is correctly set up, using the steps detailed in Chapter 3; otherwise, it will take much longer to get your bow shooting well.

## The Basics of Tuning

When you shoot an arrow out of your bow, the arrow must bend the correct amount from side to side but should have no vertical deflection.

If an arrow has too little bend, it is said to be 'stiff' and when shot will travel to the left of the

*Wietse van Alten shoots 6 Xs in Croatia at 70m.*

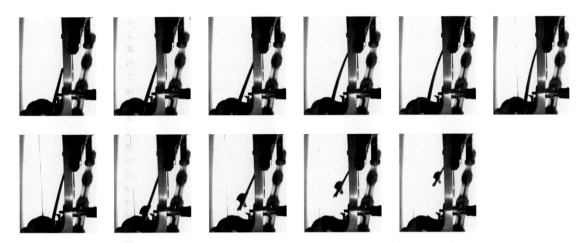

*As the arrow leaves the bow, it bends away from the bow but remains in the same plane. (Werner Beiter)*

centre line (for a right-handed archer). It will also be heavier and will reduce the range cast of the bow. If the arrow bends too much it is termed 'weak' and although it will be a fast arrow it will travel to the right of the centre line. If it is excessively weak, it may bend so much in the bow that it will break as it is shot. A weak arrow will make the scoring inconsistent, but, although it is not desirable, a stiff/heavy arrow can be set up to shoot and score reasonably well. Tuning is carried out so that the arrow is made to bend the correct amount and take a path to the target in line with the true centre of the bow.

There are two factors to consider when the arrow does not travel down the centre line to the target. These are the spine of the arrow and the bracing height. The bracing height determines the point at which the nock of the arrow becomes detached from the string. If the arrow detaches at the correct point, the nock and string part company smoothly, allowing the arrow to exit from the bow uninterrupted. If, however, the bracing height is too high or too low it will flick the nock as it leaves the string, causing its potentially central course to be altered. A low bracing height will cause the arrow to be flicked to the left of the

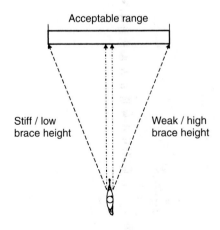

*If the arrows are stiff, they go to the left; if they are weak, they go to the right.*

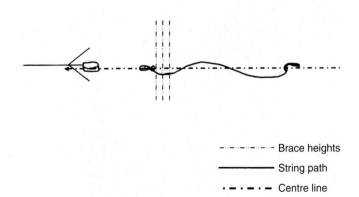

*The height of the string from the bow determines the point that the nock detaches from the string, adding twists will raise the bracing height.*

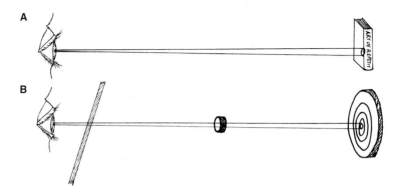

*The point of focus is the small area that the mind focuses on. (A): objects, string and sight, placed along the line between the eye and the point of focus are on the line of focus: (B).*

centre line, and a high bracing height will flick the arrow to the right of the centre line.

### Point of Focus

Understanding the eye and how vision works is one of the key points to shooting consistent groups. The eye can take in all of the visual information available, but it is the brain that interprets this

*At full draw, the string, sight and target should all fall along the line of focus.*

information. Once your brain is drawn to a significant visual point, you then focus on that point. The area of focus is very small and you will still be aware of the surrounding objects. If you want to refocus your concentration on another object you will have to change your 'point of focus'.

If you imagine a line drawn from your eye to the point of focus, anything placed along that 'line of focus' will stay within the area of concentration. The line of focus can best be described as a visual cone projecting from the eye to the object. For example, if you place a book at the other side of the room, as you look at it you can see all of it, but if you now focus on the top right-hand corner you will focus in detail on just a small area. By looking at objects over longer distances you will notice the same result. Even at longer distances, say 50–100m, you will still notice that the shift in the point of focus occurs over a small area. In archery you need to pick your point of focus. This tends to be called 'aiming', although aiming is not really the best term for pointing the bow at what you want to hit.

When tuning, you will need to pick a calm day with no wind, or carry out your tuning indoors. The point of focus when tuning will be the centre of the gold or a 1in spot made on the back of a target face with a dark marker pen. The spot is easy to focus on because it covers only a small area and a 1in spot at 18m is covered by the area of focus. If, however, you are using a target face to tune, you must look at the centre of the gold, as the gold is larger than the area of focus. The body will follow where the eye takes it. If the eye remains focused on one place and you focus your mind on that same spot the body will stay still. If your eye or mind wanders to another part of the target as you are about to shoot, the body will be induced to move, thus throwing the flight of the arrow towards where you are looking at or thinking about.

In setting up the bow (see Chapter 3), the string has been aligned through the true centre of the riser and the sight is set in place so that if you line the string up with the right-hand side of the sight ring and focus on the centre of the gold the bow will point along the same line. The string, sight and gold now all lie along the 'line of focus'. This enables the archer to concentrate on the point of focus while maintaining the alignment of the bow. If, however, the string is aligned with the bow outside the line of focus, the focus on the gold will be broken as the alignment is checked. If the alignment is not checked and the focus is maintained on the centre of the gold, variation in alignment will take place, leading to bigger groups.

The lining up of the string with the bow/sight as you shoot is referred to as the 'string picture'. Unless your string picture is a reasonably consistent alignment, tuning will be hard to determine. You have now got to the stage where you will be looking at the centre of the target and pointing the bow at it. Now you need the arrow to impact on the centre of the target.

## Method of Initial Tuning

I use the 'bare shaft' method for the initial tuning of any bow. This involves shooting four arrows that are fletched and at least two arrows that have had the fletchings removed (therefore they are bare shafts). The purpose of the fletchings is to spin the arrow to give it a more stable flight and also to straighten the rear of the arrow if it has been launched out of the bow at an angle from the axis. Bare shafts, not having any fletchings, will continue in the direction they have been originally shot. This means that if the fletched arrows and the bare shafts impact in the same place in the target, the fletchings are working only to rotate the arrows and not to alter their trajectory. This is what we are looking for at the completion of the initial tuning phase. Shooting two or more bare shafts ensures that you are not tuning with a damaged arrow. If both bare shafts are in good condition they will impact at the same point in the target. If you use two shafts and they impact in significantly different areas of the target, a third will have to be used to find the matched serviceable shafts.

The tuning schedule enables you to get the bare

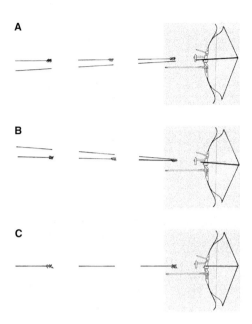

*(A) With the nocking point set high, the bare shaft impacts the boss lower than the fletched group. (B) With the nocking point set low, the bare shaft impacts about the fletched group. (C) With the nocking point set in the correct position, the bare shaft impact on the boss level with the fletched group.*

shaft and fletched arrows in the best relationship to each other. Throughout the schedule we will be looking at the group size, its position and the relationship of the bare shafts to the group. The group size will depend on your level of shooting; if your group size is 2ft or 6in at 18m, this is the size of your group. If your group is 2ft in diameter and your bare shafts fall within this area, you will have realized the requirements of initial tuning. The accuracy of your tuning will be dependent on your level of shooting, but the better you tune the bow, the better your groups. The smaller your group sizes, the finer the adjustment to the tuning. Tuning is a continual process of improvement.

Throughout this tuning schedule the sight must only be moved vertically to compensate for different distances; adjustment to the arrow's deflection left and right must be adjusted by tuning. The steps for initial tuning are explained in detail below.

1. Adjust the button pressure.
2. Adjust the nocking point.
3. Match the arrow's spine to the bow.
4. Adjust the equipment to the best match of the arrow and the bow.

## 1. Adjust the Button Pressure

Start your tuning at 18m, or shorter if that feels more comfortable. Using your fletched arrows only, sight on the gold and shoot your arrows. If the arrows go to the left of the gold, reduce the plunger pressure, making the spring pressure lighter. If the arrows go to the right of the gold increase the plunger pressure, making the spring pressure stiffer. I always rationalize these adjustments by visualizing the increase in the button pressure pushing the arrow to the left and the decrease in button pressure letting the arrow come back to the right. There is a limit to how light you can make the button at this point. If you make it too light the arrow's weight will overcome the spring pressure and will push the plunger back into the button. Once the group is roughly centred on the gold or as near as you can get to it, you can move onto the next stage. Do not spend too much time making fine adjustment to centre the group at this point as this will be carried out later.

## 2. Adjust the Nocking Point

This is carried out to ensure that any bend imparted to the arrow is on a horizontal plane. With the target at the same distance, shoot your fletched and bare-shafted arrows in a random order, just as you pull them from the quiver. This randomness will help to give a truer reflection of how the arrows come out of the bow – otherwise, archers tend to shoot the fletched arrows first, meaning that they

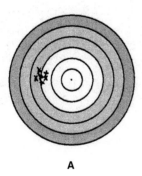

A

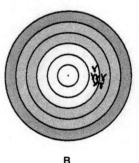

B

*(A) With the fletched group left of the gold decrease the button spring tension. (B) With the fletched arrows impacting right of the gold increase the button pressure.*

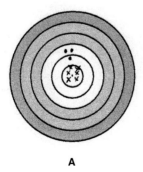

A

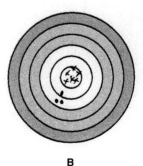

B

*(A) With the bare shaft impacting above the fletched group raise the nocking point. (B) With the bare shaft impacting below the fletched group lower the nocking point.*

are slightly tired when they come to shoot the bare shafts, which can lead to inaccurate data.

At this point, all we are looking at is whether the bare shafts are going higher or lower than the fletched arrow group. If the bare shafts go higher, it indicates that the nocking point is too low and needs to be raised; conversely, if the bare shafts go lower than the fletched arrow group the nocking point is too high and will need to be moved down.

As the flight of the bare shaft is not being corrected by the fletchings it will continue in the direction that it is launched, hence if the nocking point is high on the string the arrow will be pointing down and will go below the fletched group. If you are using a temporary nocking point it can be easily moved. Once you have adjusted the nocking point so that the bare shafts impact at the same level as the fletched group, you may need to adjust the button pressure again to get the centre of the fletched arrow group around the gold again.

### 3. Match the Arrow's Spine to the Bow

Now that the arrows are leaving the bow with only a horizontal bend, you can match the arrow spine to the bow. When this is completed, the bare-shafted arrows and the fletched arrows will be in the same group, indicating that the fletchings are only spinning the arrows and not stabilizing their course, thus giving you a good initial tune.

Continue to shoot at a distance of 18m. Now that the bare-shafted arrows are level with the group, you will be able to see whether the bare shafts are right or left of the group. If the bare shafts are to the left of the fletched group this indicates

**Moving the Nocking Point**

If you are using a permanent nocking point you can move the centre serving using the square-edged part of a multi-knife or the edge of your bracing height gauge. Care needs to be taken as some of the bracing height gauges have quite sharp edges. Do not be concerned about a little damage to the serving, as once you have finished adjusting the tuning the centre serving can be replaced.

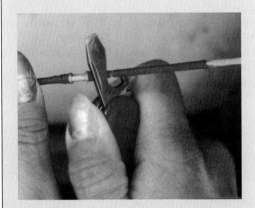

*The serving can be 'walked up' the string to move the nocking point to the correct position.*

that the arrows are stiff and do not bend enough, and/or that the bracing height is too low. If they are to the right of the fletched group it indicates that the arrows are weak and bending too much and/or

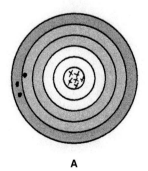

**A**

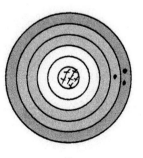

**B**

*(A) With the bare shafts left of the group, it indicates that the shafts are stiff or that the brace height may be a little low. (B) With the bare shafts right of the group, the shafts may be a little weak or the brace height set too high.*

the bracing height is too high. Note that if an arrow's spine shows stiff or weak, adjusting the button will not change this. The button compensates for an arrow's spine that is not fully matched to the bow, but it does not actually alter the spine. That can only be done by adjusting the equipment's dynamics.

Adjustments can now be made to the bow and the arrows to match them to each other.

*Adjusting the Bow*
Major adjustments to match the bow and arrows are made by adjusting the bow.

**Changing the Poundage** This will make the biggest adjustment to the arrow's spine. Increasing the poundage will make the arrow weaker, but it will also increase the amount of weight on the fingers, which may damage your style. Decreasing the poundage will make the arrow stiffer, but the lighter you make the bow the slower the arrow will fly, which will lower the cast (the distance the arrow flies) of the bow.

**Adjusting the Bracing Height** As you have already adjusted the bow to the manufacturer's

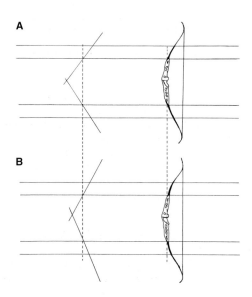

*Limb geometry. (A) With the limbs set to the lightest setting the cross point of the line of the limbs is further in front of the riser, making it more stable. (B) As the bow's weight is increased the bow becomes less stable.*

suggested mid-range, raising or lowering it will make a difference to the position and size of the group. The better the nock detachment, the smaller the group and the more forgiving the shot. Once I have set my bow to the correct bracing height, shooting 60 arrows at a 40cm face at 18 metres. An 18m FITA (International Archery Federation – the worldwide governing body for archery), I would expect to score 580+ out of a possible 600, but if I lower my bracing height by 3mm (0.2in) the score will drop below 570, however well I try to shoot. This is quite a drop at this level of shooting. If it is raised by 3mm, I will still shoot about 580 but it will not be quite as forgiving and I will have to work harder to maintain the score.

**Changing the Composition of the String** More strands in the string will make it heavier, potentially making the bow work slower and increasing the arrow's stiffness. I say 'potentially', as increasing the number of strands can actually increase the arrow's speed slightly, as the efficiency of the bow is optimized, but any further increase will then slow the arrow speed as the limbs have to move the arrow plus the increased mass of the string. Reducing the amount of strands will make the bow work faster, weakening the arrow. However, if there are too few strands, the shot will become erratic and may also damage the bow. Further minor adjustments to the string can be made by changing the weight of the serving material and the length of the servings.

*Adjusting the Arrow*
There are limited options available to adjust the spine of an arrow, as can be seen below (see also Chapter 10).

**Making the Shaft Shorter or Stiffer** The shorter a shaft is made, the stiffer it will become, but then you are limited by draw length. It is better to buy arrows that are a little longer than you require as they then can be trimmed down when tuning the bow. As you want at least 1½in in front of the button this limits you to cutting 1½in from the arrow, which will only give you a fine adjustment. Making the arrow too short moves the button position on the shaft at full draw away from the nodal point of the shaft. This makes the set-up less forgiving as the plunger movement is increased on the initial release of the string.

**Changing the Point Weight** (Note that not all arrows can have the point weight changed.)

**Adjustment Factors**

| Adjustment | Advantage | Disadvantage |
|---|---|---|
| Increasing poundage | Makes the arrow travel faster so that it is less affected by the weather and maintains the down-range velocity. | May increase the poundage past the level that the archer can cope with, leading to poor style and possible injuries. Increasing the poundage adversely changes the geometry of the limbs in the riser making the bow less stable. |
| Decreasing poundage | The bow weight may be more controllable if it was set at the archer's previous upper limit of strength. Improves the geometry of the limbs in the riser, making the bow more stable. | Reduces the arrow's speed, lowering the sight marks and giving bigger groups in inclement weather. |
| Increasing string strands | Makes the bow more forgiving. | Slows the arrow flight. Will also increase the diameter of the string, which can lead to a less positive finger position on the first joint of the drawing fingers. |
| Decreasing string strands | Makes the bow work faster, increasing arrow speed. The thinner diameter of the string may lead to a more consistent placing on the draw fingers. | Makes the bow more crucial to the shot. |
| Increasing point weight | Moves the FOC towards the point, helping to stabilize the arrow's flight. | Lowers the arrow's speed, decreasing the cast. |
| Decreasing point weight | Increases arrow speed, increasing the bow's cast. | Makes the arrows less stable, leading to bigger groups. |
| Shortening arrow | Matches the arrow to the bow better. Less shaft to be affected by shear force when shooting in windy conditions. | Moves the point of the arrow closer to the button, with 1½in in front of the button being optimum; less is not desirable |

Increasing the point weight will make the arrow's spine weaker, but the more weight you add to the point the heavier it will become and the slower it will fly. In decreasing the point weight, you are limited by the manufacturer's recommendations, as an arrow that does not have enough weight in the point becomes unstable, which will result in bigger groups. The arrow's specifications will usually give recommended point weights. It is best not to go much lighter than the recommendation as an arrow needs to have the centre of gravity forward of centre in the shaft (known as FOC: Forward of Centre). The analogy commonly used to illustrate this is trying to throw a piece of string. With no weight on it, the string is difficult to throw accurately or to any great distance. However, tie a small weight on the front of the string and accuracy and distance are improved. Tie a big weight to the front and the string again becomes unwieldy, with the distance once again reduced. Using different types of fletch-ings and nocks can also produce small differences in an arrow's spine characteristics.

Only small variations in the arrow's spine can be accomplished by making adjustments to the arrow; if greater adjustments are needed it will be necessary to purchase another set of arrows of a different spine. This is why adjusting the arrow is left to the final part of the initial tuning.

*4. Adjust the Equipment to the Best Match of the Arrow and the Bow*

For each adjustment you make, and you should only make one adjustment at a time, shoot to see the degree to which each adjustment influences the position of the bare shaft to the group. While you are making these adjustments, the fletched group may move to the side of the gold; you will need to move it back to the centre by making adjustments to the button pressure. The sight's lateral position should not be moved from the initial set-up position. The nocking point may also need to be adjusted to maintain the bare shafts' level position with the fletched group. Once the bare-shafted group is reasonably close to the fletched group at 18m, then move to 30m, which will better show the deviation of trajectory between the fletched and unfletched arrows. I feel that the longest distance to carry out accurate bare-shaft tuning is 30m; longer than 30m and the bare shaft can give erroneous.

If the bare shafts land to the left of the group (stiff), the options available are:

- Increase the poundage while maintaining the tiller adjustment.
- Increase the bracing height. (If it does not alter the position of the bare shaft, return it to the previous setting.)
- Decrease the amount of strands in the string.
- Increase the point weight.
- Maintain/increase arrow length – some nocks types and fit make the arrow slightly longer.

If the bare shafts land to the right of the group (weak), the options available are:

- Decrease the poundage while maintaining the tiller adjustment.
- Decrease the bracing height. (If it does not alter the position of the bare shaft, return it to the previous setting.)
- Increase the amount of strands in the string.
- Decrease point weight.
- Shorten the arrow's length (refer to Chapter 10 before cutting).

## Summary

Depending on the level of shooting you are at and the match of the equipment you are using, you may not be able to adjust the set-up enough to make the bare shaft enter the middle of the fletched group. The steps taken in initial tuning are designed to make the best of the equipment that you have. The closest that you can get the bare shafts to the fletched group at this stage of tuning is acceptable, and will enable you to shoot the equipment you have well.

If you want the tuning to be more accurate at this point, the next step could be to change the limbs or arrows. Increasing the poundage of the bow may not be an option, therefore you may have to find a better match of arrow spine to your current bow set-up. But before you rush out and buy new equipment first read the chapters on arrow selection (Chapter 10) and fine-tuning the bow (Chapter 13). There are other methods of tuning the bow that can be used, but I find that the bare-shaft method is quick and reliable and gives good results. Parts of the other methods of tuning are utilized in Chapter 11, 'Making Bowstrings'.

Now that you have completed the initial tuning you can get on with your shooting. Depending how close the match of your equipment is, you can now move the sight windage in or out as required to get the arrows to hit the centre of the target.

# Chapter 5

# The Biomechanics of Shooting

Whenever you use the body to carry out a task, there are a number of ways in which any particular task can be done. For example, if you are carrying a heavy bag, you could carry it with your arm held out to the side, although this would take great strength and cause imbalance. If you carry the same bag but with your arm bent by your side, this would be easier but your arm would still tire out. If, however, you hold the arm carrying the bag straight with the inside of the wrist towards the body, you will be able to carry the bag much further as you are using your body more efficiently. This is because the weight is carried on the shoulder socket and ligaments of the arm. The only muscles involved are the hand muscles gripping the bag. Furthermore, if the bag's handle is designed ergonomically, the hand will tire less quickly. However, bag handles would have to come in a range of sizes to match the range of hand sizes. You could of course, put the contents of the bag in a rucksack and carry it on your back. This is even more efficient, although the legs and back still take the same load as carrying it with your arms. The weight is now mainly supported by the backbone and leg bones in compression, with the associated muscles supporting the skeletal frame in an upright position.

Remember:

- Small muscles tire more quickly and are not as strong as big muscles; the skeletal frame can take more load when used efficiently and therefore less muscle is involved, allowing the task to be carried out for a longer duration.
- Shooting form and style is about using the body efficiently, allowing the archer to perform every shot consistently with little fatigue.

In this chapter, we will look at various aspects of the body, its alignment, operation and interface with the equipment.

*This is not an efficient way to carry a load, as many muscles are involved and so you will tire easily.*

*Fewer muscles are involved, but there is a strain on the wrists.*

*With the back of the hand and fingers in line with the arms, very few muscles are involved and the load can be carried for longer without tiring.*

## Position of the Feet

The rules of the sport state that your feet must be astride the shooting line – lining up your toes with the target is a good start. As you progress and your shooting improves, the position, stability and placement of your feet can be modified to suit your particular requirements. When you stand astride the line, the right foot can be brought closer to the line and the left foot closer to the target at about a shoulder-width apart. This will position you slightly closer to the target. This can give you a good psychological advantage (especially when shooting at 18m). The feet need to be kept facing forward from the body, as this ensures that the feet give the body maximum stability.

The weight distribution between the heel and toes needs to be approximately 70 per cent on the front of the foot and 30 per cent on the heel. If there is too much weight on the heel you will not able to regulate your balance. If you deliberately put your weight on the heel area, you will be able to feel the instability resulting from the body's weight being transferred directly to the heel. Fewer muscles are involved in holding the body upright, so there is less control. If you now transfer more weight onto the front of the foot you will feel the muscles in the front of the leg, ankle and foot coming into play. Place too much weight on the front of the foot and you will become unstable again.

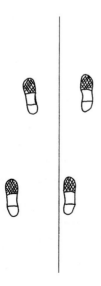

*Standing slightly closer to the target can give a psychological advantage.*

### Shoes

A much neglected area of standing on the line is what you are wearing on your feet. A few years ago, I was told a story about an archer from Europe. He did not have much money but was determined to shoot well. He spent his money on equipment and made it to the top with good international results. He was then awarded a reasonable amount of money to help further his development. Shortly after this, his score level dropped and he and his coach spent months working on technique, style and equipment but with no change to the results. After a lot of work, they found the explanation for the low scores. Now that he had more money available he had bought a good, comfortable pair of trainers in which to shoot. These new trainers had soft soles and produced an instability in his stance that caused the loss of results.

If you try standing on your bed, you will find that you become less stable and it can become quite tiring standing on a soft surface.

Your footwear for shooting should therefore have a firm, flat base, with the laces tied tightly to help support the foot. Some top archers shoot in footwear that supports the ankle as well, increasing stability. Running shoes are designed for running and have the toes and heels angled to help you run. This decreases the area of shoe in contact with the ground, making you more unstable. Tennis shoes tend to be flatter with a firm base. Some rifle shooters wear special shoes that have a flat base and a thicker sole on the outside to help support the foot for greater stability. Although the weight should be on the front of the foot it needs to be kept steady during the shot. There is a tendency to keep increasing the weight on the front of the foot, leading to a forward overbalance. A simple way to improve the stability of the shot is to shoot from a balance platform. This can easily be made by using a skateboard with the wheels taped so that it will not roll, or by taking a piece of 2in by 3in baton and attaching a piece of plywood centrally over it, which is wide enough to stand on. Using either of these, you can carry out the shot and maintain your shooting position while standing on the platform. This is a good exercise to help maintain your centre of gravity throughout the shot.

## Alignment of the Body

To get the body into a position to shoot is quite simple. Stand astride the shooting line facing forwards with your arms at your sides. Keeping the

*Position one: relaxed the arms by the side of your body. (Karen Henderson)*

*Position two: raise the arms with the palms facing forwards, leaving the shoulders down and relaxed. (Karen Henderson)*

*Position three: turn the head and fold the right arm to the face; this will give you a good position for shooting. (Karen Henderson)*

shoulders in place, raise your arms to the side with your palms facing forward, turn your head to the target, bend the right arm towards the face placing the hand under the chin. This is the shooting position.

The torso needs to be kept upright with the backbone straight; the natural tendency is to lean back away from the target. This puts an unwanted curve into the spine that can lead to damage as the discs between the vertebrae are squeezed on one side. Leaning away from the target also makes the clearance of the string from the chest harder to achieve. This usually stems from the initial days of starting to shoot, as it is quite natural to lean away from a lifted weight. If not corrected, it can be compounded if a bow that is too heavy or has too many stabilizer weights is later used.

This alignment of the shoulders and arms must be kept in the same relationship, whatever the distance and angle of the target. A change of angle is accomplished by inclining the hips. Many archers struggle with the 18m three-spot vertical faces, finding that their scores drop from shooting the single full 18m face. This is usually because the alignment between the arms and shoulders differs with the different angles of the target faces and the change in the dynamics of the bow which results.

## The Alignment of the Feet

Finding a better alignment of the feet in relation to the target can be carried out once you are shooting reasonably consistently and with confidence (all in the red at 18m). A closed stance describes the position of the feet when a line drawn from toe to toe lines up with the centre of the target. I believe that this is the best way to start as it encourages the

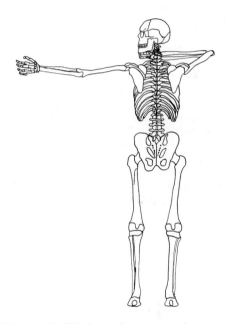

*The spine should be kept in line to prevent damage to the discs.*

### Becoming Aware of Body Alignment

To become more aware of body alignment, try shooting with the feet together, touching heel and toe. This exercise will allow you to feel your balance better, as this foot position will make you more aware of your centre of gravity. Once you have feel of your body alignment, return to a wider foot base once more.

*The string must be clear of the chest at full draw, as any deflection of the string will cause inconsistent groups.*

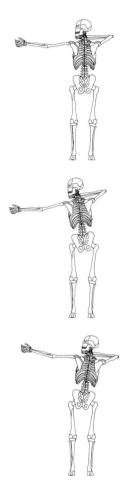

*To shoot at different distances the bow needs to be at different angles. This is achieved by keeping the spine alignment while changing the angle of the hips.*

rest of the body to take their proper alignments and allows for better progression in shooting. An open stance describes the foot position when a line drawn from toe to toe would pass the target to the left; how far to the left would depend on how open the stance is. You may find that when you shoot, every time you come to the line the arrows either go to the left or right of the previous shot. This can be caused by a different alignment of the feet every time you come to the line. This can be alleviated by putting down foot markers or pins for outside, or insulation tape stuck to the floor when you are inside. From this, you will see that the position of the group can be adjusted just by moving the feet to a slightly more open or closed position.

I believe it is best to find your body's natural alignment. If you have a very open stance, you need to twist the legs and lower the torso to make the top body alignment correct. This style is advocated by some coaches, as the twisting action can help to stabilize the body. Unfortunately, as the archer gets tired the twist 'unwinds' during the shot, leading to wider groups.

### Finding your Natural Alignment
Practising shooting with your eyes closed will help you to discover your natural alignment. Once you have discovered your natural alignment, you will find that your shooting becomes more consistent

and you will be able to maintain this consistency for longer.

To shoot with your eyes closed, carry out your draw as normal with your eyes open, look at the target concentrating on your point of focus, close your eyes and shoot the arrow. Do this first at a distance that you are comfortable with. Even if this means moving to a distance of 3m at first, you will find that you will soon become confident, as it is a lot easier than it seems. Closed-eye shooting is used for other aspects of shooting and training and will be referred to and used again.

Once you are used to closed-eyes shooting, move to a slightly longer distance. As you close your eyes, imagine that you can still see the sight on the target. As you shoot, you will find that the arrows may tend to group to one side of the gold. Now make small adjustments to your feet's alignment with the target, opening or closing the stances to realign the group in the target centre. The more consistent your shooting, the closer you will get to the ideal. When you are using your natural alignment with the target, even as you get tired, you will remain in line with the target maintaining your consistency.

## The Bow Hand and Arm

When the bow is drawn and shot, the bow is pulled into the 'V' made between the thumb and index finger. The pressure the hand imparts to the bow as it is drawn keeps the bow in place. As the bow is drawn back the bow hand needs to be kept relaxed, which should be consistently achievable shot after shot, as it is easier to keep the hand relaxed rather than at a fixed tension. If there is tension in the bow hand, either induced by trying to grip the bow or through raising the wrist, it will alter the dynamics of the bow as it is shot. Changing the wrist position up and down will make the group taller because as you change the pressure points on the grip this alters the bow's pivot point. If, however, you keep the wrist relaxed and the pressure behind the bow, the pivot point will remain consistent and so will the groups. Do what is more repeatable. If the hand 'grips' the bow this can lead to wider groups as varying tensions in the hand's grip and will impart a twist into the alignment.

To make a good consistent hand position, in the pre-draw with a little tension on the string, slide the hand up to the throat of the grip and then let it relax down onto the grip. The tension in the pre-draw needs to be enough to keep the hand in place; this relaxed hand position needs to be maintained until the arrow has hit the target. When looking at top archers shooting it appears that the wrist of the bow arm flicks the bow forward as the arrow leaves the bow. This is not the case. The hand is pulled forward by the finger sling as the bow leaves the hand.

The reason for maintaining the relaxed hand position until the arrow hits the target is to ensure that the hand and arm stay steady. One of the brain's

*Olena Sadovnycha at the 2000 Olympics, in a classic closed stance.*

*At full draw, the hand should still be relaxed into the grip; Natalia Nasaridze (Turkey).*

*At full draw, the hand is relaxed into the grip. W. Null. (Andrew Callaway)*

*As the arrow is shot from the bow the hand and arm remains in the same position. (Andrew Callaway)*

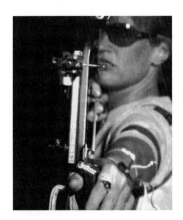

*The bow hand relaxed at full draw. (Werner Beiter)*

*The bow hand is in the same position after the arrow has left the string. (Werner Beiter)*

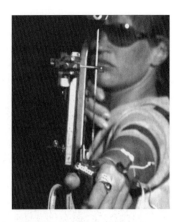

*The hand relaxes as the forward movement of the bow relieves the pressure on it. (Werner Beiter)*

specialties is to anticipate the next required movement, especially with repetitious movements. If you allow it to, the brain will have you finishing the shot before you have shot it. The muscles will fractionally start to relax just prior to the shot. In mild cases the groups will be bigger and variable; with more extreme cases the body position will collapse on the shot. To ensure that you are in control of your movements, finish the shot when the arrow hits the target at whatever distance you are shooting, even 90m. To that end, the time interval between the clicker going and the arrow hitting the target should be maintained at whatever distance you shoot. This will give you a reliable consistency as your bow arm will stay in place on all your shots, whatever the distance.

The bow arm needs to be held straight, with the bones of the upper and lower arm aligned with the shoulders. Owing to the physical differences between people, the arms will take on different shapes, bending up, down and in towards the string. The best way to explain the position of the arm is to compare it to leaning casually against a wall, holding yourself off with your arm. When doing this, you will naturally keep the arm aligned as this is less fatiguing. The pressure to keep you away from the wall comes from the shoulder girdle. When the arm is straight, the bones pressing end to end support the arm and the shoulder muscles hardly need to work as they press towards the wall to support the body. When at full draw, the arm should be used in the same manner, with the bone alignment holding the bow away from the body and the shoulder girdle pressing the bow towards the target.

*The position of the bow arm needs to be in a similar extension as when leaning against a wall. (Karen Henderson)*

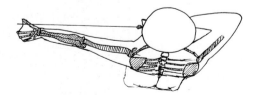

*With the arm and shoulder aligned, the bone structure takes the weight of the draw.*

*Forward Pressure*

The importance of maintaining the forward pressure on the bow throughout the shot becomes more apparent when we consider Sir Isaac Newton's third law of motion, that for every action there is an equal and opposite reaction.

When a bullet is fired from a gun equal and opposite forces are exerted on the bullet and the gun. They will move in accordance with Newton's second law of motion: 'The rate of change of momentum of a body is proportional to the applied forces and takes place in the direction in which the force acts.' They acquire equal and opposite momenta. The backward momentum of the gun is shown in the gun's recoil. The momentum is a vector quantity that has direction and magnitude. The momenta of the gun and bullet are conserved in a closed system. The gun and the bullet are motionless before firing so the momentum sums to zero as the bullet leaves the gun:

$$\text{mass of bullet} \times \text{muzzle velocity}$$
$$= \text{mass of gun} \times \text{recoil velocity}$$

The differences of mass between the bullet and gun take into account the differences of velocity of the two parts.

When shooting a bow there are a few more factors to consider but the effects are the same. During the shot, whilst the arrow is attached to the string the bow recoils towards the archer. As the string is released and the arrow is driven out of the bow, the riser comes back (recoil) towards the archer. This is why the forward pressure of the bow arm is so important.

The additional factors involved are that the string has mass which is added to the mass of the arrow being shot, therefore the heavier the string, the slower the shot and the stiffer the arrow. Also, the limbs have mass, which moves forward as the string is released, adding to the forward mass. This forward limb mass is proportional to how much of the limbs moves; the tips of the limbs move the most, with the base of the limbs being stationary and being considered as part of the riser reaction mass. This is one of the reasons why limbs are made with light materials, so as to reduce mass. In reducing mass, they also accelerate more quickly:

$$(\text{mass of arrow} \times \text{exit velocity})$$
$$+ (\text{mass of string} \times \text{forward velocity})$$
$$+ (\text{mass of moving limb} \times \text{forward velocity})$$
$$= (\text{mass of riser and fittings} \times \text{recoil velocity})$$

This recoil can only be seen when viewed in slow motion from a high-speed video.

It is the forward momentum of the limb and string once the arrow has become detached from the string, combined with the forward pressure from the bow arm, that imparts the forward motion of the bow after the shot. Therefore you can see that by altering the mass of any of the parts, it will consequently alter the velocity of the other parts. This can be utilized when fine-tuning the bow.

*Finger Placement*

The placement of the string in the first joint of the fingers has already been dealt with in Chapter 2, and keeping the forearm of the draw arm relaxed as though cords or chains were attaching the finger hooks to the elbow. The distance of finger placement above and below the arrow must remain consistent to ensure that the angle of the limbs and the pressure on them is also consistent, keeping the vertical group tighter. I place my fingers on the string so that the index finger is just touching the arrow and the middle finger is below the nock, but not quite touching. As the string is drawn back, the fingers are lightly pressed against the nock with the top finger touching slightly harder than the middle finger. This keeps the angle at the centre of the string as small as possible. The fingers touching the nock ensures that the placement on the string is consistent.

The bow's vertical alignment is mainly dependent on the draw hand keeping the string vertical. With the bow hand relaxed and the bow arm resisting forwards, any alteration to the bowstring's vertical alignment will result in an inclination of the

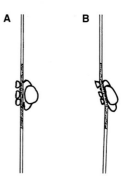

*(A) The string should be drawn back, maintaining its vertical alignment. (B) If torque is induced into the string, the riser will twist in the hand.*

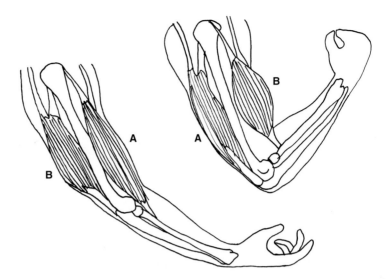

*The muscle that initiates the reverse movement of the working muscle is the known as the antagonistic muscle.*

riser. If the bow hand is used to try to compensate for the torque placed on the string by the draw hand, two unwanted outcomes will occur: first, that the counter-torque between the bow and the draw hand will result in a twist in the vertical alignment of the string, inducing inconsistent horizontal oscillations as the string is released; and, second, that on the release of the string the torque in the bow hand will assert itself unhindered, rotating the riser as it is shot. Both of these contribute to an increase in group size. As you draw the bow, feel the vertical alignment of the string in the fingers and try to maintain it throughout the draw and loose. This will enable you to maintain the vertical alignment of the riser throughout the shot, leading to more consistent groups.

### Drawing the Bow

Bringing the string to the face prior to the shot needs to be carried out consistently, smoothly and simply. According to Confucius: 'When you carry something heavy, carry it as though it is light. If you carry something light, carry it as though it is heavy.' This may seem like odd advice, but when you look at how the muscles work it makes sense. Virtually all the muscles in the body are 'paired', which means that there is one muscle or group of muscles to move, for instance the arm in one direction, and then there is the paired set to move the arm in the opposite direction. The opposite muscle to the one doing the work is called the antagonistic muscle.

When you follow Confucius's advice of lifting a

heavy object as though it is light, it means that you should only bring the muscles required to lift the object into operation, keeping the antagonistic muscles relaxed. For example, if you are going to lift an object weighing 4kg, the muscles required to do this will have to lift 4kg plus the weight of the arm, approximately 1kg, so about 5kg in total. If, however, you tense all your arm muscles prior to lifting the 4kg weight, you will make the antagonistic muscles start working, thus exerting a force of 1kg against the working muscle, so the working muscle will now have to move 6kg and will tire more quickly.

When drawing the bow you need to use the working muscles, while keeping the antagonistic muscles relaxed. In the pre-draw position your bow arm will be straight, and the drawing arm and shoulder will be forward to hold the string, with the forearm and wrist relaxed and the fingers hooked onto the string. The bow then needs to be lifted so that the bow arm is parallel to the ground.

The string is then drawn straight back to the face, by bringing the drawing shoulder back into line and rotating the upper arm of the drawing arm back and round using the shoulder (scapula) and back muscles. It is important that the draw shoulder is brought back into alignment with the bow arm and front shoulder, as there can be a tendency to leave it in the forward position. This draw is usually known as the 'T' draw; the benefit to this type of draw is that it is simple and helps to ensure that the muscles are loaded in the same way and therefore release in the same way.

*The hand reaches forward to place the fingers on the string, bringing the shoulder with it. (Karen Henderson)*

*With a little tension on the bow, the bow hand is settled into the grip. (Karen Henderson)*

*As the bow is drawn, the front arm is raised and the right shoulder starts to rotate back into position. (Karen Henderson)*

*With the string most of the way back, the right shoulder is almost in the correct position. (Karen Henderson)*

*At full draw, the right shoulder forms a line through the shoulders and front arm. (Karen Henderson)*

From the start of the 'T' part of the draw to full draw you are loading the muscles that you are going to release with. There are at least six sets of muscles in the back that are used to draw the bow. If you either have a long pre-draw or carry out a rotation of the shoulder joints near to full draw you will bring the load onto the muscles out of line with the release, giving you a less consistent release. Another disadvantage of big alignment adjustments at full draw is that it can lead to unwanted tension building up in the shoulder and neck muscles and possible strains to joints, as at full draw you will have the full pressure of your bow's weight through the torso.

Whilst drawing the bow, the draw hand needs to follow the same path every time to the full draw position. A simple way of making sure that the draw starts the same every time is to touch the fingers of

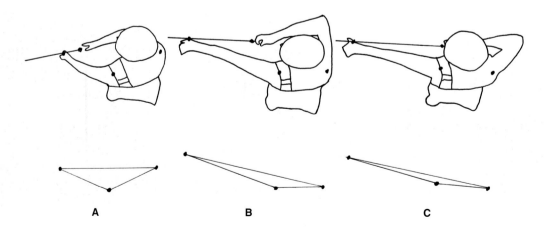

*(A) To put the fingers on the string, the right shoulder comes forward. (B) As the bow is drawn, the shoulder comes back into line. (C) At full draw, the shoulders are properly aligned.*

the draw hand against the inner arm of the bow arm. This will ensure that the angle of the shoulders and the relationship between the angle of both arms are consistent at the start of every shot, helping to make sure that the muscles are loaded in the same pattern every time.

There are several reasons for wanting to utilize primarily the back muscles to draw the bow. Back muscles are bigger, therefore they will sustain the shooting for longer than the arm muscle, but the main reason is to bring the 'draw force line' behind the arrow, so that on releasing the string the arrow can only go directly towards the target.

When seen from the side, the draw force line is the alignment and balance of forces between the elbow of the draw arm and the hand of the bow arm connected through the equipment. The hand of the bow arm is pressing towards the target and the elbow of the draw is arm moving away from the target. When they are correct, the axis of the arrow will line up with the centre of the target to the front and through the arm/elbow to the rear.

Ideally, if the line of the arrow is extended away from the target, the line would exit through the back/centre of the elbow when seen from the side. The ratio of length between your upper and lower arm will determine how close you can get to this ideal. When viewed from above, you may be able to get the body into this alignment and look good. The muscles you are using, however, will determine if the draw force line is also along the line of focus. If you mainly use your arm muscles, the draw force line will be in front of your body position and will

*The shoulder blade is kept flat to the rib cage, drawing the upper arm round; Alison Williamson (GBR).*

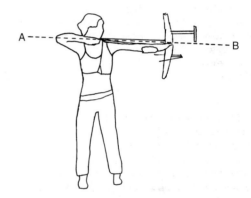

*Although the line of the arrow goes through elbow, the line of force (A–B) goes from the draw arm elbow to the pivot point in the bow hand.*

*At full draw, with the string aligned through the centre of the limb, the elbow position gives the line; Wietse van Alten (The Netherlands).*

*After the shot, the bow remains lined up with the target; Anna Karaseova (Belarus).*

*The line of the bow through the body and elbow; Katia Muliuk (Belarus).*

83

be aligned with the left side of the target. When observing archers shooting in this manner, you can see that they tend to lean forwards as though trying to reach the line at full draw; as they release there is little or no follow through, with the draw arm looking very stiff.

Using the back muscles, as opposed to the arms, will enable you to get the draw force to come to the correct alignment. You will then start to have the feeling of being behind the arrow and 'in line'. You will feel more in control. The draw force line

follows the same line as the line of focus, when viewed from above.

On releasing the string, the draw hand will flow back past the neck (follow through), as a result of the correct muscles being used, rather than because it is artificially flicked back after the shot.

Three ways of reinforcing this feeling of line are:

1. Use the 'shooting with eyes closed' technique, as this will remove the visual distractions and allow you to feel the shot.

*The line of the arrow aligns through the lower part of the elbow as it draws. A line drawn from the centre of the right elbow through the nock should align with the pivot point of the bow hand. (Barry Eley)*

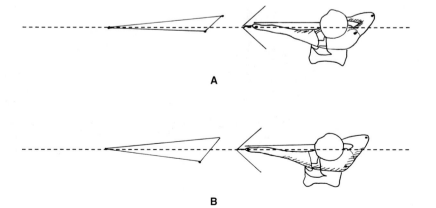

**A**

**B**

*Vectors of force. (A) If the arm and chest muscles are primarily used to draw the bow, the force line is not through the centre of the triangle. (B) When the back is used to draw the bow the force line runs through the triangle, giving the feeling of being behind the bow.*

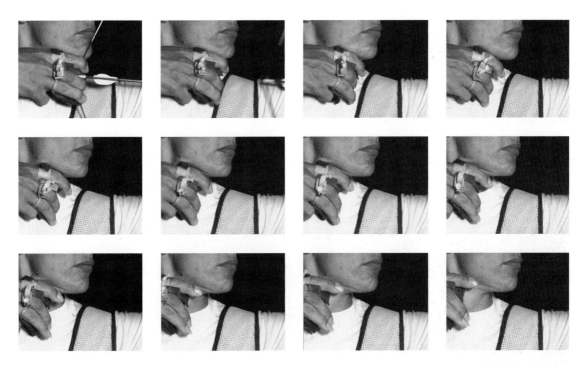

*As the string is released, the hand moves back along the jaw line, drawn back by the contraction of the back muscles. (Werner Beiter)*

2. Grasp the fingers of both hands in front of the chin, then practise focusing on how you use your muscles. When carried out using the back muscles both arms will mimic the release. This exercise can be done at home
3. The use of an elbow sling (Formaster) helps you to work on using the correct muscles and also allows you physically to see the draw force line.

The reversal sling is fitted onto the elbow of the drawing arm, with a cord joining the elbow sling to the bowstring at the nocking point. The length of the cord needs to be adjusted so that when the bow is drawn back, the fingers of the draw hand are in the same juxta-position to the string as though the fingers were on the string. When the bow is drawn with the

*You can practise using the correct muscles while at home or at work without a bow. (Karen Henderson)*

85

*The elbow sling needs to be adjusted so that it is the correct length to ensure that the body is in the correct position when exercising. (Lana Needham)*

elbow sling, you can only use the correct back muscles to draw the bow as the muscles of the forearm are kept relaxed. At full draw, the chord of the elbow sling will be directly along the draw force line when seen from the side. This is the position that the body and arms should be in when the fingers are on the string.

## Maintaining the Line

If you imagine shooting the bow without a head or neck, the draw force line (line) would be easier to maintain but the arrow needs to be given direction, so the head needs to be used to point the bow in the right direction and to give the string a central location. When the string is brought back to the face, the line must be maintained. Archers tend to place the hand under the chin then force it upwards. This leads to the elbow of the draw arm moving upwards, breaking the line when seen from the side and leaving the right elbow out from the body when viewed from above. As the shot is executed the arrow will take the resultant vector of the forced line, leading to bigger groups. When the draw force line is maintained, the line feels as though it is directly behind the arrow. On release, the arrow can only go directly towards the target, meaning that even with slight inconsistencies in shooting form consistency is maintained.

## Balance of the Draw Force Line

This is the balance of power/stretch in front and behind the string at full draw. The concept is that at full draw the string is central and stationary. The pressure of the bow shoulder pressing forwards and the back muscles drawing around the upper arm gives the expansion to draw the arrow through the clicker. If you watch top archers shooting, at full draw you cannot see how the arrow is drawn through the clicker; this is due to the balance of pressure. In theory, the string can be placed at the anchor point on the face prior to the draw, then the bow drawn around it, but this would be a very inefficient way of drawing the bow and would cause many other problems. Therefore, the string needs to be brought back to the anchor point with the 'T' draw.

If you examine the shooting of world-class archers, you will see that the string is positively placed on the face while retaining the line, and once in that position does not move or slide across the face. The head remains in the same position relative to the neck. Consequently, the arrow's final movement through the clicker is achieved through equal expansion and is *not* attained by means of breathing in and expanding the lungs. The airways to the lungs at full draw should be open, allowing the chest to be relaxed.

The analogy I use to illustrate the feeling

*Throughout the shot the pressure from the draw arm elbow and the pivot point needs to be maintained.*

you should have at full draw is to compare it to Samson standing between two pillars that are within arms' reach, with the arms nearly fully outstretched. By pressing evenly on both pillars, trying to push them over, if the pillars were to start moving the centre line of your body would stay still because of the even pressure that you are exerting.

### Setting the Clicker

The setting of the clicker to its correct position ensures that the balance prior to the shot can be achieved correctly. Full draw is the position achieved when the string has been brought back to the anchor point and there is only 2mm (0.08in) to the end of arrow before the clicker operates; the even expansion of pressure can then begin. If, however, there is too much arrow left under the clicker, the expansion will become uneven and slow. Setting the clicker requires an observer and the archer needs to be reasonably consistent with his shooting. Initially, the archer needs to shoot arrows without the clicker being used. The observer needs to check that the archer is shooting with good style and should be in a position to observe where the end of the arrow, on average, is drawn to in relation to the riser. The more consistent the archer is able to shoot, the easier it is for the observer to see the

*To push both pillars evenly, Samson had to press evenly from the centre. With the arms outstretched there must still be room for expansion. At full draw, the pressure must be even either side of the body with room for expansion – the 2mm to get the arrow through the clicker.*

average position of the end of the arrow. The clicker can then be set to the archer's average length of draw. From this position, small adjustments may need to be made to achieve the final clicker position.

The clicker is a very useful tool if used correctly. The arrow must be shot as soon as the 'click' is felt/heard. This ensures that the body is expanding

*The string is placed firmly on the face; Michele Frangelli (Italy).*

as the string is released. If a pause is left after the 'click', inconsistencies in the shot will ensue. When first using the clicker, you will need to work on this, but as you progress you will find that whenever the clicker activates you will shoot the bow. When you set the bow up and check the clicker length, always point the bow at a boss. Many arrows have been shot accidentally around living rooms when showing friends what a clicker does. Once you have passed this stage, you will find that you will only shoot the bow when the clicker operates and it is pointing at the target. This second stage can only be reached by working through the first stage to gain full clicker control.

In working with the clicker to time the release, the consistency of the release will be improved, the consistency of the release leads to consistency of arrow velocity. This can be shown in two ways: first, by using high-speed video footage to show the consistency between the clicker hitting the riser and the release of the string in thousandths of a second. For this you would need access to a top shooting facility like the Beiter Center (proper name:

Werner & Iris Center) in Germany. The second, less accurate but more accessible, method is by using an arrow speed machine (a chronograph). The more consistent the release, the more consistent the arrow speed shown on the machine. With arrow speed machines costing around £60 (at the time of writing) the purchase of one would be a good investment as a training aid to check the consistency of the release.

## Summary

The position at full draw is with the end of the arrow just short of the clicker. It will therefore consist of the combination of the position of the body and arms in relation to the draw force line and the line of focus. The body is upright with the weight distributed evenly between both feet, 70 per cent on the toes, with room for even expansion to execute the shot. Once the clicker strikes the bow, the fingers release the string, the torso remains in position until the arrow strikes the target.

Chapter 6

# Fitness

Neglect fitness at your peril. Fitness is one of the aspects of archery that is generally paid lip service, but it is as important as setting up the bow. You may have all the best equipment, set up perfectly, and shoot with a good technique, but unless you are fit for the sport your scores will still be lower than you would expect.

Fitness in archery has two aspects: shooting and general fitness. Shooting fitness is self-apparent, as you need to be physically fit enough to shoot the bow for 150+ arrows in a competition, so that the last arrow is shot as strongly as the first. To do this, not only does the upper body have to be strong, but the lower body also must be strong enough to support the upper body making the shot. The shot should ideally take place between one beat of the heart, just prior to the next beat. Therefore the more consistent the heartbeat, the more consistent the shooting. Shooting within the beat of the heart is not something that you can do consciously; it

comes with shooting a high quantity of quality shots over an extended period. I was invited to take part in a study on anxiety in sport at Manchester Metropolitan University. I was wired up to an EEG (electroencephalograph) heart monitor and microphone to pick up the sound of the bow as it was shot. I was pleased to see that just prior to each shot my heart rate dropped, giving more time between beats, then I released the string just before a beat. This phenomenon is subconsciously controlled and improves with your shooting experience.

It is also worth noting that the fitter you are, the more resistant to illnesses you will be. Also, should you fall ill, your fitness levels will still be higher than if you were unfit. Along with fitness comes confidence. You will feel better in yourself knowing that you have done the training required to give you the best chance possible.

Being fitter also brings you a better quality of life – you will be able to do more without feeling tired,

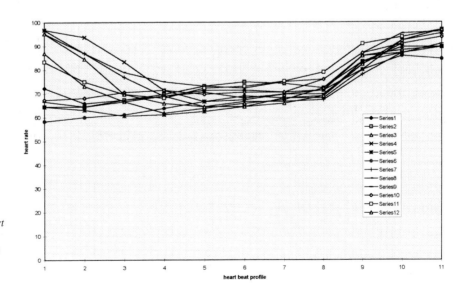

*Prior to the shot, the heart rate stabilizes. The shot takes place just before the heart beat at 8, then the rate rises after the shot.*

89

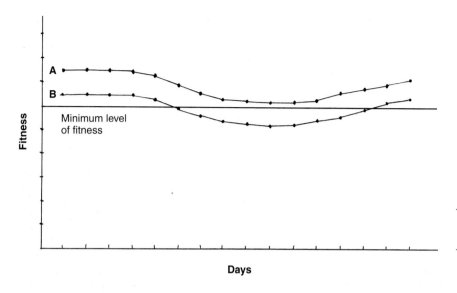

*The graph shows the levels of fitness. (A) is of a fit archer and (B) is of an unfit archer. If both are affected by an illness, the fit archer will still be able to maintain a reasonable level of shooting.*

be more alert and so on. As my old Sgt Major, Ted Greenbury, used to say: 'Make the blood boil once a day', as it invigorates the body and mind. You will have more friends as fitness usually involves interacting with others, even if it is just saying 'hi' as you run past them. Exercise also has the advantage of enabling you to eat more of what you like, as diet and exercise go hand in hand.

Regular sleep patterns also play a major part in maintaining a healthy body and mind. If you exercise well but maintain poor sleep levels, your performance will undoubtedly suffer.

## General Fitness

Taking regular exercise will help you to keep fit, whatever form of exercise that is. Regular exercise means three times a week, not regularly once a month. You must think about where you want to go with your archery. If you want to do well but still carry on doing whatever pleases you for exercise that is fine, but if you want to excel at archery, there are some sports that do not lend themselves well for preparing to shoot. Archery is a sport of fine motor control and thus you are using the mind to make controlled, specialized repetitious movements of the body. Some other sports, such as tennis, badminton and squash, use muscles in an explosive, dynamic way that is contradictory to the muscle and body movements in archery. If you do this type of sport as part of your fitness training, it will inhibit your full potential in archery.

You need to do good cardiovascular exercise, for example walking/hill walking, running, cycling and swimming, or use the machines in the fitness suite at the local health centre or gym, such as the cross trainer/skier and step machine. You must first look at your present level of fitness and health; it is always advisable to see the doctor for a check-up before starting on any exercise regime. Take it easy to start with and work up to the level that you feel you need to maintain. If you have not exercised before, you may well feel a little strange as your body adapts to the new regime. If the body is under threat it will deal with the situation by making you feel faint and dizzy, so stop if this happens and consult your doctor.

Cost can be a major factor in getting fit. The local sports centre or swimming pool may have the facilities you want to use, but may be too expensive. However, there are plenty of ways to get and stay fit without incurring a great deal of expense.

## Planning

Healthy living requires planning, otherwise it will not happen. Start by working out your weekly/ monthly timetable of what time you have available. One way of doing this is to make up a weekly sheet showing the twenty-four hours of each day. Then shade in your work, sleep and shooting times and see what is left. You need to adjust your lifestyle so that you find time to carry out your exercise for the week. Once you have adjusted your timetable to encompass exercise, it will become part of your normal routine and will not require a special effort. If there is little time available to you outside work times, see what can be done at work. Take the stairs rather than the lift, park the car away from work and walk the remainder of the way. Exercise should be part of your life, and not just for the archery. Buy a pedometer and see how many steps a day you take at the moment, then find a way to increase them. Being healthier is not necessarily about spending an hour a day at the gym; the exercise routine you embark on should be of a maintainable duration and frequency.

## Exercising

Walking and running are both good ways to start your fitness programme. Plan for four times a week if possible. Running is an impact exercise because the weight of the body is jolted from one leg to the other as you run, so ensure that you have suitable footwear. If hard-soled shoes are worn, you may find that you will impart undue strain on the joints which can lead to injury. Start with brisk walking and then move onto a combination of walking and running, for example run a lamp post, walk a lamp post. When you are ready, move on to the full run. The distance does not need to be long: 3km, for example, and within a few weeks this should be easily completed within fifteen minutes. Include an incentive to run – for example, I run to the beach and back. I like looking at the sea and this provides me with an incentive to do the run, as every day the sea is different. If you have problems with knee or hip joints, try low-impact exercises such as cycling, cross-trainer, rowing machine or swimming.

If you want to use weights or multi-gym equipment, work on doing varied exercises with light weights and a high number of controlled repetitions, as opposed to heavy weights and few repetitions – you are trying to build stamina, not muscle bulk.

My routine at the gym is twenty minutes on the cycle machine, thirty reps on each of my selected multi-gym machines, twenty minutes on the cross-trainer, thirty reps on the multi-gym, twenty minutes on the running machine, then 500m on the rowing machine. I vary the type of aerobic machines depending on what is available and what I feel like doing. All gyms should run induction sessions, when you are shown the equipment and how to use it. Make sure you understand how the equipment works and the required body position when carrying out the exercise – adopting the correct posture means you will perform the exercise injury-free.

*How to Breathe When Exercising*

Most people are not aware of the need to harness their breathing patterns as they exercise. This is easiest to illustrate with running. Match your respirations to the steps that you take; breathe in for two steps then out for two steps. Regulating the breath with the beat of the steps enables the exercise to be carried out without going into oxygen deficit. In addition, the regular breathing will help to regulate and maintain the pace of the exercise. The breathing pattern technique can be used to regulate all exercises, for example three breaths when cycling, single breaths when using the rowing machine and so on. Find out what suits you – it will make your exercising easier to carry out.

## Sleep Patterns

Most people do not get enough sleep – they 'make do' with less than they require. Making do is not good enough when trying to shoot well, or even when trying to carry out a job efficiently; efficiency drops off dramatically when a person is deprived of sleep. The amount of sleep an individual requires per night will differ from person to person, but as a rule of thumb it is one hour of sleep for every two awake. In everyday life being a little tired is not really noticeable, but if you are tired while doing archery you will lose the fine motor control required and your concentration levels will go down. Finding the right level of sleep can take some time, but eight hours is a good place to start, although children and teenagers will need approximately ten hours, to help with growth and adjusting to new levels of hormones.

I became aware of how much lack of sleep can affect you when about twelve years ago my shooting started feeling 'fuzzy'. I initially thought it was a poor diet, because when I came home from work, I had a quick sandwich, went out to shoot, then came back at about nine o'clock, had another quick bite to eat and then went to bed around eleven. When I went to see the doctor and he suggested that perhaps a vitamin supplement may help, I tried this but my shooting was still off. I sat and thought about what it could be; I like reading and used to read every night before going to sleep. I realized that, although I went to bed at a reasonable time, I would read until around one o'clock in the morning, ending up with approximately six hours sleep a night. I decided to make sure that the light was out by eleven o'clock every night, giving me eight hours sleep, and within a few days my shooting came back on form without the 'fuzzy' feeling. Through trial and error I found that nine hours seems to be the optimum amount of sleep for me to aim for every night.

A recent survey on sleep patterns showed that approximately 40 per cent of people suffer from serious sleep deprivation, which can lead to accidents within the home and when operating machinery, including driving. Lack of sleep will definitely make your shooting suffer. You are not able store sleep; it is like filling a glass with water. Once it is full, pouring more water into it will not make it store more. If you will drain it at the same rate every day, if it is not refilled enough every night, the level in the glass will remain low.

If you require eight hours sleep a night to fill your sleep glass to its optimum sleep level, and you only get seven hours, you will need an extra hour of sleep the following night to refill the glass. If, however, you only have seven hours of sleep Monday to Friday, by Saturday night you will need an extra seven of sleep. But as it is Saturday night you may well go out, so you may get to bed even later than usual. It is unlikely you will be able to sleep for the fifteen hours required to refill the sleep glass on the Sunday, so you start the next week with a sleep deficit and so it goes on.

You will need to experiment with your sleep periods to see what is best for you. A good place to start is to look in the mirror – if you have dark lines under the eyes it is an indication that you are not getting enough sleep. You can also try lying on your bed with a spoon held in your hand, over the side of the bed with a plate underneath. Check the time on the clock, relax and try to sleep. When you go to sleep, the spoon will slip from your fingers and hit the plate, waking you up. Check the clock; if it has been less than five minutes you are severely deprived of sleep. Five to ten minutes is a sizeable sleep debt; ten to fifteen a manageable sleep debt. More than fifteen minutes indicates that you are getting enough sleep. (For further details, *see* Dr William C. Dement, *The Promise of Sleep*). Once you have found and are maintaining your personal sleep level, if you were originally sleep-deprived you should find that both your archery and general alertness

improve. It is also worth noting that if you do have a late night the effects seem to miss a day, so a late night on Friday seems to affect the Sunday more than the Saturday, which is useful to know when planning competitions.

## Shooting Fitness

Before starting any exercise you should follow a warm-up routine, carry out the exercise, then warm down with a full stretch of the areas most used during the exercise. When running, after an initial warm-up routine, you should start with a walk then graduate with wider strides to a run, finishing the run with a walk and finally a hamstring stretch.

In archery, you do not normally get out of breath when shooting, but you still need to warm up the muscles and joints prior to shooting. This is to ensure that there is a good blood flow around the parts of the body used to shoot the bow. Either follow a formal warm-up routine, or help to set out the range prior to shooting by rolling out the bosses, putting up the stands and so on.

Full, strong stretching should only be carried out at the end of a shooting session. This is because when you stretch the muscles you also stretch the ligaments that hold the muscles to the bone. The muscles go back to their normal length quite rapidly after being stretched, but the ligaments take far longer. This means that if you carry out strong stretching prior to shooting, the ligaments will be elongated. As you start shooting, the muscles will have to work harder as they will have to contract more to make the same body movement. As you continue shooting, the ligaments will slowly contract back to their normal length. This will mean that, as you are trying to complete the shot the same way, you are using the muscles differently every end that you shoot. Therefore the full/strong stretching should only be used at the end of your shooting session, when it will ensure that the ligaments do not shorten and restrict normal movements.

Shooting large quantities of arrows is the best thing for improving shooting fitness. This is something that needs to be worked up to. I would not suggest you go from shooting 120 arrows a week to 300 arrows a day, as something is bound to break. The important issue with shooting large quantities of arrows is that they must be shot well. Each one needs to be shot the best that you can. Your limiting factors are then how much time and what facilities you have available. Some clubs are only able to shoot once a week at their venue, so here are some recommendations on how to increase your shooting strength at home, starting with the most basic.

### Rubber Exerciser Band (Clini Band)

These are lengths of clinical rubber bands normally used in rehabilitation from injury under the direction of physiotherapists. They are available in varying colours, which correspond to the elasticity of the band, black being the strongest. These are good for doing warm-ups on the field but at home they can be used to improve strength. A band can be left on the end of the sofa and picked up of an evening to start working the muscles for shooting. The strength of the exercise depends on the length of band that you take up – the shorter the length, the stronger the exercise.

The following exercises can be used to work the muscles at home and as a warm-up prior to shooting. Pay particular attention to how the band is gripped in the hand. The band under tension should come from the palm of the hand with the free end extending between the thumb and index finger; this will avoid undue strain on the wrist. Start with the tension in the elastic low and do not overdo it on your first session. The band can also be used to simulate shooting.

*Ensure that the Clini band runs over the palm of the hand so that undue strain is not put on the wrist.*

### Reversals

The elbow sling/Formaster can be used at home. Fit it with a cord for this exercise. It must be set up so that at full draw the fingers of the draw arm are in the same relative position to the string as when you are shooting. The bow is then drawn using the Formaster. Initially, the head must to be in the correct position for shooting, that is, looking over the left shoulder. Once the full draw position is attained and the draw force line felt, the head should be turned to face forwards, keeping the neck muscles relaxed. This is intended as strength training for the

*Some exercises that can be carried out with the Clini band at home. Most of the exercises should be done with straight arms as it is the back and shoulder muscles that need to be strengthened.*

arms and torso, rather than to teach the subconscious to hold the bow at full draw for extended periods. To start with, try to maintain this position for fifteen seconds then come down and relax. I find that it is easier to work around a one-minute interval for this exercise regime.

Therefore, draw for fifteen seconds, relax for forty-five seconds and repeat until you are unable to complete the fifteen-second hold. You may only manage this six times on your first attempt, but do this every day and quite quickly you will be able to complete more repetitions, with the target amount being for thirty minutes. Once you can complete this comfortably for thirty minutes, the hold time can be increased to twenty seconds. Your eventual aim should be thirty seconds hold per minute for thirty minutes, the equivalent to shooting 180 arrows in only thirty minutes. I have an electric clock with the hour and minute hands removed, leaving only the second hand for doing this

*Only a short distance is needed to shoot at home. It allows you to shoot arrows in comfort and in a short period, making the most of the time available.*

exercise. This is a good exercise to do while watching television, so long as it is not a comedy, as laughing is not so good at full draw. Once you are able to complete the thirty-minute session, you can raise the bow weight if you want to work harder. Reversals can be extended for longer periods, but they are best used as a short exercise to build strength and fit into the time you have available.

The reversal sling can also be fitted with elastic instead of a cord. This can be used for practising the shot to make sure you are maintaining the pressure throughout the shot, as explained in Chapter 5. It is not a good device to use for long periods. This is because as you release, the bow pulls the bow arm back into the body, which can cause unwanted jarring of the elbow and shoulder joints.

### Exerset Trainer

This air-cushioned training device bolts onto the front of the bow. It allows you to shoot the bow, with the bow falling forward out of the hand after the shot. This is a good way to shoot at home, without the concern of shooting arrows into the wall, although you should put a representation of a target onto the wall so that you can aim properly. It is important when shooting like this that you make every effort to shoot the bow well every time. As there is no feedback regarding the accuracy of your shot it is very easy to just pull it back and let go, without executing a good shot.

### Shooting at Home

Depending on the layout of your house or the availability of a garage, it may be possible to set up a target in your home. The distance does not have to be great – 3m is adequate – but it does have to be in a position where no one can walk between you and the target when you are shooting and must have a good solid wall behind. The 1m foam boss is the best for short-range work, as it is big enough to move the groups around the target so it wears evenly. With a target at home you can shoot a good quantity of arrows in a short period, for example 130 arrows in one hour at ten arrow ends. Because the target is foam, rather than straw, you will not experience so much wear of the arrow shaft, especially with carbons.

For each session you carry out you must have a plan and you must maintain well-executed shots throughout the session – if you just shoot 150 arrows without maintaining control of the shot, your shooting will not improve. As you are shooting at such a short distance, you need to maintain a gap between the arrows, otherwise you will damage them quite quickly. Even at 3m you can control where the shot lands and the following exercises will help to maintain your form and concentration. First, place a target face on the boss with the face towards the target, to give you a white background; this will give you a clearer string picture. Then:

- Adjust the sight so that as you focus on the first arrow you shoot, the second arrow lands 2cm above or to the side. Shoot again, this time focusing on the second arrow and so on. You will end up with a line across the target. When shot well, the gap between each shaft will be the same distance.
- Draw ten black spots on the back of the face; hit the black spot every time.
- Draw a vertical line on the back of the face with a thick marker; make every arrow hit the line.
- Draw a horizontal line; with a horizontal line you must adjust your foot position as your group moves across the target face, otherwise you will twist your body on the shot.
- Make a small target face and shoot at it with your eyes closed, feeling the shot and imagining that every shot goes into the ten ring.

You can make up many versions of these exercises; the trick is to keep control of the shot and to make it as interesting as possible. These exercises will help to build strength, but you must always try to shoot your best shot. The other benefit of shooting at home is that you can listen to music as you do it.

### Shooting at Distance

If you have the time and facilities, shooting at competition distances is probably the best practice you can get, in order to both build up fitness and to gauge your performance. For strength building, do not restrict yourself to a competition quantity of arrows. You need to train with a good quantity of arrows while maintaining your style. Shooting ten arrow ends has two main benefits. Firstly, you are there to shoot, not walk, so increasing the amount of arrows per end means that you will shoot a greater amount of arrows per hour. Secondly, it will get you out of the habit of thinking that the third or sixth arrow is the last arrow. Every arrow should

be shot the same, as though it were the only arrow you have to shoot. However, if ten arrows per end becomes too tiring, reduce to six arrows – you are there to improve the quality of your shot as much as to build your strength.

### Volume Shooting

One of the exercises I carry out to keep a check on my fitness involves shooting ten arrow ends at 60m (due to the length of our range). The idea is to shoot the arrows smoothly and quickly and get into a flow of repetitious shooting. Three minutes are spent shooting the ten arrows, followed by a quick walk down to the target, retrieving the arrows, then coming back to the line and repeating this for two hours. I shoot about 300 arrows during this period. The focus must be on quality rather than quantity, so using a shorter time period is the best way to start this exercise. Do not use a telescope as it slows down the shooting and interferes with the flow of the shots. You will be surprised at how good the groups will be; this is because you are keeping the conscious mind busy, letting the subconscious control the shot. The exercise can also be carried out at shorter distances but you must put up a number of faces so as not to damage your arrows. Remember to adjust your feet alignment to allow for the faces being next to each other. This is an exercise which should not be carried out if it interferes with the shooting of the other members of the club, so you will have to plan to do it when the range is quiet.

## Summary

'The more you shoot, the luckier you will get.' It is the amount of arrows shot well in a week that will improve your shooting; fitness will enhance the improvements. Your fitness levels will reflect in the scores that you shoot. If you want to get to the top in archery, consider building up to at least the equivalent of 1,000 arrows per week. Listen to your body, there may be slight aches as you change your routine to include exercise but ease off if you are having problems. The reversals and jogging are very good to start with, as reversals encourage you to use the correct shooting muscles, and jogging/walking can be done anywhere, so you are more likely to start doing it.

Chapter 7

# Competitions, Training and Practice

Too many times I have heard from archers at clubs that they are not good enough to enter competitions. In my opinion, there are two main reasons for attending archery competitions. The first is that it they are a good place to meet other archers and enjoy an activity with like-minded people. After all, you do have a picnic at lunchtime and you get to see different fields around the country – my favourite venue is the shoot at Glamis Castle. The second reason is to measure the content of your training, by shooting a score at a competition and

*Glamis Castle lawn is a great venue for a shoot, with the piper playing at lunch break.*

seeing how you compare to the other competitors. When shooting with others. they will invariably give you a good idea of what frequency and content of training they have been doing, which can help you to evaluate your own training. The score you shoot is a reflection of the training that you have been doing. If you train only one day a week, you will not be going to the Olympics, so you need to be realistic about the score you will obtain. To that end, if you want to win a competition you will need to train at least as much as, if not more than, any other competitor.

This chapter will look at the competitions and the training for them.

## International Archery Federation (Fédération Internationale de Tir à l'Arc) (FITA)

This is the world governing body of archery. The competitions run under the FITA rules are all shot in metric distances and will have the same rules and regulations wherever in the world that round is shot. The main indoor rounds are either 25m or 18m, with the 18m being the more prevalent as it is the round shot for the World Indoor Championships. With sixty arrows being shot, a score of 580+ out of a possible 600 is a score good enough for selection for the GB team.

The main FITA outdoor round consists of thirty-six arrows shot at each distance of 90m, 70m, 50m and 30m for men and 70m, 60m, 50m, 30m for women – 144 scored arrows in total, with a total possible score of 1440. A score of 1300 or above for recurve shooters is deemed a good score – currently the world records for men and women are 1377 and 1405 respectively. The target

| Round | 122cm face | | | | | | 80cm Face | | | | |
|---|---|---|---|---|---|---|---|---|---|---|---|
| | 90m | 70m | 60m | 50m | 40m | 30m | 50m | 40m | 30m | 20m | 10m |
| FITA gentlemen | 36 | 36 | | | | | 36 | | 36 | | |
| FITA Ladies | | 36 | 36 | | | | 36 | | 36 | | |
| Metric 1 | | 36 | 36 | | | | 36 | | 36 | | |
| Metric 2 | | | 36 | 36 | | | | 36 | 36 | | |
| Metric 3 | | | | 36 | 36 | | | | 36 | 36 | |
| Metric 4 | | | | | 36 | 36 | | | | 36 | 36 |
| Long Metric gentlemen | 36 | 36 | | | | | | | | | |
| Long Metric Ladies | | 36 | 36 | | | | | | | | |
| Short metric | | | | | | | 36 | | 36 | | |
| Long metric 1 | | 36 | 36 | | | | | | | | |
| Long metric 2 | | | 36 | 36 | | | | | | | |
| Long metric 3 | | | | 36 | 36 | | | | | | |
| Long metric 4 | | | | | 36 | 36 | | | | | |
| Short metric 1 | | | | | | | 36 | | 36 | | |
| Short metric 2 | | | | | | | | 36 | 36 | | |
| Short metric 3 | | | | | | | | | 36 | 36 | |
| Short metric 4 | | | | | | | | | | 36 | 36 |
| FITA 900 | | | 30 | 30 | 30 | | | | | | |

*Outdoor FITA rounds.*

score area is divided into ten zones, ten being in the middle and the highest score value for one arrow. The size of the face will depend on the distance being shot. Juniors (depending on their age) and novices (archers in their first year of competitions) can shoot at shorter distances, but will shoot a comparable round in terms of arrows shot, although novices in their first year of shooting may shoot rounds of fewer arrows.

Competitions are of different standards, the lowest being a club competition and the highest being world record status. If a shoot is world record status it will be run to the highest standard. This ensures that wherever you are in the world the status of the shoot is such that if you break a world record it will be recognized. It also assures you that another archer shooting the same competition the other side of the world will be shooting to the same standard. A club shoot can be run with three people, but the assurances that the shoot is run to the same standard is not there.

*The target zone is divided into ten scoring zones. 70m at the Werner & Iris Center. (Lana Needham)*

*Although the same face is used for GNAS and FITA rounds, the value of score zones differs. (A) GNAS scoring five zone. (B) FITA ten zone.*

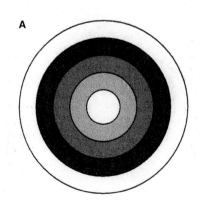

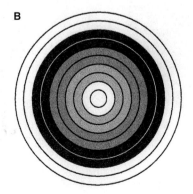

# Grand National Archery Society (GNAS)

This is the governing body of archery in the UK. As archery has a long history in Great Britain there are a lot of competitions unique to GB. These rounds are usually measured in yards. The score zone is by colours, with the gold scoring nine, red seven, blue five, black three and white one. The number of arrows shot in most of the full rounds is still 144. At the British outdoor championships, the round for men is the York round and the Hereford for women. These are shot at distances of 100yd, 80yd and 60yd for men and 80yd, 60yd and 50yd for women. Six dozen arrows are shot at the longest distance, four dozen at the middle distance and two dozen at the shortest. The York/Hereford shoot is supposed to be a representation of the Battle of Agincourt of 1415. A top score in Great Britain for this shoot is around the 1200 mark out of a possible 1296.

The popular indoor British shoot is the Portsmouth round, which is shot over a distance of 20yd (approximately 18m), but the face is larger than the 18m 40cm face, as a 60cm face is used. Although this round is shot over an imperial distance, the ten-ring score zones are used. A top score for this is 590+ out of a possible 600. My best so far is 599.

So the shoots in Great Britain can be of two types and come under either FITA or GNAS rules.

These are on the whole similar rules, with some variations. One of the more relevant rules is the amount of time allowed to shoot your arrows.

In a FITA competition you can have up to forty-five minutes of practice prior to the competition. The timing of shooting an end in practice is the same as the competition, but you are allowed to shoot as many arrows as you like within the timing. The timing for a FITA competition is as follows. You will get four minutes to shoot a six-arrow end at the longest two distances and two minutes to shoot a three-arrow end at the shorter distances. The two minutes for three-arrow ends is also used for the FITA indoor rounds. The timings for FITAs are regulated by whistles and 'traffic lights' (light signals are used to indicate the timing periods), and may also include a count-down clock. The archers will be allocated a target number and a position on the score sheet: A, B, C or D.

As there is only space on the shooting line for two archers per target to shoot at a time, A and B shoot their arrows together and then C and D will shoot their arrows. When the shoot starts, the whistle will sound and A and B will go to the line; the traffic lights will be red. After twenty seconds. a second whistle will signal the start of the four minutes to shoot the six arrows and the lights will change to green. After three minutes and thirty seconds, the lights will change to amber to signal that there is thirty seconds left to finish the shoot. At four minutes, the judge will sound two whistles and the lights will turn to red. If any archer shoots outside the four minutes they will loose the value of their highest scoring arrow. This also signals archers C and D to go to the line. They will be given twenty seconds to get ready prior to their four-minute shooting period. Once all the archers have shot they will go to score and collect their arrows.

On subsequent ends, A and B will alternate with C and D when going to the line first so that both groups get an equal opportunity to shoot at an empty target. At the shorter distances, 50m and 30m, the format remains the same but with two minutes to shoot three arrows.

In the GNAS rounds, although you still shoot six arrow ends, the format is different. Timing by lights is not normally used in GNAS rounds (apart from a British record status Portsmouth round). When the whistle sounds, A and B go to the line and when they are ready shoot three of their arrows. They then come back to the equipment line and C and D 'filter' (walk on when their space is available) onto the line to shoot three arrows, draw back and then A and B come forward shoot their remaining

| Rounds | 100 YDS | 80 YDS | 60 YDS | 50 YDS | 40 YDS | 30 YDS | 20 YDS |
|---|---|---|---|---|---|---|---|
| York | 72 | 48 | 24 | | | | |
| Hereford/ bristol I | | 72 | 48 | 24 | | | |
| Bristol II | | | 72 | 48 | 24 | | |
| Bristol III | | | | 72 | 48 | 24 | |
| Bristol IV | | | | | 72 | 48 | 24 |
| St George | 36 | 36 | 36 | | | | |
| Albion | | 36 | 36 | 36 | | | |
| Windsor | | | 36 | 36 | 36 | | |
| Short Windsor | | | | 36 | 36 | 36 | |
| Junior Windsor | | | | | 36 | 36 | 36 |
| New Weston | 48 | 48 | | | | | |
| Long Weston | | 48 | 48 | | | | |
| Weston | | | 48 | 48 | | | |
| Short Weston | | | | 48 | 48 | | |
| Junior Weston | | | | | 48 | 48 | |
| Short Junior Weston | | | | | | 48 | 48 |
| American | | | 30 | 30 | 30 | | |
| St. Nicholas | | | | | 48 | 36 | |
| New National | 48 | 24 | | | | | |
| Long National | | 48 | 24 | | | | |
| National | | | 48 | 24 | | | |
| Short National | | | | 48 | 24 | | |
| Junior National | | | | | 48 | 24 | |
| Short Junior National | | | | | | 48 | 24 |
| New Warwick | 24 | 24 | | | | | |
| Long Warwick | | 24 | 24 | | | | |
| Warwick | | | 24 | 24 | | | |
| Short Warwick | | | | 24 | 24 | | |
| Junior Warwick | | | | | 24 | 24 | |
| Short Junior Warwick | | | | | | 24 | 24 |

*Outdoor GNAS rounds.*

three arrows, then C and D do likewise. Although there are no timing lights, the three arrows still need to be shot in two minutes and thirty seconds. If someone takes longer than this they will first be given a verbal warning and, if they persist, a written warning. The penalty after this is to loose the highest scoring arrow of that end, followed by disqualification.

The field layout will be similar to that of a club's, with a shooting line and a waiting line, but there will be a few extra lines. At a FITA round there will be a line 3m in front of the shooting line. If you drop or shoot your arrow and any part of the shaft remains within the 3m line, on calling the judge you will be able to shoot another arrow. This is to stop archers reaching forward of the line during shooting. At big shoots there may well be a photography line, which is a 1m-wide path between the shooting line and the equipment/waiting line. Behind the equipment line is the tent line, with the tents placed behind this line. Invariably, there are at least two rows of tents, so it's a case of first come, first served with regard to being on the front line. There are usually paths marked along this line to

ensure that the archers of the tents that are behind the front row can come forward to shoot. It is normal for the tents put on the front row to leave gaps for the archers from behind to come through.

## Entering Competitions

Competitions are not for everyone and it is the club archers that keep the club running, as they are the regulars that turn out every week. But if you do decide to enter competitions all you have to do is put your name down and pay the entry fee. The entry forms may be sent to your club secretary, or the secretary may download the forms for the club members, and will usually deal with the entry fees for the competitions and will tell you of the venue and time that the competition starts.

I have shot since I was eight years old and for many years enjoyed going to various clubs, meeting people and enjoying my shooting. It was not until I joined Links Archers in Montrose, Scotland, that I had the time and inclination to go to competitions. When the other archers came back from

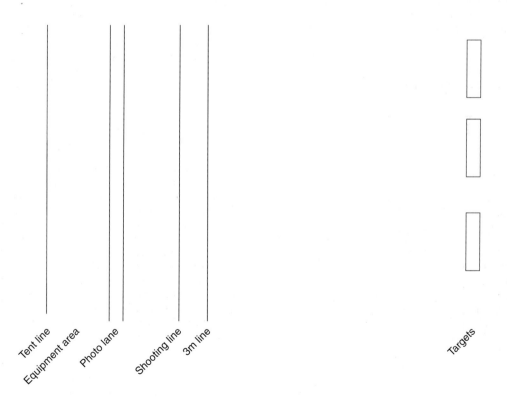

*In competitions, lines marked on the field will show you the areas around the shooting line.*

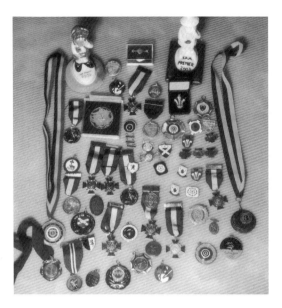

*Some of the badges that can be won at competitions.*

the shoot at Glamis Castle with a suntan and a tale of a good day's shooting I decided it would be good to join in. I thought I would have to pass a shooting test before I could go. I did not realize that it was for anyone who wanted to join in. I found that I really enjoyed competitions. It is always said that it is the taking part and not the winning that counts, which to some extent is true, and if you enter a competition with that attitude, you will have a good time. I have found that, on the whole, the people who enjoy shooting tend to be sociable. To shoot, you have to work on being calm and controlled, so you do not seem to get the 'lager lout' archer. There are usually four archers to a target and I always seem to end up with interesting target companions.

When you go to competitions, use them to help you to evaluate your shooting. Where you end up in the results will help to show you the areas and distances to work on. Once you have been to three competitions, the scores will be used to give you a classification. This will enable you to shoot against your peers in the same classification, so not only can you work on moving up classifications, but, if you are so inclined, winning your class.

For those who are badge collectors, there are plenty of badges to win, not only as medals but also for gaining certain score levels and for getting all six arrows in the gold in the same end at either of the longest two distances.

If, however, you are the competitive type, competitions will give you the benchmark of your training. The mental mechanism of doing well at competitions is to shoot every arrow the best you can. At the end of the competition, evaluate what percentage of your arrows was shot well and plan to work on ways to improve that percentage. If you go to a competition intent only on winning, you will not be focusing on shooting the arrow – you will be too busy looking at what the others are doing and trying to get tens. That is not focusing on the shot. If you endeavour to shoot every arrow the best you can and focus on each arrow one at a time, you will get the score that you deserve for the shooting you are doing.

### Equipment for Competitions

In the UK almost all competitions require you to wear specific clothing and this will be stated on the entry form. It will either be a combination of white or dark green or your registered club colours. If you are not in the correct clothing you may well be asked to leave the field, if the tournament is of British record status or above.

You will need to take food and water for the competition, plus a chair is a good idea as it gives you the opportunity to rest between shooting and as the targets are being moved between distances. If you start going to more competitions, a small tent can be a good idea for shelter from the weather. Competitions are only usually only cancelled due to lightning or severe winds, although a shoot in Glasgow was cancelled a couple of years ago when the field turned into a bog! Otherwise, the shoot will continue, rain or shine, so it is useful to have somewhere to shelter and put your equipment.

Waterproof clothing and an umbrella are essential due to the average British weather. An umbrella will help to keep your score sheet dry if nothing else. It is important that you try out during your training the clothes that you intend to use at a competition. I have seen, even at international level, archers trying on clothing for the first time and finding that the string catches their arm, causing the arrows to miss the target. You need to shoot in clothing that will not interfere with the shot, so even though it may look a little strange trying out waterproof clothing on a dry day, it is best to be prepared. Once the judges declare inclement weather, any colour of clothing can be worn. Once you start going to competitions you will see what sort of clothing the other archers are using and they will let you know where you can buy it.

*The shooting line at the seeding round, 2000 Olympics. Plenty of room on the line for archers and scopes. (Barry Eley)*

A good telescope is useful, especially at competitions – as there are four archers on every target it can be very difficult to see which arrows are yours, especially at the longest distance. There are many 'scopes available but it is worth getting one that has a larger front lens. It is not just about the magnification factor but the amount of light the object/front lens lets in. 'Scopes and binocular object lens and magnification are normally given as multiplication, for example 22 × 60. The 22 is the magnification and the 60 is the size of the object lens. On a bright day, a 20 × 50 will work well, but on a rainy or dull day you will find that it can be quite difficult to identify your arrows clearly, as not enough light enters the front lens to be magnified. If the magnification is too great it can be difficult to keep the 'scope trained on the target. 'Scopes are not only used during competitions, they are also very useful for training.

## Training and Practice

Going to the club and shooting arrows without a plan for what you want to achieve in that session is not training or practice, it is just 'plonking' arrows and

*At the Golden Autumn in Lvov, Ukraine, the space on the line is more restricted.*

will be of very little benefit to you. Go to the club with an idea of what you want to achieve in that session. Training and practice go hand in hand. In training, you make adjustments to your shooting style, shoot lots of arrows to build and maintain strength, tune the bow and teach the subconscious what you want from the shot. Training is about perfecting the shot and improving your archery to get more arrows in the middle of the target. Practice is about shooting arrows as though you were at a competition and letting your subconscious shoot the arrows. In practice, set yourself a task, say to score 50m, then shoot and score every arrow with the same accuracy as at a competition. Your must score every arrow; if you miss arrows or ends out, you are not being fair to yourself as it will give you false data for your records.

## Keeping a Diary

One of the best aids to improving your shooting is to keep a record of all your shooting, physical and eating activities. This can be done by using a diary into which you put all the details/notes that you feel are necessary for that day's shooting. You do not have to write a lot – how many arrows shot, where, score, distance and any adjustments you made to your equipment. Note any exercise that you did, running or even walking around the shops. The idea is to see what patterns of activities help to improve your shooting. It is easier to evaluate how your shooting is going if your transfer the details into a computer spreadsheet. The details on the sheet need to be kept simple, I usually highlight all competition results in red and perhaps results from practice in yellow. On the spreadsheet it is much easier to pick out trends.

In keeping a spreadsheet of your daily activities, you may also be tempted to do more to keep the day's entries filled, helping to improve your shooting.

## Training

Training is when you work on improving your shot, while at the same time teaching your subcon-

| Date | Day | Activity | Arrows | Distance/ score | Duration in Hours | Remarks | | hours sleep |
|---|---|---|---|---|---|---|---|---|
| | | Malting Shed | 159 | 70 | 3 | | | 9.5 |
| 1-Mar | Sat | Sports Centre | 36 | 295 | 2 | sat morn round | | |
| | | Malting Shed | 120 | 18m | 3 | 298 for 30 arrows checked strings and tabs | | 9 |
| 2 | Sun | travel to marks | | | 10 | | | 5 |
| 3 | Mon | Travel to Nimes | | | | World indoor champs | | 7 |
| 4 | Tue | unofficial practice | 103 | 18m | | | | 5 |
| 5 | Wed | Official Practice | | | | | | 5 |
| 6 | Thu | comp | 66 | 577 | | | 290,287 | |
| | | team round | | 89 pass | | 266 pass for team | | 7 |
| 7 | Fri | head to head | | 171 pass | | tsrempelov Baljimina 29th place | | 8 |
| 8 | Sat | no shooting | | | | | | |
| 9 | Sun | finals | | | | | | 8 |
| 10 | Mon | Travel to UK | | | | | | |
| 11 | Tue | travel to Scotland | | | | | | |
| | | Fitted grip extension | | | | | | 10 |
| 12 | Wed | Malting Shed | 247 | 30m | 5 | Adj Tiller on INF | | 9 |
| 13 | Thu | Malting Shed | 267 | 18m | 4 | | | 9 |
| 14 | Fri | Drive to Lillishall | | | | | | |
| | | reversals | | | 30 min | | | 8 |
| 15 | Sat | British champs | | 581 | | Qualif score | | 8.5 |
| 16 | Sun | Reversals | | | 20 min | | | |
| | | British champs | | 578 | | 4th place | | 7 |
| | | Drive to Scotland | | | | | | |
| 17 | Mon | Multi gym | | | 1 | | | |
| | | opened new Multi Gym | | | | | | 8 |
| 18 | Tue | Multi gym | | | 1 | | | |
| | | Malting Shed | 181 | 30m | 4 | tiller tuning TP | | 8.5 |
| 19 | Wed | Multi gym | | | 1 | | | |
| | | Malting Shed | 140 | 70m | 4 | beiter v' easton rod TP tab slipped | | |
| | | Sports Centre | 66 | 590 port | | | | 9.5 |
| 20 | Thu | Malting Shed | 210 | 30m | 3 | 355 @30m | | |
| | | School club | | | 1 | | | |
| | | kit | | | 2 | Cut new X10's | | 6 |
| 21 | Fri | Multi gym | | | 1 | | | |
| | | Malting Shed | 114 | 50,60,70 | 3 | 1357 Ladies FITA | | |

*A sample of a simple diary on a computer spreadsheet, which gives you the information you need to track your progression.*

scious how you want the shot to go. Work on one area at a time, starting on areas that will lead to the most improvement. It is no good spending a whole session working on where your little finger should be on the bow hand, if every time you shoot you do not keep the bow arm up and steady. Work on the big things first, then move on to the minor areas that need your mind's focus. Training should be about improving your archery. For every improvement you make, it will take about 1,000 good shots for that improvement to become part of your subconscious. This means that if, for example, you want to improve your loose, you may need to spend a few weeks just working on that one aspect to get it right; shooting two or three ends will not be enough.

Your telescope is a valuable asset when training, as it allows you to evaluate your individual shots to work out what it takes to shoot a ten. If, after shooting your six arrows, you find that three of your arrows are in the gold, you need to know how this was achieved; just knowing it was three of the last six shots is not good enough. So shoot the shot, *feel* the shot, then look to see where the arrow landed. When using a telescope on the line keep it set low, so that it will not interfere with your body position. If you have the 'scope set high when you are shooting the arrow, although your head will be facing the target you will find that the 'scope is in your peripheral vision and your natural preservation reflex will tend to make you lean away from it.

> ### Pacing your Preparation
>
> A few years ago I was shooting approximately 1,500 arrows a week. I noticed, looking at my spreadsheet, that the scores for one competition seemed to be higher and more stable than usual. On close evaluation, I found that three weeks before the competition I shot 1,500 for the week, the next 850 and the week prior to the competition only 600 arrows. The drop in arrows shot was due to work commitments, but showed a good result. I tried to reproduce the formula for another competition and found that it gave me better results. The rationale I deduced from the results was that the 1,500 arrows helped with strength and training, the 850 were part-training, part-practice, and the 600 were all practice, while also helping to conserve my energy prior to the competition. This pattern has proved to be one that assists in my preparation for a big shoot.

Keep in mind that the shot finishes when the arrow hits the target. I have seen archers start leaning to look into the 'scope as the arrow is leaving the bow, which will not help your shooting, as your body needs to stay in a stable position. The 'scope should not be used in all aspects of shooting, especially

*'Scope heights need to be set for the individual's needs but out of the line of sight. (Barry Eley)*

when carrying out volume shooting (ten arrow ends in three minutes), as it will distract you from the flow and rhythm of shooting.

As it takes 1,000 arrows to make the aspect of the shot you are working on part of the subconscious, you can now understand one of the benefits for shooting larger quantities of arrows. At a seminar in America, Mr Ki Sik Lee, the Korean coach working in Australia at the time of writing, stated that the junior archers of high school level are expected to shoot ten hours a day, up to 1,000 arrows. When you are working your way up to the top, it is the volume of arrows you shoot that will help to get you there. In training, you combine the elements of reversals, shooting at a short range of 3m and going to the club to shoot the full distances. The rest is exercise, both mental and physical. All of this should be all entered into the diary.

*Practice*

Anything that you use in a competition, you must also use in practice. To determine the areas you need to practise, look at the results from either previous sessions or competitions. Work on the distances that you need to improve to bring up the scores. At clubs it is very easy to shoot the distances that are set up when you get there, but if you know you need to work on 90m then you need to set up that distance. When practising, you bring together all aspects of your training in order to shoot the arrow into the middle. You need to be able to let your subconscious shoot the shot, to be able to focus without trying. If during practice the groups and scores are going well, stop and think about what has been going through your head. You will probably find that you were thinking about what you were going to eat after the session, or some other mundane thing.

You can either score the distance, shooting it as though you were at a competition, or you can shoot for groups. Give yourself a parameter, for example all the arrows within the eight ring. Shoot ends of seven, eight, or ten arrows when shooting for groups outside and look at the group size and not the score. If you shoot six- or nine-arrow

groups you will be tempted to score the arrows as they are in multiples of three, which will distract from your session. Whether shooting for groups or scores use the telescope to evaluate each of the shots.

Practice is the place to learn to shoot in the wind and the rain, and to make sure that you have clothing for poor weather that does not affect your shooting. I find that if I have any clothing on my bow arm the string tends to catch and make the groups bigger.

Shooting in the wind is relatively easy – it just takes practice. Remember to keep your shooting form and use everything around you to your advantage. Everyone else is experiencing the same wind, so it is what you can make of it that will give you the advantage. Look at the flags across the field and listen to the trees blowing in the wind, as these will give you an indication of when and how strong the gusts of wind are. If it is a light, steady wind I may move my sight to keep the point of focus on the gold. One of the most interesting places to shoot in the wind is in a stadium, as the wind does not generally follow a pattern, so you will probably only have the flags on the top of the targets to give you an indication about how the wind is behaving. Similarly, if you shoot in a very sheltered field, you will need to visit a club that has a more open field to gain experience of shooting in the wind. See Chapter 12 for more on shooting in the wind and rain.

## Summary

With good training and practice your competitions will go well. If you carry out a post-competition analysis you will realize the areas that you need to work on during your practice and training sessions. Competition is about shooting every arrow the best you can. Leave the work on your style changes and improvements for during your training.

Even if you are not a competition archer you can use the information in this chapter to take you to the level for which you have the time available.

Chapter 8

# Nutrition

When I first started going to competitions, it was because of the interesting venues and the picnics at lunch times. I have subsequently found that if you have a good picnic at lunch time, the results in the afternoon drop. This chapter is therefore about looking at your eating and drinking habits and adjusting them if necessary. As there is so much information available on sports nutrition and nutrition in general, this will only be an introduction to food and eating habits.

Nowadays when you mention diet, it seems to be connected with some form of weight loss. To me, the word 'diet' is about what you eat and drink on a regular basis to fuel your body. If you maintain the proportion of input to output your weight will remain reasonably constant. Therefore it stands to reason that if you change the proportion between input and output your weight should also change accordingly.

We need to eat carbohydrates, protein, fat, vitamins, minerals, water and fibre in the right balance.

The energy from food comes from four components:

- carbohydrates – energy, stored as glycogen
- proteins – tissue growth and repair
- fat – concentrated energy source, excess stored as fat
- alcohol.

These components are broken down by the digestive system and taken into the bloodstream, although alcohol goes directly into the bloodstream without having to be broken down. Carbohydrates come in two forms: simple (sugars) and complex (starches) and are broken down into single sugar units. Fats are broken down into fatty acids and protein into amino acids.

It is a balanced intake of three of these power sources at the right times that will help you with your shooting. Alcohol is a banned substance in archery, so it may not be consumed prior to or during competitions.

A recommended balance of energy intake from the three permitted sources is: 70 per cent carbohydrate, 20 per cent fat and 10 per cent protein. Easy to say, but how do you work this out and what does it look like? On the whole, most dinner plates contain too much fat and protein and not enough carbohydrate. One way of working out the balance is to use the interactive nutrition section from Encarta 95 or 96. (Although Encarta 2002 has a calorie counter it is not as comprehensive as the earlier versions.) Using this interactive program, you can select the food you have eaten for a meal or for a day and it will calculate not only the balance of carbohydrates, proteins and fats, but also intakes of vitamins and minerals. If you use this for a few weeks to evaluate the proportion of intake, you will soon be able to adjust your eating habits to a better balance.

Another way of calculating the proportions is to work them out from the information given on the packet. All food products will give the amounts of carbohydrate, protein and fat per gram on the packaging. This information in grams needs to be recalculated as the energy released by a gram of fat is twice as much as released by a gram of

---

**The Benefits of Bread and Jam**

Bread and jam contain mainly carbohydrates, simple in the jam and complex in the bread. Carbohydrates are easily broken down into glycogen, which is one of the main energy sources that the muscles need to operate when shooting (although it is the creatine energy system used to shoot the bow, which is replaced via glycogen and fat stores).

carbohydrate or protein. For example: 1g of carbo-hydrate or protein releases 4kcal of energy; 1g of fat releases 9kcal of energy; and 1g of alcohol releases 7kcal. 1kcal is the heat required to raise 1kg (litre) of water by 1°C.

To find the proportions of energy in a tin of mushroom soup you would calculate it thus:

*Information given on the tin*

100g provides 54kcal:

Protein 0.9g        $0.9 \times 4 = 3.6$kcal
                    $100/54 \times 3.6 = 6.66\%$

Carbohydrate 4.6g   $4.6 \times 4 = 18.4$kcal
                    $100/54 \times 18.4 = 34.07\%$

Fat 3.5g            $3.5 \times 9 = 31.5$kcal
                    $100/54 \times 31.5 = 58.33\%$

                    Total = 53.5kcal

To do this calculation is to multiply the proteins weight in grams by its substance multiplier protein × 4 this will give you the amount of kcal for pro-tein for 100g serving. To then find the percentage of protein, divide the 100g by the total kcal given for the 100g portion 54kcal 1.85 then multiply this by the 3.6 this will give you the percentage of protein that makes up the soup. You can see from this that fat makes up for 58 per cent of the soup and is higher than you want, if you have bread with the soup you will change the proportions per meal.

*Information on an average loaf of bread*

100g provides 215kcal:

Protein 9.6g        $9.6 \times 4 = 38.4$kcal
                    $100/215 \times 38.4 = 17.86\%$

Carbohydrate 39g    $39 \times 4 = 156$kcal
                    $100/215 \times 156 = 72.55\%$

Fat 2.3g            $2.3 \times 9 = 20.7$kcal
                    $100/215 \times 20.7 = 9.6\%$

                    Total = 215.1kcal

The carbohydrate content of bread is high and the fat low, so bread and soup go well together.

Once you start looking at labels and doing some calculations you will soon have a good idea of what percentages of energy the package holds without having to do the calculations. As you look closer, you will find that some foods have a higher percentage of fat than you first thought. As with exercise, eating is about adjusting the proportions and rhythms of what you eat to maintain a healthy body.

# Drink

Maintaining your body fluids to the correct level will contribute to maintaining your performance, because as you dehydrate your performance levels will drop significantly, no matter how strong you are. The performance loss by both dehydration and sleep deprivation are two areas that cannot be over-come by mental or physical strength or fitness. Keeping your body hydrated is the only way to maintain performance. A loss of 2 per cent of your body's weight through dehydration can affect your muscles strength and performance by up to 20 per cent. A loss of 4 per cent of your body weight will lead to nausea, dizziness and possible fainting. Dehydration will also increase body temperature and increase heart rate.

Drink comes in three categories: hypotonic, iso-tonic and hypertonic:

- Hypotonic fluids are less concentrated than your bodily fluids, therefore they are absorbed into the body quickly, leading to faster rehydration.
- Isotonic fluids are of the same concentration as your body fluids and will be absorbed at about the same rate as water.
- Hypertonic fluids are more concentrated than your body fluids, therefore they are absorbed more slowly. If you need to rehydrate, this fluid will do it the slowest, but it may contain more carbohydrates which will help to maintain or boost the blood sugar levels.

If you are thirsty, this means you are dehydrated and your performance will have already been affected. So keep yourself hydrated.

*Finding Your Hydration Level*
The easiest way of finding your hydration level is to look at the colour of your urine. It should be rel-atively clear. The darker the colour of your urine the more dehydrated you are. If your urine is dark, drink a hypotonic drink as this will rehydrate you faster than water. Being well hydrated all the time is good for the body as it helps the flow through the

kidneys. Work on keeping the body well hydrated by looking at the colour of your urine. There are 'pee charts' available that give you a colour index you can match to your urine. These are available from Dietitians in Sport & Exercise Nutrition (DISEN), P.O. Box 176, Stockport SK7 1XZ, or can be found on the web by searching for 'pee chart'.

If you travel to hot countries you will dehydrate quicker, so you will have to drink a larger quantity to compensate

*How to Maintain Your Hydration Levels*

Ascertain the temperature both inside and outside where you live. When you are away from home try to keep your accommodation at a similar temperature to your home, especially the bedroom, as you still sweat when you are asleep but will be less aware of this fluid loss. Keep a drink by the bed when you sleep, so that you can drink at night if you wake up thirsty. In the morning, finish the drink, as this will ensure that any fluid loss overnight is immediately replaced and you start the day by maintaining your fluid levels. Be aware of any changes in the outdoor ambient temperature. If it is warmer than at home, drink a little more to compensate. Make sure you have drink available throughout the day – get into the habit of having a bottle of drink in your shooting bag whenever you go training and also have drink available at work. Two litres of fluid a day is a good intake to start with; if you exercise, you will need to take more. The current thinking on 'drink' seems to be that it is covered by any sort of fluid intake of a non-alcoholic variety. Therefore to keep yourself hydrated you do not have to drink just sports-specific drinks – tea, coffee, juice and so on are fine. In archery, there is no excuse for becoming dehydrated, as you have plenty of time between shooting to drink.

*Caffeine*

Up until January 2004 caffeine was a banned substance in competitions over a certain level. It is a stimulant and can alter how you feel and your arousal levels, so can negatively affect your shooting. This varies with the individual so you will need to experiment to see how much impact it has on your shooting. I find that it is quite easy to be caffeine-free in the UK – I take a small jar of decaffeinated coffee around with me. However, it can be difficult sometimes to get decaffeinated

coffee or tea abroad. So I now have caffeinated coffee occasionally, but try as much as possible to be caffeine-free before and during the competition. The other benefit to cutting back on caffeine is that after the shoot with a long drive ahead of you, a coffee really keeps you awake. The other downside of caffeine is that it is a diuretic, so it will make you go to the toilet more often, which can make you dehydrate quicker. Needing to go to the toilet more often can also be disruptive if the competition toilets are not nearby.

*What to Drink*

Drinking 'still' water is fine, but you may find that you need to have a little extra in it. Drinking too much water and not eating enough seems to wash out the salts from the body and may leave you feeling nauseous. So it is a good idea either to eat a small amount between drinks, or take drinks with a little sugar and salt in to help replace the lost minerals. These drinks can either be bought ones, such as Lucozade Sport and the like, or made up. It is usually beneficial to add a little flavour to the water as this will tend to encourage you to drink more than if it was just water.

*Homemade isotonic drinks*

- 1ltr water
  60–70g sugar or glucose
  1g salt
  + sugar-free squash to flavour
- 500ml water
  500ml unsweetened fruit juice
  1g salt

Personally, I prefer Lucozade Sport as a hypertonic drink as it contains maltidextrin, which helps to give an even release of carbohydrates; alternately, I drink carbonated water with a little 'Hi-Juice' mixed in an isotonic drink. It is not always recommended to take carbonated drinks, so try it out in practice first, but I find them more refreshing.

## Food

Awareness of what you eat and drink starts in the practice field. By keeping a training diary, you will start to see if there are any patterns developing regarding what you eat and your results. Large meals prior to shooting are quite likely to lower the level of your shooting. If you decide to enter competitions, you will most likely need to take

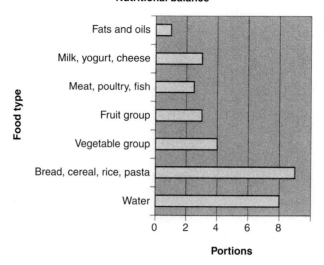

*The chart shows a reasonable daily balance of food stuffs.*

food with you, so take along the sort of food that you normally eat. Indoors, you may be shooting in the morning session so will be able to eat after the session, but do make sure you eat then. If you feel that you will need a little sustenance during the competition, take some bread and jam (lightly flavoured) sandwiches cut into little squares, or fruit – these can be taken just after you have shot your arrows, followed by a little drink.

This allows time for you to clear the mouth while scoring your arrows, as it can take at least ten minutes between ends, especially if you are shooting first on the end that you take the snack. Strong flavoured foods, and especially salty, spicy foods, will change how the glands in the mouth work. This in turn changes the shape of the mouth, in so doing altering the position of the nock in relation to the eye, which will then change the centre of your group.

At outdoor competitions you will be there all day so you will need to refuel during the day, otherwise by the end of the day your scores will suffer. You can eat little bits during the day, much the same as at indoor competitions, but try to maintain the rhythm of your normal eating, in particular eating at lunchtime. At some competitions you may get an hour for lunch, but it is likely to be shorter. The trick is not to eat too much and to eat food that is easily digestible. If you have your rolls prepared, you can, as at indoor events, eat your rolls on the way to the

target after shooting the last end prior to the lunch break. This will give you as much time as possible to start digesting the food prior to shooting again.

When going to events either overnight or abroad, try to stick as far as possible to your normal eating habits. Bed & Breakfasts and hotels always seem to put on nice cooked breakfasts, but if you do not normally eat them, stick to cereal or toast. You will have invested time and effort into your training and spent money on accommodation and travel to a competition – eating the foods that you normally eat will maximize your chances of getting the results you deserve.

Once you have finished the training session or competition, carbohydrates will be absorbed at a higher rate within the first one and a half hours of completing the exercise. So prepare some food for the end of the competition, especially if you are competing over more than one day. This will help to replenish your energy levels more quickly. The food needs to be mainly carbohydrates but a little protein will help with the absorption.

### Dairy and Calcium
A study into maintaining a regular intake of dairy-product calcium found that one of the side effects was to switch the cells in the body to store less fat. This is partly due to the hormone

called calcitriol – if the level of calcium is low, calcitriol is released, telling the body to store more fat. If the levels of calcium are sufficiently high, the body burns fat instead of storing it. The original data came from a study in osteoporosis. Women especially can suffer from a weakening of the bones, osteoporosis. A study group was set up, with one of the groups taking a good intake of dairy calcium, such as milk, yoghurt and cheese, to help maintain bone density, while the other group just took a calcium supplement. The group that maintained its calcium supplement through dairy products not only ensured that its calcium levels were maintained but also lost weight. This was not reflected in the group that just took the calcium supplements. Two cups of yogurt or the equivalent a day should be sufficient to keep your levels up.

## Summary

This is only an introduction to nutrition – there are many good books on the subject if you wish to find out more. Diet is not only about the balance of foods that you eat but also ensuring that you eat the full variety of food stuffs – fruit, vegetables, dairy products, meat, fish, fats. The variety in a balanced diet will ensure that you get the full range of vitamins and minerals necessary to maintain a healthy body. It is the portions on your plate that will determine a rising or falling weight level. In this way, you can maintain or adjust your weight and strength while ensuring that your body gets the right nourishment. This will allow you still to eat all the foods that you like – there is no need to feel guilty about having a chocolate mousse when it forms part of a balanced food intake.

# Chapter 9

# Making the Most of Your Mind

Because most people do not understand how their brain operates, they underestimate their potential and tend to underachieve in life. If you can understand how your brain/mind operates, you can modify the way you think to improve your chances of achieving whatever you want.

There are many books and tapes on psychology and self (mental) improvement. The ones I use are listed in the Suggested Reading section. In the space available here, I will suggest the key areas to work with in order to improve your shooting. One aspect that you must be aware of is that men's and women's brains are wired differently. The female brain is the original pattern and it is the amount of testosterone released while the foetus is in the womb that modifies the female brain into the male type. The levels of testosterone and oestrogen will determine how much the brain is modified. This leads to better spatial awareness and concentration in men and more empathy and multitasking abilities in women, to illustrate a few of the differences.

## Making You Believe

Psychology only works once you believe in the power of the mind; once you do believe, the rest is easy. The trick is to prove it by showing that in some areas of life you use psychology without knowing it. If I can make you aware that it works in some areas, it will encourage you to utilize it further, enabling you to use these tools to make the most of your mind. Why do you think that successful people tend to be successful in all they do? It is their attitude to how they approach challenges in life that gives them the opportunity to succeed.

How do you tie your shoelaces? You do not even have to think about how to tie the bow. The mental mechanism works like this:

- You are made aware that your lace is undone.
- You bend down to catch hold of the lace in both hands; for this you need to see where the laces are.
- Once you have the lace in your hands, you will carry on talking or thinking about what you were doing previously.
- You then tie the lace, without having to engage the conscious mind.

When I was a young boy I remember the first time that I tied a bow. It was on my dressing gown belt, and I was congratulated by my parents for being so clever. Now I do it without thinking – using the subconscious.

To learn a new task, first you decide that you want to learn something new, then you use the conscious mind to teach the subconscious how to do it; once the subconscious has learned, it will take over and you will perform the task automatically. For example, if you undo your shoelace and then try to talk yourself through every movement and placement of the lace in the fingers to tie it again, you will probably go wrong. This is because if you let the conscious mind 'help' with a subconscious routine, this disrupts its sequence and the task is no longer a routine. Once you understand this mechanism, you will catch yourself, at other times, disrupting a subconscious routine and having to start at the beginning of the sequence again.

Another aspect of shoelace tying is that it is quite likely that you tie your laces differently to me. If you try to learn my method of tying shoelaces it will probably take one month to relearn the different way of doing it. This is because one month is normally the amount of time it takes to teach or reteach the subconscious. For those of you who wear a watch, try putting it on your opposite wrist every morning

*On turning the book upside-down the distortion leaps out at you, as the brain processes inverted faces as objects. Only when the 'face' is the correct way up is the distortion more apparent. (Exploratorium)*

– you will find that it will take about one month before you automatically put it on the alternative wrist and even then, if you are tired you may unintentionally go back to putting it on the original wrist. Using the techniques of mental rehearsal and repetition, this one-month period can be reduced.

Many of you will either drive cars or play console games. If you remember what was it like when you first started – three pedals, a steering wheel, indicators, lights, mirrors, a gear stick or a game pad with loads of buttons and controls – lots of things to think about and not enough arms and legs to do them. Now that you have gained experience not only can you drive or play easily, you can put a CD on, hold a conversation and relax while doing these tasks. Drivers will probably find that sometimes, when travelling a regular route to work, they will forget where they are on the journey. This is because the subconscious has taken over the driving and it is like being on autopilot. However, if anything out of the ordinary were to happen, the subconscious would alert the conscious mind to make decisions to deal with the situation.

Watching Jay Barrs' video, *The Mental Game*, was the key to opening my eyes to the huge advantages of mastering the mental aspects of my life. Jay set out to prove that the mental practices he was given to do while he was at the US national team training would not work; but, in doing them, he found quite quickly that his archery improved and that the mental training did in fact work. It led to him winning the gold medal at the 1988 Olympic Games.

## The Conscious and the Subconscious

Although the conscious mind can only think of one thing at a time, the subconscious can multitask; it is the conscious mind that lays the pattern for the subconscious to follow. If the subconscious pattern is disrupted by the conscious mind, the pattern will falter. If the conscious mind is engaged on another subject, the subconscious takes over with the task in hand. This can be illustrated when driving, especially when following a regular route. If when driving home you decide you will detour from your normal route to go to the shops and before you get there your conscious mind should happen to be distracted by, say, a careless driver, invariably the subconscious will take over and you will find yourself following your regular route, having missed the turn to the shop. Most will put it down to being forgetful; it is not that you forgot, but the subconscious took over and set you on your normal route. Consider the amount of repetitive activities you carry out every day – getting dressed, brushing your teeth, making coffee, brushing your hair, putting your keys in your pocket, putting the milk in the fridge and so on. The list is endless of what your subconscious does for you, allowing you to think consciously about more immediate matters. This is one of the systems of the brain that we can use to our advantage when shooting.

Use the conscious mind to teach the subconscious how you want to shoot (training). Then distract the conscious mind to let the subconscious mind shoot the shot (practice). Training involves taking the part of the shot that you want to improve and then consciously working to improve that aspect. During the practice session, you need to distract the conscious mind to allow the subconscious to shoot the shot. There are a number of ways to achieve this, but what must be understood is that during the practice period the conscious mind will want to 'help'. It will want to be involved with getting that better score and making you try harder. Therefore you need to give the conscious mind a task that will enable the subconscious to be able to get on with the task of shooting.

It is necessary to utilize a number of mental 'tools' to keep the conscious mind engaged. If you only have the tool of keeping the hand relaxed, this will eventually be taught to the subconscious, then the conscious mind will start to 'help' in other dynamic areas. So you will need to find a selection of mental tools to use on your conscious mind. The conscious mind needs to be distracted, but kept within the sphere of what you are doing, for example by:

- keeping the alignment of the string picture
- concentrating on the point of focus
- keeping a long stretch in the forearm of the draw arm
- feeling your feet on the ground
- thinking about food.

You will need to discover what works for you. When you are shooting very well either in the training or practice cycle, stop, go and sit down and quietly think about what was going through your mind. If you find something useful, add it to

---

**Keeping the Conscious Mind Busy**

I discovered while I was training was that if I worked on my bow arm, or release, or any part involved with movement, the conscious mind would tend to exaggerate the movement, causing inconsistencies in the group size. When I worked on keeping my bow hand relaxed, I would shoot very consistent groups. This, I realized, was because I had given my conscious mind a task, to work on keeping the hand relaxed, a useful job for it to do because if I tensed up the bow hand muscles, the arrow would go 3cm above the group at 18m. It also allowed the subconscious to shoot the shot without interference.

---

your tools. (Originally, the analogy of 'tools' was to keep them in a mental 'toolbox', but I find I have a mental 'cupboard' with lots of shelves on which to keep the tools and spare pieces of the mental jigsaw.)

You may well see in others, and yourself, a pattern while shooting. You start off scoring well, realize that you are 'on' for a good score and then start to try. As a result, you do not end up with the result you expected halfway through. Your conscious ego wanted to 'help', but interfered with the flow of the subconscious.

*Recognizing Erroneous Subconscious Routines*
If you think closely about the different areas of the shot, then examine the results of your training, practice and competition using your diary, you will start to notice trends and patterns, but some of them will be errors in the subconscious routine.

*Example One*
Many archers shooting indoor rounds will notice a trend that the first two arrows go in the middle, but the third always tends to go off. This pattern may well initially stem from not being strong enough to shoot three arrows consistently in a row without getting tired. The fitness levels in archers just starting out tend to be slow to increase because they are only shooting once a week. The subconscious therefore becomes programmed not to shoot the third arrow quite so well. On another level, the conscious mind becomes aware that the third arrow is not going in the middle, so it tries to 'help' and consequently the confidence of the third arrow hitting the middle is low. The first two arrows are expected to go in the middle, so they do. To get the third arrow to go into the middle, you have to trick the mind. Put the third arrow in the bow and come up to full draw. Then come down, take the arrow out of the bow and put it back into the quiver. Now take it or another one out of the quiver and shoot it as the 'fourth' arrow, saying to yourself that 'The fourth arrow always goes into the middle' – and it will. Once you have done this for a couple of weeks, you will get bored of it and realize that the third arrow always goes in the middle anyway.

*Example Two*
While shooting a double FITA near Belfast a few years ago, one of the team at the start of the lunch break on the Sunday said 'I shot over a 1200 FITA score yesterday. I have shot well this morning but I

will tire after lunch and not make 1200 again today.' He had never shot a double 1200 before as he said that he always tired on a Sunday afternoon. On one level he was talking himself out of shooting well, on another his subconscious had got into the routine of not shooting well on the Sunday as he usually worked a full week and was tired by the weekend. On this occasion he had had a couple of days off work and so there was no reason to be tired as he had slept well and been doing all the training. Once he realized that his subconscious was verbalizing why he wasn't going to shoot so well in the afternoon, he was able to turn it around by giving himself a pep talk. He achieved his first double 1200 that afternoon.

### Teaching and Reteaching the Subconscious

You can teach the subconscious not only through repetition of the shot and the movements and positions you want for it, but also by the amount of emotion attached to the shot. For example, if, after five good shots, you make a poor one and react by cursing and shaking your head negatively, this will not only reinforce the bad shot but the excess of negative emotion will cancel out the five good shots. When you make good shots, give yourself a mental 'pat on the back'. If it is a good group tell yourself how great it was and remember how it felt to shoot such good shots. The positive emotion for shooting a good shot must far outweigh any disappointment for a shot that didn't go how you wanted it to. By reinforcing the good shots, you are indicating to the subconscious what you expect of it. Remember that once the arrow is shot, there is nothing more you can do about it. In the words of Lanny Bassham in *With Winning in Mind*: 'feast' or 'forget'. Learn what it takes to shoot an arrow into the ten –'feast'. If it does not go how you want: 'forget'. Just think about how to shoot the next arrow into the ten and shoot it well.

If you want to change some aspect of a shot, by starting normally and following through until you get to the aspect you want to change, it will be a slow process. If, however, you modify the whole start and draw and include the new aspect of the shot, you can learn the new bit quite quickly. Once you have become consistent with the new aspect of the draw, return to your normal start and draw, incorporating the new aspect. If you do not do this, your subconscious will want to continue with your normal routine. If you use your mind well, this will help you to make quicker progress with your archery.

## Neurolinguistic Programming

Neurolinguistic Programming (NLP) pertains to adjusting the way you think and the words that you use, and also how you, or another individual, perceive the meaning of these words. In essence, NLP is about studying the methods and practices of people at the top of their profession in whatever field and then copying the best practices. NLP is not only useful for the archer but for the coach as well. Some of the areas it covers are:

- goal setting
- body language and confidence
- eye-accessing cues
- sensory perception preferences
- verbal communication.

If you copy the practices of a 1200 shooter that is what you may become. If, from the start, you follow the practices of a 1350 shooter you will go a long way in achieving your ultimate goal.

### Goal Setting

All top performers will have a plan. Their plan will be set up around what they want to achieve – their goal. Once you have an ultimate goal, you can plan for reaching that goal, but the first step is to work out what your goal is.

Your goal is what you ultimately want to achieve or acquire. This will then need to be broken into short- and long-term goals to ensure that you are on target for your ultimate goal. The first step is to ensure that you have the correct ultimate goal. For example, a boy's dream was to own a Porsche. He left school early and wound up in a low-paid job. He saved his money over many years and eventually bought a second-hand Porsche. He was a clever man but had the wrong goal. If he had studied hard and done well at school, he would have perhaps become a doctor or an accountant, had a well-paid job and been able to buy himself a new Porsche and a house as well. So his goal perhaps should have been to become as well-educated as possible to lead on to getting a highly paid job that would allow him to buy whatever cars he wanted.

My goal to start with was to become a world-class archer. Once I was competing at world-class level, I realized that the goal was not correct, because I had achieved it. I revised it so that my goal was to be the best archer in the world. Maybe I will reach my goal, but as long as it is leading to the top, I will be aspiring in the right direction.

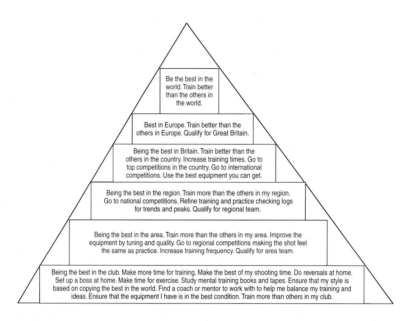

Be the best in the world. Train better than the others in the world.

Best in Europe. Train better than the others in Europe. Qualify for Great Britain.

Being the best in Britain. Train better than the others in the country. Increase training times. Go to top competitions in the country. Go to international competitions. Use the best equipment you can get.

Being the best in the region. Train more than the others in my region. Go to national competitions. Refine training and practice checking logs for trends and peaks. Qualify for regional team.

Being the best in the area. Train more than the others in my area. Improve the equipment by tuning and quality. Go to regional competitions making the shot feel the same as practice. Increase training frequency. Qualify for area team.

Being the best in the club. Make more time for training. Make the best of my shooting time. Do reversals at home. Set up a boss at home. Make time for exercise. Study mental training books and tapes. Ensure that my style is based on copying the best in the world. Find a coach or mentor to work with to help me balance my training and ideas. Ensure that the equipment I have is in the best condition. Train more than others in my club.

*Once you have decided on your goal, it is much easier to plan how you are going to achieve it.*

You need to set short- and long-term goals that will be ultimately attainable but will force you to work hard while keeping you on target for your ultimate goal. Aim to become the best archer in your region, then in Great Britain, followed by Europe and finally the world. The first goal would be to make the regional team. Find out what level you need to be at to make this team. As you are working towards that goal, you need to have your eye on the next step, to be the best in Great Britain. To achieve this, what score levels will you need, what shoots will you have to go to?

How are you going to be the best and what will make you the best? When striving to achieve these goals, there are various mental methods that you can employ, for example setting a 'task' or an 'outcome' goal. Task-setting within archery means working on shooting every arrow as best as you can, focusing on how you carry out the task of shooting the arrow. With outcome-setting, your plan is to win the shoot at all costs, which tends to lead to the focus being on what the other archers are doing and trying to beat their scores. Outcome-setters are therefore more likely to cheat, either by deliberately putting other competitors off by words or actions, or by mis-scoring the arrows to their advantage.

I feel that 'task over outcome' is the preferable mindset. If you carry out the task of shooting the arrows better than everyone else, you will win. It also means that by concentrating on the task in hand, you will be much less affected by what is going on around you. You will be better able to 'control the controllables', which will allow you to manage your physical movements and mental routine far better than an 'outcome over task' orientated archer. So you are then more likely to reach your goals.

How to achieve what you want:

1. Decide on what you want – your ultimate goal.
2. Devise a plan to achieve your ultimate goal – intermediate goals/training plan and so on.
3. Stick to the plan.
4. Assess your progress – are you achieving your goals?
5. If progress is good, carry on. If it is not, modify your plan.

### Body Language and Confidence

Body language and confidence go hand in hand. If your body language is good, your confidence will be good. Look at how top players in any sport hold themselves – upright, strong, with positive, controlled body movements, perhaps keeping their focus close, on a spot on the ground a metre or so in front of them or on a piece of equipment. In tennis, do the racquet strings always need adjusting, or is the player finding his focus? The loser will let the body sag, look at his feet or stare into the distance as though watching his dreams fly away.

Body movements affect how your confidence waxes and wanes. If you see your opponent shaking his head from side to side and looking glum, your game will improve because you can see that your opponent is visibly struggling. He is sending a signal to his subconscious via his body position to say that things are not going well, so in turn his game will falter.

Use body language to your advantage; when you are shooting well, feel how you hold yourself and how you act, then try to be that archer all the time, whatever the scores. This will mean that other archers will not know if you are having a bad day, and in any case because you are giving your subconscious the 'good shooting' body movements, you will naturally shoot better.

Building confidence is about doing everything in your training plan to succeed. If you go to the competition having followed your plan, shot the arrows required, eaten the right things and had the right amount of rest, your confidence will be high and using your body language to look good will bolster that confidence both outwardly and inwardly.

*Eye-Accessing Cues*
Have you ever noticed when you are talking with someone that their eyes look to one side or the other as they try to remember what they want to say or decide what they want to do? As you access and use certain areas of the brain, your eye movement is linked to those areas. This is known in NLP as 'eye-accessing cues'.

According to this concept, when you remember sounds, pictures or feelings you will look to one side and when you construct sounds, pictures or feelings you will look to the opposite side. In the greater percentage of people, looking to the left will be for remembering and the right will be for constructing. Looking up, level or down will indicate what sensory area your thoughts are taking you. To ascertain what an individual's eye-accessing cues are, you can ask deliberate questions to evaluate them.

Remembered questions:

- What colour is your front door?
- How does your couch feel when you sit on it?
- What does your doorbell sound like?
- What did you last say to your best friend?

Constructed questions:

- What would your front door look like painted tartan?
- What would sitting on the moon feel like?
- What sound would a piano make when it is hit by a train?
- What would you say to the Queen if you met her?

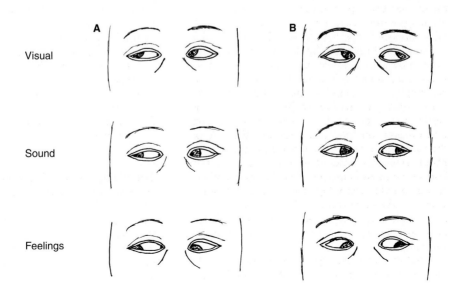

(A) *Remembered cues.*
(B) *Constructed cues.*

Alternatively, you can chat to people, including particular questions in the normal conversation and following their eye movements.

What, you may ask, has this got to do with archery? The answer is that once you have established your own eye pattern, you can deliberately look in the appropriate direction when you want to remember how a shot felt. Or, if you want to construct a new shot sequence, you can look to the 'construction' side in order to work out how to improve the draw quicker, so it is a useful aid when carrying out mental rehearsals.

*Sensory Perception Preferences*
1. Visual – pictures.
2. Kinesthetic – touch.
3. Auditory – sounds.
4. Olfactory – smells.
5. Gustatory – taste.

Most of us possess the five senses with which to sample and interact with the world, and the steps listed above are the perception paths by which most people carry out this interaction. When thinking about a car, for example, the usual first impression will be a picture in the mind, followed by how it will feel, sound, then smell.

So, for many people, if they talk to each other about, say, a couch, a picture of a couch will be in the mind of the speaker, while the listener, on hearing the words, will form a picture of a couch in his own mind. As the speaker goes on to describe the couch, the picture is reformed and clarified in the listener's mind to fit the words.

The next biggest group of people will have touch as their primary input, with perhaps visual as the secondary sense, so when they talk about the couch they will be initially thinking and talking in feelings, concentrating on the smoothness of the material and how it feels to sit on. For those with auditory as their primary input, it will be how it sounds. Olfactory types will have smell as the first impression with which they sense the world. But in all types, as the conversation continues, the other senses will be brought into play. There are also differences in the balance between the senses, for example some will be very visually orientated, to the point where it almost overpowers all the other four senses. Some will experience less difference between the primary and secondary senses, usually between kinesthetic and visual, so there will be a blurring of the primary sense.

So now we understand that different people sense the world in different ways and at different levels. Not being aware of this can lead to a breakdown in communication, especially between coach and archer. If the coach is visual and the archer kinesthetic, misunderstanding in what one is conveying to the other can occur. If the coach ascertains that the archer is kinesthetic, he can then change his descriptions to use feelings and 'feelings words' to convey the content of the coaching, thus improving mutual understanding. This will take a little thought on the coach's behalf as he will have to access his secondary sense input, but it will be well worth it in the end.

To ascertain the primary and secondary inputs of individuals you can use a direct-question method, by asking them to give first impressions of random familiar words, for example by asking them what they first think about when you say: car, sofa, bed, house, front door, chair, food and so on. Or you can listen to them as they talk about the sort of day they have had, making a mental note of the words and phrases they use:

- visual – I see what you mean, looked in on, picture this, visualize and so on
- kinesthetic – I have a feeling, I'm touched and so on
- auditory – loud and clear, sounds good and so on.

The phrases and words individuals use will give you a good idea of how they are thinking, which will enable you to communicate with them more efficiently and effectively. You may know people who speak the English language well and are intelligent, but just do not seem to make sense when they talk, or you may have noticed, at school, a pupil that just cannot follow the instructions on the blackboard, to the exasperation of the teacher. In the end, the teacher reads aloud what was written to the pupil and then the pupil understands without any problems. In both cases of misunderstanding, it could possibly be due to differences in primary sensory input.

Shooting is about how the shot *feels* – it is kinaesthetic. When a visual person thinks about the shot, he will see the shot. When you consider what you can actually see in shooting, it is very little. You should be focusing on the point of reference and in doing so some areas of the visual cortex will in fact be closing down. So, unless you are a kinesthetic person, you will need to engage fully your kinesthetic sense. If you are a visual person, this is quite easy to do. For example, when you shut your eyes, as soon as you disrupt the primary sense the secondary sense takes over and the other senses become sharpened to support the secondary sense's new role. This is why shooting the arrow at the target at all distances with your eyes closed helps to reinforce the feel of the line and shot. For distance shooting, come up to full draw as normal, look at the point of focus, close your eyes, visualize what you saw when you were looking at the point of focus and shoot. If you want to feel the full draw with your eyes closed, do it at a close distance of 3m, but still visualize how the target looks at full draw. For auditory people, you can try shooting with headphones on in practice, perhaps with your eyes closed as well. When you are doing this exercise, feel the draw, the body position and weight distribution on the feet.

*Verbal Communication*

The key area in NLP is verbal communication – both communicating with others and with yourself. The internal and external dialogues require the same care and attention to produce positive results.

Don't think about pink elephants! Over the next few lines I want you to stop thinking about pink elephants. I don't want you to think about pink elephants, especially the big pink elephants. Put pink elephants right out of your mind. Now I have told you not to think about pink elephants they should be clear from your mind! Or not? If you now think about green giraffes, with big green eyes, they will replace the other big pink jungle animal that you were thinking of. The mind does not recognize 'don't' and will continue thinking about the action or object that follows the word 'don't'. So if you are told not to think about pink elephants, all that happens is that the pink elephants are reinforced. To supplant the elephants think about the green giraffes. In other words, think about what you want to do, not what you do not want to do.

A good example in archery is the cry often given by coaches: 'Don't drop your bow arm.' The mind will be left thinking about dropping the arm. What should be said is: 'Keep the bow arm up.' Think about want you want to achieve, keeping the arm in place after the shot. When the coach is listening to the archer talking about what he is working on, listen to the words the archer uses, for example 'I keep dropping my arm and am working on that'. Your internal dialogue is as important as the words you use to other people.

'Can't' should be another banned word; it is like a road block across the path of any progression: 'I can't cook', 'I can't draw', 'I can't drive', 'I can't work the computer' and so on. For example:

- 'I can't cook.' – So you don't, or do not try because you know already that you can't.
- 'I can't draw.' – So, again, you don't try.
- 'I can't change what I do.' – So you won't.

How about instead:

- 'I am not as good as I would like to be at cooking, but I am working on it.'
- 'In the past my drawing has been rudimentary, but with practice it will get better.'
- 'I can do anything – so I will give it a go!'

Change the words you use. If you say to yourself and others, 'I am not very good at the moment at [drawing, cooking, skiing …] but I will give it a go,' it will enable you to start working on the task at hand, at least letting you try to become the best you can be at whatever you do. Aim to say:

- 'I will do that.'
- 'I will see what I can do.'
- 'I will work something out.'
- 'I will try to improve it.'
- 'I will give it a go.'

Encouraging advancement of a goal or task is a combination of phrasing things in a positive manner and using the right words, which will allow

| Negative phrases | Change to positive statements |
|---|---|
| I can't do it. | I will try it, and see how it goes. |
| I have a problem. | I have a challenge. |
| Don't drop your arm. | Keep your arm up. |
| Can you look at me and tell me what I am doing wrong? | Can you look at me and tell me how I can improve? |
| I don't like this bow, it feels strange. | The bow feels different; I will work with it and see what I can do with it. |
| It is difficult to change my draw. | This is a different draw and I can get used to it. |

*Think about what you think and say – use positive statements.*

you, or the person you are helping, the opportunity to complete the task to the best of his or her ability.

NLP covers a large area of self-improvement, enabling you to reach your goals, giving you the mental and physical tools to make the best of all your abilities, improving and speeding up your learning techniques and ability to communicate with yourself and others. As you master NLP, you will be able to incorporate changes and improvements to your technique, allowing you to progress faster.

## Positive Attitude

A positive attitude is about finding the good in every situation. To some people this seems to come naturally, but it is only a learned trait. Some learn it early in life, but it can be adopted whatever life stage you are at. For example, if your house is flooded, you can take the attitude that at least you will be able to get new carpets. In archery, a positive attitude is about finding the good arrow that you shot even if there was only one arrow throughout the whole competition. Look at the good group in the black – this group is good, which means that

you are shooting consistently and well but they are in the black. In that case, all you have to do is move the sight and they will all go into the gold! These are very simplified illustrations of being positive, but it is about finding the good in what has happened, even if it is just learning from the experience.

Try to find the good in others, in what they say or do. If you look for the bad in people or situations you will find it. Turn that around and look at the good. By doing so, you will reinforce what you want to achieve, but, as with all other aspects of the mental process, this needs to be part of what you do every day and not just for archery. I know a few people who try to be positive in archery, but are negative in everything else they do. This holds them back from what they are trying to achieve. To enable you to embrace this concept, listen carefully to the words that you and others use and try to find better ways of phrasing them. It is easier to do this if you have two or more people who want to work on improving their mental outlook, as you can work together to improve each other's external dialogue, which in turn will help you to retune your own internal dialogue. Success in this area is directly connected to the concept of the use of words in NLP.

---

### True Story Time

A few years ago, the vehicle mechanics were deployed on exercise in north Norway. A vehicle came in with an electrical fault behind the dashboard. The only available mechanic, we knew, was poor at working out electrical faults. He immediately said, 'I can't do electrics', but we told him to get on with it. He stood next to the vehicle for three hours, telling everyone who passed that he could not do this. Yes, this is an extreme case, but true to life. If he had told himself and others, 'I am not very good at electrics, but I will give it a go', he would at least would have got into the vehicle and managed to take the six screws out of the dashboard!

Another story: my clerk was a keen golfer; I don't know much about golf, but we had occasion to discuss our sports. During the conversation, he started telling me that he could not putt: 'That's where it all goes wrong, I just can't putt,' he said. After a little questioning, it transpired that his handicap was seven, which is not too bad. He said he could drive the ball

no bother, but he was rubbish at putting. I suggested that his putting must be reasonable as his handicap was seven. He simply needed to improve his putting to bring his game up. It ended up as a two hour re-evaluation exercise on his putting ability. Because he had already told himself that he could not putt, when he got to the green he did not even try. On re-evaluation, he realized that he needed to take as much care in preparing himself for a putt as he did for his drive. He came back after the weekend having taken five off his handicap.

Both these stories illustrate that once you start using the 'can't' word it impedes your progress and stops you trying things that you might end up being good at. If you say you can't cook, you won't cook; 'can't' will stop you going into the kitchen and opening a cook book. If you say you can't draw a picture, you won't even pick up a pencil. Most tasks that you embark on require work, effort and time for you to become competent at them.

# Mental Training

As the brain is fed by electrical impulses and has no direct connection with the outside world, it is unable to tell if an action has actually been done, or if the same action has just been imagined. Mental training or rehearsal enables you to play and replay in your mind what you want to achieve using remembered and constructed sensual (visual, kinesthetic, audio) replays.

Many people talk about 'visualization', but what they are actually referring to is 'mental rehearsal'. As already discussed in NLP, with the greater amount of the population being visually orientated they will tend use the visual aspect of mental rehearsal, when they are actually trying to influence all the senses.

A study was carried out in the USA a few years ago using students. The study took a group of students and asked them make a penalty shot with a basketball through the hoop. The success rate was recorded. The main group was then divided into four groups. Group one was told to go away and carry on with life. Group two was asked to spend half an hour a day practising throwing the ball. Group three was told to think about how to throw the ball through the hoop. Group four was asked to practise throwing the ball through the hoop and also mentally to rehearse taking the shot.

When the groups were brought back and retested, group one showed no improvement. Group two, which had been physically practising throwing the ball, improved by 90 per cent. Group three, which only had to think about it, improved by 85 per cent. Group four, which did both, improved by 95 per cent. The results from this study indicate that there is very little difference between doing something and just thinking about doing it. Mental rehearsal does need to make use of all the senses, especially how the shot feels in archery, because when you consider how little you can see when you are shooting, you will understand how important the feel of the shot is.

Mental rehearsal exercises – mental training – should always be carried out in first person in real time. This means that as you rehearse the shot, you should feel, hear and see it as though actually carrying it out 'in your body' at the speed you would be doing the shot if you were really shooting.

Some coaches suggest that you should carry out mental rehearsal as if watching a video, which can be useful at some stages of your training. The downside is that it can start to divorce you from the feelings of the shot. For example, individuals who

have suffered a traumatic incident, such as a car crash, can suffer from traumatic episodes as they relive the incident in first person. In regression therapy, the individual is made to relive the event out of the body as though standing at their own shoulder, then over time moving further away from the crash, finally making the 'video' smaller, turning the sound down and making it black and white. Unhappy incidents are dealt with by making them small and black and white. Good incidents are encouraged to be imagined in full colour, loud and in first person.

When you first start carrying out mental training, the best way to get the sequence correct is to stand on the shooting line ready to shoot. With a friend at hand, have them write down what you say. You can then talk through the shot. The first time you try this, break each sense down and talk through your shot using each individual sense.

## *Visual*
- Look at the quiver.
- See your hand select an arrow and lift it up over the bow and place it in line with the nocking point.
- Spin the arrow to see the alignment of the nock.
- Place the nock on the string.
- Place fingers on the string.
- Make sure the tab plate is hard against the string.
- Look at the bow hand and settle it into the grip.
- Pull the string back a little.
- Check that the arrow is on the arrow rest.
- Watch the arrow sliding past the button and clicker.
- See the point of the arrow just under the clicker.
- Look up at the target.
- Look at the point of focus.
- See the arrow hit the gold.

## *Kinesthetic*
- Feel the shaft of the arrow in your finger and thumb.
- Feel the arrow slide out of the quiver.
- Feel the arrow spin between the finger and thumb.
- Click the nock onto the string.
- Lift the clicker with the finger and slide the arrow onto the button.
- Feel the tab in the hand and the first joint of the finger on the string.
- Feel the bow hand settle into the position in the grip.

- Straighten the front arm.
- Rotate the draw shoulder to draw the bow.
- Feel the balanced increase of pressure on the grip and the fingers.
- Feel the string on the centre of the nose and chin.
- Bring the rear shoulder into line.
- Expand.
- Feel the clicker.
- Feel the bow shoot forward and the tab on the neck.

*Auditory*
- Hear the fletching's click in the quiver.
- Hear the arrow sliding against the other arrows.
- Hear the click of the nock on the string.
- Hear the sound of the clicker being placed on the arrow.
- Hear the clicker sliding over the arrow as the bow is drawn.
- Hear the noise of the clicker.
- Hear the thrum of the bow as it is shot.
- Hear the sound of the arrow hitting the middle.

Mental rehearsals can be played through as individual senses, then amalgamated into a replay that combines them all. They can either be practised over a half-hour period or throughout the day. I find that if I try to run through mental rehearsals as a package, my mind wanders, so I prefer to do mental shots throughout the day, when waiting for a bus, queuing at the supermarket, having a shower and so on. This way, my shooting remains with me throughout the day. Once you have started doing mental training you can then include venues and situations, practising in your mind shooting and beating the best in the world. When you are putting together your mental training package, include your best shots from training or competition and how you felt when your shooting was going well.

Mental reinforcement should take place before every shot. Look at the target, feel the wind, look at the flags, listen to the rustle in the trees. Pick your point of focus; rehearse your shot with the arrow hitting the ten, then shoot the rehearsed shot. I find that the 'mental rehearsal shot' is played faster than real time, but the feeling is the same as if it was a real-time shot.

Whatever you are doing, make sure that you say and hear the right words. When you are shooting, concentrate on the good shots only. Make sure that the people around you are saying things that you want to hear. I can listen all day to archers who are talking about the good shots. The more you talk, think or listen to other archers talk about getting tens, the more likely you are to score them yourself. But more often than not, archers will tell you about the bad shots, how they missed and so on. When this happens, switch off mentally and think about shooting good shots. If necessary, walk away and mentally rehearse how to shoot the arrow into the middle.

Words are very powerful; their influence can be either negative or positive. An example of the negative influence of words would be to mention to a friend that he does not look well. Get others to make the same unfounded observations of illness to the same friend. He will soon be feeling unwell, just through the use of words. Choose to use words positively. While watching someone shoot, if you mention that his shooting is looking better, and a few others from the club do the same, the archer's form and stance will ten to improve. This is because the individual's self image is being improved and as a result his shooting is likely to become more consistent. Positive words that are credible and used at the right time will go a long way towards encouraging an archer by bolstering his mental image of how he shoots. Whether or not he does mental training himself, it will improve how he feels about his archery. The other side of using positive words and talking about how well an archer is doing is the reflected mental image of good shooting reinforcing your own mental training.

## Mirror Neurons

When watching an action take place, the neurons that would normally fire when doing that action are instead fired by the sensory input of observing it. The firing of the neurons mirrors the action. When watching top athletes or dancers performing, you will find your body starting to twitch as though wanting to perform the movement itself. Even when watching a film, when you are engrossed in the action you may find your body wanting to jump as the main character takes a jump. This is because the neurons in the brain fire as though you are doing the movement. If you are watching an activity at which you are competent, the firing of the neurons is stronger. It is believed that this effect of neurons firing to copy a movement initially stems from learning to mimic actions as part of childhood development.

Mirror-neuron firings can be utilized as part of the learning process in archery. According to the

Korean archery coach, Mr Ki Sik Lee, archery beginners in Korea are initially given to a master, behind whom they stand to mimic his movements. As a result, when they first come to pick up a bow, the body and mind already know the movements and actions necessary to hold and draw the bow, as the neurons required to do the action have been repetitively fired while mimicking the master.

To improve your own archery and mental training, watch a video, DVD or movie clip on the Internet of world-class archers shooting; observe carefully and feel the shot as they do it. If you do this prior to a session, your shooting will probably be that little bit better for that session. If you have a permanent shooting venue, having pictures of top archers in the range will help to keep the mind firing the right muscles to shoot the shot.

It is important to understand that, when you are competing, if there are any very good archers there, you should watch only them. If you watch archers with a poor shooting technique you will be firing up the brain to shoot like that. Keep focused only on good shots. If there is no one there with a good technique, read a book or look at anything else. Competitions are not the place to help other archers to shoot better.

## Coping with Excitement and Arousal Levels

Too often, feelings of nervousness and excitement are confused. Excitement can be used as a positive value to enhance shooting. However, if you tell someone that they will be nervous, then teach them how to cope with it, it is preparing them for failure.

You will be excited when you are doing something that you really want to do, such as going to the cinema or on holiday. Going to an archery competition should generate the same excitement. You are going to something where you want to do well, so it is only natural that you will be excited. When you are excited your pulse rate will rise, which is not usually conducive to good shooting and you may also find your mind wandering off the task in hand. When you are excited, your muscles will be a little more tensed, which will restrict the flow of blood slightly and lower the amount of oxygen flowing to the muscles. Will I win? How many tens will I get? How are the other archers shooting? These will be the type of thoughts going through your mind. This is where your mental training will come in, when you draw and shoot

the arrow your body needs to carry out the same movement every time. The more you work on your mental training, the easier it will be to keep your mind on the same steps throughout the shot. Sometimes you will see a good archer come down and start the shot again; it is not always because the shot is not set up the correctly, but sometimes it is because the mental programme needs to be restarted.

### Relaxation

Relaxation is a useful tool to enable you to lower your arousal levels. If you are excited your arousal levels will be high. If you are nearly asleep your arousal levels will be low. When shooting, you need to find the arousal level that gives you the best score. Too high and your heart will be racing, too low and you will not be interested enough. Stop shooting when you are doing well in practice and think about how you feel; judge what arousal level works best for you. On the whole, it is usual for an archer's arousal level to be relatively low, allowing for greater focus, although each individual's arousal level will be slightly different. Some archers may shoot better with high arousal levels; your score will help to indicate the best arousal level for your shooting.

In order to be able to lower your arousal levels effectively, you need to learn how to relax completely and to feel what it is like to be in that state. To start with, it may three-quarters of an hour to be able to get into a relaxed state, but it will get quicker with practice. Once you know what it feels like to be relaxed, you will be able to reach this state in one or two breaths. It will also make you more aware of your arousal state.

There are a number of ways of learning relaxation. One simple method is to lie down comfortably and tense each muscle one by one, holding the tension in then letting it relax. After a muscle has been tensed, its relaxation will be deeper than before. Work around the body, starting from the feet and moving upwards; this will give your conscious mind something to focus on. This technique will help to relax the mind as well as the body. Once you become practised at this technique, you will find that by tensing the whole body at the same time, then breathing out with a long breath while pushing down on the diaphragm, you will be able to relax in just one breath. I take a slightly deeper breath than normal, hold it for two seconds then breathe out, pushing all the excitement down.

Further to this tensing of the muscles, it can be

the mind that needs the most work on learning how to relax. This part is usually best carried out for the first time with someone reading out the following instructions once you have relaxed your muscles. It should be done in a darkened room or at least with the eyes shaded.

With your eyes closed:

- Feel the floor pushing up against your body, supporting it.
- Let your body flow into the floor and relax completely.
- Think about being warm and comfortable.
- Think about a time that you were happiest and most relaxed, perhaps a beach on holiday, or a winter's afternoon sleeping by the fire.
- Take yourself to that place.
- Immerse yourself in this favourite place.
- Use all your senses to explore this place and feel the sense of well being.

Once you have reached this comforting place, bring yourself back into your body and feel the peacefulness within.

You only need to bring the arousal level down to the level at which you shoot best, but you also need to be able to bring it up again if required. A few years ago when I was shooting everyone was telling me to relax. I became great at it, so much so that I could lower my arousal level to the point where I was just about asleep. This was not what was needed for me to shoot well.

To raise or lower your arousal level to your optimum, you need to do it in a fashion that does not alert other shooters. Lowering it is relatively inconspicuous as long as you do not make blowing noises. Raising it without making too much fuss can be a little trickier. I find that by coughing a little will raise my arousal level sufficiently. If when raising or lowering your arousal levels, the breathing patterns become rapid, your opponent may think you are nervous and feel better in himself, so do not give anything away.

## Concentration and Focus

A single-day shoot can take nine hours from start to finish; some competitions are shot over six days. You need to learn to focus in short bursts, being able to switch your concentration on and off. Concentrating for short periods allows your mind to relax between shots and ends, enabling you to make every shot count. There are different levels of

concentration and if you were to try and focus all day, you would wear yourself out.

Concentration needs, to an extent, to be learnt and practised, although not necessarily just by shooting. For those of you who play chess, this is a good concentration exercise. You will need the time to play at least two games – invariably as you start the first game you will be concentrating well, but as the game continues you may find that your concentration starts to slip. At this point, try to maintain the focus on the game, with the same feeling as when you started. Once that game is over, play another game directly after, maintaining your concentration on the moves.

Another concentration exercise I use is to play Tetris Game B on a Nintendo 'GameBoy'. You can start at the lower game levels, but aim to work up to the hardest game where the blocks come down at full speed. To complete the game, you need to concentrate fully on what you are doing; any distractions will lose you the game. These types of games will help give you the feeling of what it is to maintain full concentration.

There needs to be different levels of concentration during your shooting day. On the way to the shoot you need to be thinking about the weather and mentally rehearsing the shot. Prior to shooting, you need to run through the set-up of the bow and the rest of your equipment.

The next level of concentration is when the signal to shoot goes. At this point, push all your emotions down to get to your correct arousal level, stand on the line and assess the weather and how you are going to shoot, while putting the arrow into the bow. My main concentration period for the shot starts when I place my fingers on the string and finishes when the arrow hits the target. Once the arrow hits the target my concentration level goes down one step, until I place my fingers on the string once again.

It is best to use a physical signal to start the concentration cycle. For me, the signal is putting my fingers on the string. If you watch other athletes playing tennis, golf and so on, you will usually see a movement that they always carry out prior to the concentration sequence; for tennis it may be bouncing the balls twice on the ground before the shot, for example. The start, or anchor, of the concentration period needs to be worked on as much as any other aspect of the shot. It should be deliberate, but not complicated. Some archers will adjust the chest guard, or tap their leg to indicate to the brain that it is the start of the intense concentration cycle. If you are inclined to concentrate easily,

# concentration levels

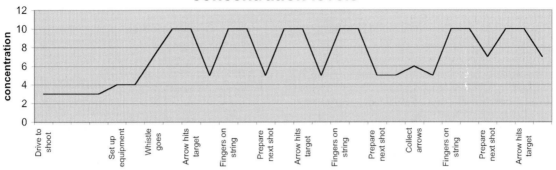

*Changing your concentration levels throughout the day enables you to concentrate fully during each shot.*

simply putting your fingers on the string should be a big enough signal, but if that is not enough to start the sequence you may need a more deliberate signal, such as tapping your side twice. The more you practise your concentration exercises, the more you will get the feeling of what it is to maintain your concentration.

Another aspect of concentrating hard is to be fully involved in what you are doing at a particular moment. If you are shooting – shoot. If you are cooking – cook. If you are relaxing with friends – relax. If you think about one activity while doing another, your focus will be lost and you will not get the full benefit out of the activity you are doing. As Lanny Bassham says: 'Be all there.'

## Situation Planning

Situation planning is part of the mental game. It involves dreaming up situations that you might come across in competition and planning how to deal with them. It may be as simple as: Question: 'What will I do if my rest breaks?' Answer: 'Step back from the line and quietly attract the attention of the judge, wait until the judge comes over and let him know what has happened. With fifteen minutes in which to fix it, take the spare rest from the blue box in the top right-hand corner of the tackle box, fit the spare rest and check that the shaft

of the arrow lies on the centre of the button. Once everyone else has finished shooting go up to the line with the judge, who will tell you how much time you have to shoot the remaining arrows.'

Your contingency plans need to cover what spares you will need to deal with all failures. Are you going to repair a tab or use your spare? Do you have a spare rest, string, nock, button, stabilizers? What will you do if the car breaks down on the way to a shoot? How will you deal with someone talking negatively to you? What will you do if it rains, snows, is very sunny, or is cold or hot? What will you do if your limbs break in training, or are lost or stolen? Or if the person you are shooting with has bad breath?

Situation planning enables you to have a game plan that allows you to deal with any situation. This is important because if you know what you will do it will be no surprise to you, and you will continue shooting your arrows into the middle as normal. Situation planning is closely linked with mental rehearsals as you will mentally rehearse every situation. Archers who do not plan for situations tend to lose points after an incident. It comes as a surprise to them and has interrupted their mental cycle putting them off their game.

## Summary

The mental game makes up 70 per cent of success in whatever you do. Having a good positive attitude and using all the mental tools available to you will enable you to reach your potential. As I stated at the beginning of this chapter, this is just a taster of using the mind's potential. A list of some of material that will enable you to pursue the mental game further is in 'Suggested Reading'.

Chapter 10

# Arrow Selection and Preparation

It is worth taking your time when selecting and matching the arrows to your bow. There are many different types of arrow available, each with different characteristics; at the top end of the market there is the X10, which can cost up to £300 for twelve arrows. Selecting the correct spine, type of arrow and correct cutting can potentially save you lot of money. With arrows you definitely get what you pay for. The top aluminium arrow is far better than a cheap carbon arrow.

## Arrow Anatomy

**Shaft** The tube that makes up the length of the arrow.

**Nock** The nock holds the arrow onto the string. These can be glued directly onto the arrow shaft. This type can take time to fit as the nock must be

checked to ensure that it is kept straight. A nock alignment gauge can be used to help in this process. The other type of nock is push-fit, some fitting into a unibush and others fitting directly onto the arrow shaft, either into, over or both (in nock, over nock and in/out nock). The push-fit type is easier to change and if the shaft is undamaged it will always fit straight. Beiter nocks must only be fitted to the string the correct way up.

**Unibush** This is fitted into the back end of the arrow shaft to locate a standard nock on aluminium arrows.

**Swage end** This is the tapered back end on some aluminium arrows where a nock is glued on.

**Point** The point is fitted to the front of the arrow to make it heavier and to allow it to penetrate the target. It can either be made in a single piece, or

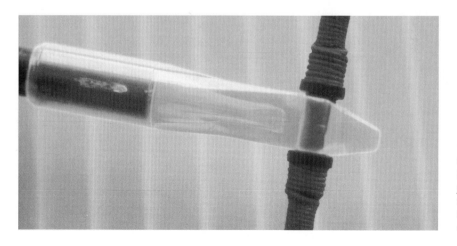

*The nock must be fitted the correct way up; as the bow is drawn, the nocking point angle changes. The nock is designed to locate the nocking point at that angle.*

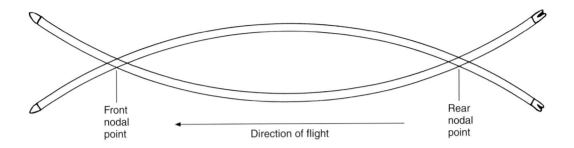

*As the arrow flexes as it leaves the bow, two points on the shaft appear to remain 'still'. Recurves would view this from the top and compounds from the side.*

used in conjunction with an insert. They are glued directly into the shaft with hot-melt glue. Special care needs to be taken when carrying out this procedure, otherwise serious damage to carbon shafts may occur. The single piece points may come in varying weights, or will come with the facility to 'break off' part of the insert to make the point lighter to aid tuning.

**Insert** The insert is glued directly into the shaft. It makes up part of the total front weight of the shaft and has an internal thread. Points of various weights can be screwed into it, allowing fine tuning of the arrow.

**Nodal points** When an arrow in flight is viewed from above, the arrow will flex. Two points on the shaft appear to be stationary along the line of the arrow's axis; these are the nodal points. If the set-up of the tuning is correct the path of both nodal points will follow the same trajectory to the target.

**Fletches/vanes** These are fitted to the back of the arrow shaft to help to stabilize the arrow as it leaves the bow and to make it spin as it flies to the target.

## Main Arrow Types

- Aluminium shafts
- Carbon shafts
- Aluminium with carbon overlay shafts

### Aluminium Shafts

These shafts range from basic to top quality. Most of the better shafts will be marked with a four-number sequence: 2013, 1816, 1615 and so on. The first pair of numbers indicates the arrow's diameter to the nearest sixty-fourths of an inch and the second pair of numbers indicates the thickness of the material that makes up the wall of the shaft to the nearest thousandths of an inch. Take 2014 – 20 indicates the diameter and 14 the wall thickness. For these types of arrows, points and unibushes must be bought to fit the shaft size, and they are not interchangeable with different diameter shafts. When choosing the arrows consider the wall thickness. A thicker wall may be a little heavier, but it will be more resistant to damage. Fitting points to aluminium shafts is relatively simple as they are held in with hot-melt glue. The points need to be warmed up on a small gas flame, so that the hot-melt glue will melt onto it without bubbling (which it will if you overheat the point). Excessive heat can melt the point or damage the shaft when the hot point is inserted.

### X7 Shafts

X7 shafts are the best type of aluminium arrow. They are made to a higher tolerance of straightness than all the other shafts. These shafts are more resistant to bend than other shafts, but if they are bent they are then harder to straighten. If the shafts are shot into tight groups, they will tend to crack before they bend, so if you are shooting well, or see that the shafts have struck each other, check them closely for cracks before you shoot them again. These are very good arrows for shooting indoors or for juniors looking for top-quality arrows but not wanting to go as far as some of the better carbon shafts. The limiting factor when shooting aluminium arrows is their weight, as they are heavier than the carbon equivalent. So reaching the longer distances may be an issue when selecting your shafts.

*Jazz Shafts*

Jazz shafts are a good starter arrow and not too expensive – most of the juniors in the club I belong to start on these arrows and they get good results. Although they are easier to bend they are a good price and simple to replace.

*Carbon Shafts*

There are several types of these on the market; some are at the basic level, giving a lighter arrow to help get the distance when shooting lighter bows. Check with the retailer before buying, as some types of shafts have an upper restriction of draw weight that they can used with.

*Aluminium with Carbon Overlay Shafts*

These arrows are constructed out of a small diameter aluminium shaft (7075 aluminium), with a high-strength carbon-fibre overlay giving a straight, light arrow. Care must be taken when gluing in the points into all carbon shafts, because if the insert of the point is too hot it will overheat the carbon, damaging the bond in the carbon itself and the bond to the aluminium tube.

*Navigators and ACC Shafts*

Both of these arrow types are made up of a parallel 7075 aluminum shaft and an even layer of carbon over the shaft, giving a shaft with a parallel finish. The difference in spine is determined by the thickness of the carbon layer over the aluminum tube. The difference between these two types of shaft is that the ACC has a larger aluminum core, giving it a larger overall diameter. The ACC is used with great success by both compound and field shooters alike; although the navigator can be shot well with the recurve target archers, the newer navigator arrows are more suited to target shooting, with its smaller diameter shaft. The navigator shafts (up to 610) have the same internal diameter as the ACE shafts, therefore they use the same point and nock system.

*ACE and X10 Shafts*

Both of these have a standard aluminum shaft for a core. The X10 shaft has a smaller diameter, but despite this they are slightly heavier than an ACE of the same spine. The difference between this type and the ACC and navigators is that the carbon layer tapers from the centre to the back of the shaft. It is this that makes this shaft more expensive to produce and gives it better performance over the other shafts. The taper allows the back of the shaft to flex more than the front of the shaft, which enhances the shaft's performance. It also enables you to tune the arrow to the bow to a closer tolerance. The X10 was designed for the 70m round; its smaller diameter and heavier weight helps it maintain its down-range velocity, minimizing the weather's effect on it.

## Selecting the Correct Spine

The arrow has to bend as it is shot. If the arrow is too rigid or too flexible, it will not shoot or group well. A rigid arrow will also be heavier than the correct arrow, slowing its speed. The 'spine' of the arrow is the amount it deflects (measured in thousandths of an inch) when a weight of 880g is placed on the centre of the shaft with the arrow resting on two 'V' supports 28in apart. The first step is to determine the length of arrow required and the actual weight on your fingers at full draw.

Determining the correct arrow length will depend on how long you have been shooting, as you will tend to have a more consistent draw length after shooting for a period of time. The most important aspect of selecting an arrow is to make sure that it is long enough. If an arrow is too short as you draw the bow back, it can be drawn past the bow and catch on the riser as you shoot, causing it to collapse and break, possibly injuring you or the person standing close by. When you start shooting, the arrow length will be determined by holding your hands in front of you with your palms together. An arrow is then placed between the palms of your hand with the nock end resting against your chest. The point of the arrow should protrude past the ends of your fingers.

Once you have been shooting long enough to have a reasonably consistent draw length, an arrow marked in inches can be used so that the length can be easily read off. If you are unsure, keep the arrow longer, as you can always shorten it later. Once you have determined your draw length, you can then determine your draw weight.

The weight marked on the limb will only give you an indication of the bow's weight when drawn to 28in. It is always best to check the actual draw weight of the bow using a set of bow scales. If there are no bow scales in your club, judges will have calibrated bow scales at competitions with which to check compound bows; if you ask, they will usually let you use them to weigh your bow. The other way of checking the bow's weight is to secure the

*If the arrow is longer than the length of the arms and the string is in front of the eye, the bow can be drawn safely and the arrow will be long enough.*

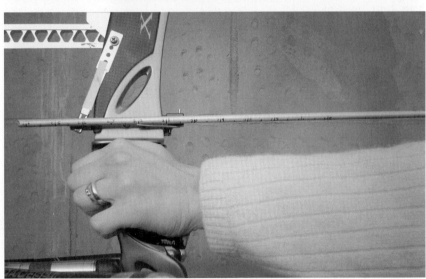

*A measuring arrow can easily be made out of an old arrow.*

bow by the grip from above. Load the string with a dead weight until the bow is drawn back to your draw length, then weigh the dead weight and find your draw weight. For lighter bows with the bow still hung from above, hang a bucket from the string and fill it with water; you can then measure the weight of the bucket on kitchen scales and measure the amount of water in the bucket. 1ltr of water weighs 1kg. This will give you a very accurate way to measure the bow's actual force at full draw.

The Easton selection chart provides the best guide to which arrow you should use. It indicates which spine of arrow you require. The chart can be found on the Easton website (www.easton.com) and in some catalogues, for example Quicks Archery. To use the chart, you must have to hand the information on the arrow's length and the bow's weight at full draw. Look at the right-hand side of the chart and select the weight, then look along the top to select your arrow length. Follow the lines across and down the chart until you find the box where they meet. This will indicate which group box to look in. The group box indicated will detail the spine of arrow that may suit you. Then,

## COMPOUND BOW - Release Aid / Correct Arrow Length for Target · Field · 3D

| COMPOUND BOW - Release Aid Calculated Peak Bow Weight - Lbs. | | | 23" | 24" | 25" | 26" | 27" | 28" | 29" | 30" | 31" | 32" | RECURVE BOW Bow Weight - Lbs. Finger Release |
|---|---|---|---|---|---|---|---|---|---|---|---|---|---|
| Soft Cam AMO up to 210 FPS IBO up to 260 FPS | Medium Cam AMO 211-230 FPS IBO 261-290 FPS | Single or Hard Cam AMO 231 FPS up IBO 291 FPS up | | | | | | | | | | | |
| 29-35 lbs. (13.2-15.9kg) | | | | | | | T1 | T2 | T3 | | | | 17-23 lbs. (7.7-10.4kg) |
| 35-40 lbs. (15.9-18.1kg) | 29-35 lbs. (13.2-15.9kg) | | | | | T1 | T2 | T3 | T4 | T5 | | | 24-29 lbs. (10.9-11.2kg) |
| 40-45 lbs. (18.1-20.4kg) | 35-40 lbs. (15.9-18.1kg) | 29-35 lbs. (13.2-15.9kg) | | | T1 | T2 | T3 | T4 | T5 | T6 | T7 | | 30-35 lbs. (13.6-15.9kg) |
| 45-50 lbs. (20.4-22.7kg) | 40-45 lbs. (18.1-20.4kg) | 35-40 lbs. (15.9-18.1kg) | | T1 | T2 | T3 | T4 | T5 | T6 | T7 | T8 | T9 | 36-40 lbs. (16.3-18.1kg) |
| 50-55 lbs. (22.7-24.9kg) | 45-50 lbs. (20.4-22.7kg) | 40-45 lbs. (18.1-20.4kg) | T1 | T2 | T3 | T4 | T5 | T6 | T7 | T8 | T9 | T10 | 41-45 lbs. (18.6-20.4kg) |
| 55-60 lbs. (24.9-27.2kg) | 50-55 lbs. (22.7-24.9kg) | 45-50 lbs. (20.4-22.7kg) | T2 | T3 | T4 | T5 | T6 | T7 | T8 | T9 | T10 | T11 | 46-50 lbs. (20.9-22.7kg) |
| 60-65 lbs. (27.2-29.5kg) | 55-60 lbs. (24.9-27.2kg) | 50-55 lbs. (22.7-24.9kg) | T3 | T4 | T5 | T6 | T7 | T8 | T9 | T10 | T11 | T12 | 51-55 lbs. (23.1-24.9kg) |
| 65-70 lbs. (29.5-31.8kg) | 60-65 lbs. (27.2-29.5kg) | 55-60 lbs. (24.9-27.2kg) | T4 | T5 | T6 | T7 | T8 | T9 | T10 | T11 | T12 | T13 | 56-60 lbs. (25.4-27.2kg) |
| 70-76 lbs. (31.8-34.5kg) | 65-70 lbs. (29.5-31.8kg) | 60-65 lbs. (27.2-29.5kg) | T5 | T6 | T7 | T8 | T9 | T10 | T11 | T12 | T13 | T13 | 61-65 lbs. (27.7-29.5kg) |
| 76-82 lbs. (34.5-37.2kg) | 70-76 lbs. (31.8-34.5kg) | 65-70 lbs. (29.5-31.8kg) | T6 | T7 | T8 | T9 | T10 | T11 | T12 | T13 | T13 | T14 | 66-70 lbs. (29.9-31.8kg) |
| 82-88 lbs. (37.2-39.9kg) | 76-82 lbs. (34.5-37.2kg) | 70-76 lbs. (31.8-34.5kg) | T7 | T8 | T9 | T10 | T11 | T12 | T13 | T13 | T14 | | 71-76 lbs. (32.2-34.5kg) |

☐ No X10 or A/C/E shafts suitable in shaded areas above.

### Group T1
| Size | Spine | Model | Weight Grs/Inch | Wt @29" |
|---|---|---|---|---|
| *920-1000R | 0.920-1.000 | A/C/E | 5.83 | 169 |
| *900-1000R | 0.900-1.000 | X10 | 5.75 | 167 |
| *880-1000R | 0.880-1.000 | Nav | 5.50 | 160 |
| 2L-04 | 1.020 | A/C/C | 6.05 | 175 |
| 2-04 | 0.920 | A/C/C | 6.48 | 188 |
| *920-1050R | 0.920-1.050 | Vector | 5.44 | 158 |
| 900 | 0.900 | Rdln | 5.83 | 169 |
| 1712 | 1.099 | X7 | 6.70 | 194 |
| 1713 | 1.044 | 75 | 7.42 | 215 |
| 1714 | 0.963 | X7 | 8.07 | 234 |
| 1616 | 1.079 | 75 | 8.36 | 242 |

### Group T2
| Size | Spine | Model | Weight Grs/Inch | Weight @29" |
|---|---|---|---|---|
| *780-850R | 0.780-0.850 | A/C/E | 6.01 | 174 |
| *750-830R | 0.750-0.830 | X10 | 6.35 | 184 |
| *810-880R | 0.810-0.880 | Nav | 5.80 | 168 |
| 2-04 | 0.920 | A/C/C | 6.48 | 188 |
| *770-840R | 0.770-0.840 | Vector | 6.26 | 182 |
| 780 | 0.780 | Rdln | 6.30 | 183 |
| 1812 | 0.879 | X7 | 7.30 | 212 |
| 1714 | 0.963 | X7 | 8.07 | 234 |
| 1716 | 0.880 | 75 | 9.03 | 262 |

### Group T3
| Size | Spine | Model | Weight Grs/Inch | Weight @29" |
|---|---|---|---|---|
| *720-780R | 0.720-0.780 | A/C/E | 6.35 | 184 |
| *700-750R | 0.700-0.750 | X10 | 6.70 | 194 |
| *710-810R | 0.710-0.810 | Nav | 6.29 | 182 |
| 3X-04 | 0.830 | A/C/C | 6.74 | 195 |
| 3L-04 | 0.750 | A/C/C | 6.95 | 202 |
| *700-770R | 0.700-0.770 | Vector | 6.38 | 185 |
| 780 | 0.780 | Rdln | 6.30 | 183 |
| 1912 | 0.778 | X7 | 7.60 | 220 |
| 1813 | 0.874 | 75 | 7.86 | 228 |
| 1814 | 0.799 | X7 | 8.57 | 248 |
| 1816 | 0.756 | 75 | 9.27 | 269 |

### Group T4
| Size | Spine | Model | Weight Grs/Inch | Weight @29" |
|---|---|---|---|---|
| *670-720R | 0.670-0.720 | A/C/E | 5.93 | 172 |
| *650-700R | 0.650-0.700 | X10 | 6.79 | 197 |
| *610-710R | 0.610-0.710 | Nav | 6.87 | 199 |
| 3L-04 | 0.750 | A/C/C | 6.95 | 202 |
| 3-04 | 0.680 | A/C/C | 7.22 | 209 |
| *700-770R | 0.700-0.770 | Vector | 6.38 | 185 |
| 690 | 0.690 | Rdln | 6.27 | 182 |
| 1912 | 0.778 | X7 | 7.60 | 220 |
| 2012 | 0.680 | X7 | 8.00 | 232 |
| 1913 | 0.733 | 75 | 8.34 | 242 |
| 1914 | 0.658 | X7 | 9.28 | 269 |

### Group T5
| Size | Spine | Model | Weight Grs/Inch | Wt @29" |
|---|---|---|---|---|
| *620-670R | 0.620-0.670 | A/C/E | 6.11 | 177 |
| *600-650R | 0.600-0.650 | X10 | 7.02 | 204 |
| *540-610R | 0.540-0.610 | Nav | 7.39 | 214 |
| 3-04 | 0.680 | A/C/C | 7.22 | 209 |
| *640-700R | 0.640-0.700 | Vector | 6.26 | 182 |
| 690 | 0.690 | Rdln | 6.27 | 182 |
| 2012 | 0.680 | X7 | 8.00 | 232 |
| 2013 | 0.610 | 75 | 9.01 | 261 |
| 1914 | 0.658 | X7 | 9.28 | 269 |
| 1916 | 0.623 | 75 | 10.05 | 291 |

### Group T6
| Size | Spine | Model | Weight Grs/Inch | Weight @29" |
|---|---|---|---|---|
| *570-620R | 0.570-0.620 | A/C/E | 6.30 | 183 |
| *550-600R | 0.550-0.600 | X10 | 7.47 | 217 |
| *540-610R | 0.540-0.610 | Nav | 7.39 | 214 |
| 3L-18 | 0.620 | A/C/C | 7.47 | 217 |
| *580-640R | 0.580-0.640 | Vector | 7.06 | 205 |
| 600 | 0.600 | Rdln | 6.92 | 201 |
| 500 | 0.500 | LSpd | 6.53 | 189 |
| 500 | 0.500 | FB | 7.10 | 206 |
| 2112 | 0.590 | X7 | 8.42 | 244 |
| 2013 | 0.610 | 75 | 9.01 | 261 |
| 2014 | 0.579 | X7 | 9.56 | 277 |
| 1916 | 0.623 | 75 | 10.05 | 291 |

### Group T7
| Size | Spine | Model | Weight Grs/Inch | Weight @29" |
|---|---|---|---|---|
| *520-570R | 0.520-0.570 | A/C/E | 6.65 | 193 |
| *500-550R | 0.500-0.550 | X10 | 7.80 | 226 |
| *540-610R | 0.540-0.610 | Nav | 7.39 | 214 |
| 3-18 | 0.560 | A/C/C | 7.82 | 227 |
| 3-28 | 0.500 | A/C/C | 8.11 | 235 |
| *530-580R | 0.530-0.580 | Vector | 7.56 | 219 |
| 520 | 0.520 | Rdln | 7.09 | 206 |
| 500 | 0.500 | LSpd | 6.53 | 189 |
| 500 | 0.500 | FB | 7.10 | 206 |
| 2212 | 0.505 | 75 | 8.84 | 256 |
| 2114 | 0.510 | X7, 75 | 9.94 | 288 |
| 2016 | 0.531 | 75 | 10.56 | 306 |

### Group T8
| Size | Spine | Model | Weight Grs/Inch | Weight @29" |
|---|---|---|---|---|
| *470-520R | 0.470-0.520 | A/C/E | 6.81 | 197 |
| *450-500R | 0.450-0.500 | X10 | 8.10 | 235 |
| *480-540R | 0.480-0.540 | Nav | 7.98 | 231 |
| 3-28 | 0.500 | A/C/C | 8.11 | 235 |
| 3-39 | 0.440 | A/C/C | 8.58 | 249 |
| *480-530R | 0.480-0.530 | Vector | 7.78 | 226 |
| 460 | 0.460 | Rdln | 7.32 | 212 |
| 500 | 0.500 | LSpd | 6.53 | 189 |
| 500 | 0.500 | FB | 7.10 | 206 |
| 2212 | 0.505 | X7 | 8.84 | 256 |
| 2213 | 0.460 | 75 | 9.92 | 288 |
| 2114 | 0.510 | X7, 75 | 9.94 | 288 |
| 2115 | 0.461 | 75 | 10.75 | 312 |

### Group T9
| Size | Spine | Model | Weight Grs/Inch | Weight @29" |
|---|---|---|---|---|
| *430-470R | 0.430-0.470 | A/C/E | 7.03 | 204 |
| *410-450R | 0.410-0.450 | X10 | 8.48 | 246 |
| *430-480R | 0.430-0.480 | Nav | 8.42 | 244 |
| 3-39 | 0.440 | A/C/C | 8.58 | 249 |
| 480 | 0.480 | Vector | 7.78 | 226 |
| 460 | 0.460 | Rdln | 7.32 | 212 |
| 400 | 0.400 | LSpd | 7.41 | 215 |
| 400 | 0.400 | FB | 7.75 | 225 |
| 2312 | 0.423 | X7 | 9.48 | 275 |
| 2213 | 0.460 | X7, 75 | 9.92 | 288 |
| 2214 | 0.425 | X7 | 10.41 | 302 |
| 2115 | 0.461 | 75 | 10.75 | 312 |

### Group T10
| Size | Spine | Model | Weight Grs/Inch | Weight @29" |
|---|---|---|---|---|
| *400-430R | 0.400-0.430 | A/C/E | 7.50 | 218 |
| *380-410R | 0.380-0.410 | X10 | 8.87 | 257 |
| *430-480R | 0.430-0.480 | Nav | 8.42 | 244 |
| 3-39 | 0.440 | A/C/C | 8.58 | 249 |
| 3-49 | 0.390 | A/C/C | 8.83 | 256 |
| 480 | 0.480 | Vector | 7.78 | 226 |
| 410 | 0.410 | Rdln | 7.60 | 220 |
| 400 | 0.400 | LSpd | 7.41 | 215 |
| 400 | 0.400 | FB | 7.75 | 225 |
| 2412 | 0.400 | X7 | 9.65 | 280 |
| 2413 | 0.365 | X7, 75 | 10.50 | 304 |
| 2214 | 0.425 | X7 | 10.41 | 302 |
| 2314 | 0.390 | X7, 75 | 10.76 | 312 |

### Group T11
| Size | Spine | Model | Weight Grs/Inch | Weight @29" |
|---|---|---|---|---|
| *370-400R | 0.370-0.400 | A/C/E | 7.91 | 229 |
| 380R | 0.380 | X10 | 8.87 | 257 |
| 3-49 | 0.390 | A/C/C | 8.83 | 256 |
| 3-60 | 0.340 | A/C/C | 9.45 | 274 |
| 360 | 0.360 | Rdln | 8.31 | 241 |
| 400 | 0.400 | LSpd | 7.41 | 215 |
| 400 | 0.400 | FB | 7.75 | 225 |
| 2413 | 0.365 | X7, 75 | 10.50 | 304 |
| 2314 | 0.390 | X7, 75 | 10.76 | 312 |
| 2315 | 0.390 | X7, 75 | 11.67 | 338 |

### Group T12
| Size | Spine | Model | Weight Grs/Inch | Weight @29" |
|---|---|---|---|---|
| 370R | 0.370 | A/C/E | 7.91 | 229 |
| 3-60 | 0.340 | A/C/C | 9.45 | 274 |
| 3-71 | 0.300 | A/C/C | 9.92 | 288 |
| 360 | 0.360 | Rdln | 8.31 | 241 |
| 340 | 0.340 | LSpd | 8.16 | 237 |
| 340 | 0.340 | FB | 8.30 | 241 |
| 2512 | 0.321 | X7 | 10.28 | 298 |
| 2613 | 0.265 | X7 | 11.49 | 333 |

### Group T13
| Size | Spine | Model | Weight Grs/Inch | Weight @29" |
|---|---|---|---|---|
| 3-71 | 0.300 | A/C/C | 9.92 | 288 |
| 2512 | 0.321 | X7 | 10.28 | 298 |
| 2613 | 0.265 | X7 | 11.49 | 333 |

### Group T14
| Size/Spine | | Model | Weight Grs/Inch | Weight @29" |
|---|---|---|---|---|
| 2613 | 0.265 | X7 | 11.49 | 333 |

| | | | |
|---|---|---|---|
| A/C/E | Aluminum/Carbon/Extreme | R | The size recommendations for recurve bows are indicated with a letter 'R' next to the size. |
| X10 | X10 Shafts (Aluminum/Carbon) | | |
| Nav | Navigator (Aluminum/Carbon) | Size | Indicates suggested arrow size |
| A/C/C | Aluminum/Carbon/Composite | Spine | Spine of arrow size shown (static) |
| Vector | Vector | Model | Designates arrow model |
| Rdln | Redline | Weight | Listed in grains per inch |
| LSpd | LightSpeed | | |
| FB | FatBoy | | |
| X7 | X7 Eclipse and Cobalt (7178 alloy) | | |
| 75 | X07s: Platinum Plus and Jazz (7075-T9 alloy) | | |

* When two sizes are listed together, the weight listed is for the first shaft.

Part of the current Easton selection chart; full charts can be downloaded from the Easton website.

using the chart, look back at the top selection box and look at the next nearest weight box. As the weight of the bow or length of the arrow may be almost between selection boxes, look to see if it then puts you up or down group boxes. You will find that arrow spines will be in two or more boxes. For example, if your arrow is 27[3/4] inches long and your draw weight is 38lb and you were selecting for ACE arrow shafts, first select the box 36–40lb then select the box 28in, as this is for arrows 27½ to 28½; this will give you group T5. T5 indicates 670 ACEs for recurve (670R). However, 27¾ is close to 27½, so reselect using the 27in box. This will give you group T4, although 670 is indicated in the box 720 as the recommendation. Again, revisit the chart, looking at the slightly higher poundage box 41–45lb; this again takes you back to T5 for 27in and to T6 for 28in. So the indicated selection would be ACE 670 shafts.

When selecting arrows for juniors, ensure that you consult the junior selection charts. I have found that if you select shafts for juniors from the senior selection chart, the juniors end up with arrows that tend to be too stiff.

Prior to buying arrows it may be possible to try out someone else's arrows at the club. This can give you a far better indication of suitability of spine as you can shoot a few fletched and unfletched arrows. If the bare-shafted arrow impacts close to the fletched arrows it will show that they are a reasonable match to your bow. If you can only find arrows that are a spine stiffer or weaker, ask to try them with a bare shaft, at a shorter distance, as this will give you an indication of how accurate your selection by the chart has been.

There are several other factors to consider prior to buying your arrows:

- Are you staying at the current poundage or thinking of moving it up or down?
- Are you established in your style as an archer? Is it possible that your draw length will change – increased draw length will increase your poundage.
- Are you still growing? If you are, your arrows will get shorter (relatively) and your poundage will increase.

When trying out someone else's arrows:

- Are you using a string with the right amount of strands for the weight on your fingers?
- Is your bracing height correct?
- Most importantly, is your bow set up correctly?

Once you have considered these factors, look at the chart again and see if your selection has changed. As a general rule of thumb, a stiffer arrow flies better than a weak arrow. So err towards stiff, but also remember that as a stiffer arrow is heavier and slower, your sight marks will be lower, so do not go too stiff.

### Type of Arrow

Consider the following points when selecting arrows:

- Your pocket – how much do you want to spend?
- What distances do you want to shoot? If you only shoot indoors, do you really need to get expensive carbon arrows?
- The cost of replacing arrows – ACEs and X10s usually come in sets of twelve shafts, although some companies do sell ACE separately. Most other shafts can be bought individually.

Along with the spine selection chart, you will also find the Easton spine and weight comparison chart. This shows the relationship between different types of shafts and indicates the difference in weight and spine between shafts for a given spine group. Remember that the heavier the shaft, the lower the sight mark.

## Cutting Arrows

When ordering arrows, they can be cut to the length you require and prepared with nocks and fletchings by the retailers. Ensure that you measure the longest length that will fit your draw length and bow. This will ensure that if you open up a little the arrow does not get too short. If you have an arrow cutter available at the club it is probably best to order the shafts full length with points, fletches and nocks separately and then put them together yourself.

Arrows are normally cut from the front of the shaft, but parallel-type shafts (aluminium/carbon ACCs, navigators and so on) can be cut from either end to get them to the length you require. The shorter the arrow, the stiffer they will react in the bow. ACEs and X10s have tapered shafts, which must be cut differently, so these will be dealt with separately in the next section of this chapter.

Although you have now selected the spine that will suit, you can further alter the length slightly to help match the arrows to your equipment. So to start with, keep the arrow as long as possible within the frame of the bow – approximately 2in in front of the button. Clicker extensions can be put onto the front of the bow, putting on 3in in front of the button. This will enable you to cut up to 2in from the length of the arrow to help make it a little stiffer if required.

*Using an Arrow Cutter*
Our club has bought its own arrow cutter. The cutter's use is limited to competent club members who have been shown how to use the equipment. If you are using an arrow cutter for the first time, either ensure that you first read the instructions that come with it or ensure you are shown how to operate it. Care needs to be taken as the cutter operates at a very high speed, so, before you plug it in, check the cutting wheel to make sure that it is not damaged and is adjusted so that it will cut through the wall of the arrow. If you have not used one before, practise on an old arrow first. Make sure before you cut your first arrow that the cutter is set at the correct distance, although it is best to set it a little longer if you are unsure. If you are cutting arrows to the same length as a previous set, you can set the distance by using the old arrow as a measure so that it fits into the holder at the base end and the other end just scuffs the cutting wheel. As I cut from both ends, I measure the new shaft against the old shaft to ensure that the same amount is cut from the back.

---

**Taper Length Compared to Overall Arrow Length**

One of the other considerations of the tapered shafts is the symmetry of how long the taper is compared with the overall arrow length. I have found that if the taper length exceeds half the arrow length (that is, the back is longer than the front), the groups are not so good. If you look at the lighter arrow spines, you will notice that the back of the arrow is shorter to start with, allowing the arrow to be just cut from the front, maintaining the proportion of the back and front of the shaft. As I shoot quite a short arrow (28in), to ensure that the taper length does not exceed half the length, I plan to cut from the back of the shaft as part of the selection.

---

As you cut the arrow the hand nearest the blade turns the arrow and the other hand covers the shaft to ensure that the base of the arrow remains in the tailstock of the cutting bed. There is a tendency for the end of the arrow not being cut to slip out of position, giving an angled cut to the other end of the shaft. Once you are satisfied with the length of the arrow to be cut, cut all the shafts at that setting as this will ensure they are all exactly the same length.

*Cutting and Tuning X10s and ACEs (Tapered Arrows)*
The spine of arrow you choose from the chart may be a little stiff or a little weak for your set-up and for the length you require. For a parallel shaft, the spine is fixed for a set length of arrow. Ideally, you could have an arrow spine made exactly to match your set-up, but this would be prohibitively expensive, so with parallel shafts you may find that the spine you need falls between two spines and you end up with a shaft that is a little stiff or weak.

With the ACE or X10 arrows you can adjust the spine for a set length. Because the arrow shaft is tapered on the rear half of the shaft, this area of the arrow gets progressively weaker towards the nock end of the shaft. As a rule of thumb, if you cut 2in from the back of a 550–X10, it will work more like a 500–X10. Therefore if you cut 1in from the back, it will be equivalent to a 525–X10, thus allowing you to adjust the spine for a given arrow length and enabling you to make the best match for your bow.

This also works for the ACE. As an experiment, I have tried cutting 2in from the back of 620 ACEs in order to make them act like 570s. They acted in tuning in a similar way to the 570s, but did not group so well at a distance, so I would not cut much more than 1in from the back of either ACEs or X10s.

*Example of X10 Arrow Selection*
I want to shoot 46lb, my draw length is 26in to the button; also, I want my overall arrow length to be 28in, so 2in of arrow in front of the button seems to work well. As an established archer my draw length is not going to change much. The arrow selection chart shows that I should be looking at a 500 or 550 X10.

I would then cut all the shafts (from the front only) to 29½, which would give me 1½in to play with (extra length over the 28in I want to end up with). Then I would fletch three arrows and use

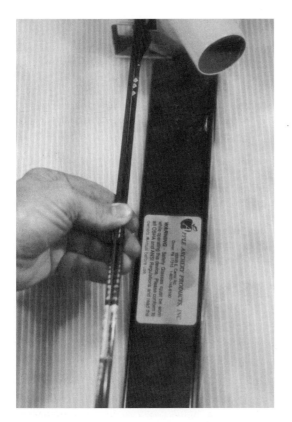

*Matching the decals on the arrow to take a cut from the back of a new shaft.*

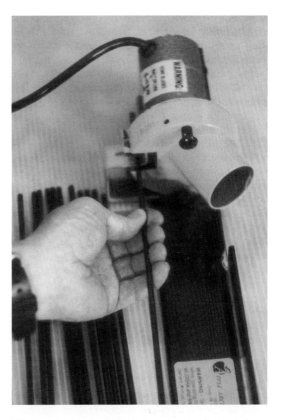

*The hand next to the cutting wheel turns the shaft; cut all the shafts at each setting to ensure that they all remain the same length.*

*The hand over the arrow shaft ensures that the back of the arrow remains in position in the tailstock.*

three as bare shafts with the recommended point weight fitted. Shooting at 30m I would see how they group, but would expect them to indicate weak. I would then cut from the back of the shaft, perhaps 4mm (0.16in) to start with, and shoot the bare-shaft test again to see how much cutting 4mm stiffened them. I would then cut small amounts from the back until the bare shafts were almost in the group of fletched arrows. Then I would cut from the front of the shaft to give me the arrow length I required, remembering that in the final cut from the front of the arrow, to get 28in it would also stiffen the arrows slightly.

This is a slow job and should not be rushed. I feel you need to cut the full set every time you make a cut, as this will ensure that they all stay the same length and spine. This will also mean that as you cut from the back of the arrow you will have to refletch each time. It is therefore better if you have the cutter at the range. Using this method, you can match the arrows exactly to your bow. Final alterations to tuning can be made with the string weight.

## Points

Although the point is fitted to the arrow to help it enter the target and to protect the front of the shaft, its main job is to balance the shaft and to give weight to the front of the arrow. It can also be used to help tune the shaft to the bow. For a selected spine, increasing the point weight will make the arrow act weaker and decreasing the point will make it act stiffer. Making the point heavier will also lower your sight marks as the arrow will fly slower.

The Easton charts mentioned above will not only enable you to choose the correct spine but will also recommend which point should be fitted to the selected shaft. The recommendation is to ensure that the forward of centre weight is maintained. If the front of the arrow is too light, it will not fly or group well.

Aluminium shafts may well come with only one weight of point or a limited range of points. It is possible to alter the weight of the point to help match the arrow to your bow by increasing the point weight by adding lead fishing shot into the back of the point. A set of grain scales will need to be used with this as it is vitally important that each of the points is the same weight, otherwise each arrow will end up with a different spine characteristic.

Carbon and carbon aluminium arrows usually come with a bigger range of points. They will either take the form of an insert and separate point or a one-piece point. The insert type is fitted into the shaft and the points screwed into the insert, as used with navigators and ACEs. Both the inserts and points come in a range of grain weights, giving good versatility to tune the arrow shaft. With screw-in points, the points tend to come loose as you shoot them. I have found that putting a little beeswax on the thread of the point prior to fitting it into the insert keeps the point from coming undone. For ACE type fittings, there are also one-piece points available. The X10 shafts only come with one-piece points that have break-off sections; as the name suggests, to make the point lighter you break off part of the insert. Once it has been broken off, new points will have to be purchased to increase the point weight again, so do plenty of tuning before breaking off the insert. With the X10s, there are tungsten points available with a full unbroken weight of 120 grains and a price of £11.50 for one point, so they are not to be broken off lightly.

Although the ACE arrows and the X10 arrows appear similar, remember that the X10 is a heavier shaft and therefore needs a higher point weight than a similarly spined ACE shaft. Within reason, try to maintain a higher point weight when setting up the arrows, as this will give you more FOC weight and help with grouping and arrow flight in windy conditions.

### Running Repairs

As the shaft enters the boss, the friction heats up the shaft and even if the points are glued in well they might pull out slightly as they are pulled from the boss. Taking care that the shaft does not have any carbon splinters, squeeze the area of the shaft where the insert is between the thumb and forefinger, then with the other hand pull the area of the shaft with the insert in, backwards and forwards between your fingers. The arrow shaft will heat up with the friction, which will make it hot enough to melt the hot melt slightly, then push the point back in by pressing it against a hard surface, like the leg of the target stand.

*Slide the point into the shaft and quickly put it into the water, stirring the shaft to keep it cool.*

## Fitting Points

When fitting points to shafts, ensure that the points are glued in well. Running out of points during a good performance at a shoot will crimp your score; even if you carry spare points and are able to glue them in as you go, it can distract from the flow of your shooting.

Hot melt is the best method of holding in the points. To work, hot-melt glue has to be heated enough so that it is still liquid when the two parts are in position. If the point is not hot enough it will adhere to the point and not the shaft, which will lead to the points falling out. If the point is too hot, and therefore the shaft is too hot as you insert the point into it, especially with carbons, the carbon to aluminium bond will be damaged. This will lead to the carbon splitting from the aluminium shaft. With both aluminium and carbon arrows I use the same method, which requires a large jam jar filled with cold water ,a blowtorch (or gas cooker), hot-melt glue, pliers, arrows and points.

Holding it with pliers, I heat the insert part of the point so that the hot-melt glue melts onto it readily but does not 'hiss'. I cover the insert with glue, then slide it into the shaft. I then immediately put the end of the shaft into the water to cool it down. This ensures that the glue is hot enough to adhere to the inside of the shaft, but

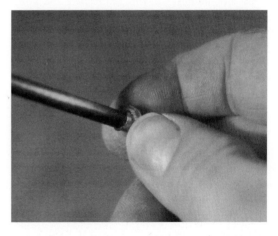

*Peel the glue towards the point of the arrow so that carbon is not stripped from the shaft.*

cooling the shaft quickly ensures that the shaft itself is not damaged. Once all the points have been glued in, the shafts can be removed from the jar of water and the excess glue removed from the point and shaft. With carbon shafts it is important that when you do this the glue is peeled away from the shaft. If the glue is peeled away from the point, carbon can be lifted from the shaft by the glue.

133

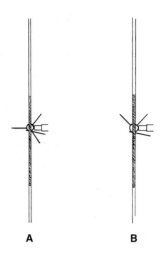

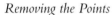

*The angle between the nock and fletch can be changed to give you the best clearance. The arrow does not start to spin until it is well clear of the riser. (A) is the initial position. (B) is where the fletch may end up.*

*The fletch angle must be set so that when viewed from the front the face of the fletch can be seen. This ensures that the arrow spins in flight.*

### Removing the Points

With aluminiums, you can gently heat the point and shaft, but with carbons you must heat the point only. Keep pulling on the point with pliers until it slides out. This needs to be carried out carefully, especially with carbon shafts, as heating the shaft too much will damage it.

## Nocks

A nock's primary job is to hold the arrow onto the string. Some types also incorporate a design to help protect the back of the shaft from damage when another arrow impacts on the nock:'A Robin Hood'.

There are many types of nock on the market. The type of nock used may change the tuning and grouping, so it is worth trying different types to see how each affects the groups. When selecting nocks, look at the length of the nock grooves as some are longer than others. With the longer nocks, the string will stay in the groove longer, which may affect the tuning. Personally, I like the Beiter nock system, using both the Beiter nock and nock reel. I get the same nock fit on the string every time and the same nock fit from string to string. Beiter also makes long and short nocks, which can be useful when adjusting your tuning.

If you use small G-nocks you may find a difference in your group size dependent upon colour type. I have found that the opaque white and black give a different tune to the clear coloured nocks. So try to keep to the same type and colour when buying new nocks; if you change, recheck your tuning.

The nocks will need to be aligned on the arrow when they are fitted so that once the arrow is attached to the string the fletchings should be initially aligned as shown at point (A) on the illustration above. This will help to ensure that as the arrow leaves the bow the fletches do not touch the rest or button. After the arrows have been shot from the bow a few times you may find that the fletches touch the button, so try adjusting the fletch position by rotating the nock slightly. You may find that the fletch position may end up as at point (B).

## Fletches

The fletches both stabilize the flight of the arrow and make it spin to increase its accuracy. The larger the surface area of the fletch, the quicker the arrow will be stabilized in flight. However, a larger surface area creates more drag on the arrow, which will slow it down quicker – a disadvantage over longer distances. This, in turn, will give you lower sight marks. At the longest distance if the arrow slows too much the group size can disproportionately increase because the arrow loses 'direction' as its momentum drops off.

There is plenty of choice of fletch on the market, but whatever type you choose, the fletch should be attached to the arrow at a slight angle to ensure that the arrow spins in flight. When viewed from the front, you should be able to see the face of each fletch. When all the fletchings are set at the same slight angle, the group size will be smaller. Finding the best angle for the best groups may take a little testing but will be worthwhile. If the angle of the fletch is too great, although it will make the arrow spin faster, it will also slow the arrow down quicker.

If even one fletch is on 'straight' with the rest at an angle, this arrow will tend to leave the group. It is therefore worth spending time ensuring that the fletches are at the same angle.

### Plastic and Feathers

Plastic vanes are more durable but heavier than the spin-wing type and there is a much bigger selection of sizes available. Although you can buy arrows already fletched, you will still need a fletching jig to renew any fletches that are damaged or fall off. To get the best results, it is preferable to fletch your own arrows. Most fletching jigs come with a clamp that holds the fletch. Glue is applied to the base or foot of the fletch, then the fletch is held onto the main jig with clamps or a magnet to ensure that the fletch is glued at the same position and angle on the shaft. Most jigs will come with a straight clamp, but some will have a helical clamp, which, although more expensive, may yield better results, as it makes

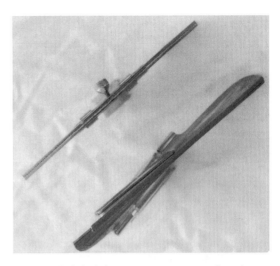

*Although the helical clamp is more expensive it places the fletch on the arrow shaft in an alignment that ensures that the arrow spins but does not cause as much drag as a straight clamp. (Karen Henderson)*

the fletch spin better for less drag. The jig will have a facility to adjust the angle of the fletch on the shaft. It will also have a simple system to space the fletches evenly around the shaft of the arrow, which will include a setting to allow the 'cock' fletch to be set on the shaft so that when the arrow is placed on the string it will be in the correct position.

There are several types of fletching glues available. A good all-round glue is the Bjorn F-type.

*There are many types of fletching jig, but they all work in a similar manner – a clamp holds the fletch onto the arrow at a set angle.*

When using this type of glue, you need to leave enough time between each fletch to let the glue dry. If you take the clamp off too early, the fletch will tend to lift off the shaft. This is more relevant if you are using feathered fletchings for shooting indoors. I take one day to fletch one arrow. I put one fletch on in the morning before work, the second when I get home and the third one before I go to bed. This allows the glue to set properly. Some of the newer fletchings such as the Easton diamonds come with a superglue gel, which allows you to fletch the arrows much more quickly. The disadvantage with this type of glue is that when you come to change the fletch, it can be very difficult to remove the glue, especially from carbon shafts, so great care has to be taken not to damage the carbon.

Initially, you will have to guess the position and angle of your first fletch. It needs to be far enough from the back of the shaft so that when you release

the string the fingers do not touch the fletchings. Once you have glued on the first one, you will be able to see if you have adjusted the jig so that the vane is on at a reasonable angle, enough to see the face of the fletch. If it is not, remove the fletch, reset the jig and try again until you are satisfied with the result. You will then be able to fletch the rest of the arrows.

### Spin Wings

Spin-wing vanes are both light and stiff. There are several different types on the market and when making your choice, go by your group size as opposed to colour. I have known a number of archers change to a nice colourful vane and then struggle to get their previous score levels.

The best way to mark the shafts for fitting these vanes is to use a gold or silver marker pen. Put the arrow into the fletching jig or Beiter Tri-liner with the jig set at a slight angle and run the pen along the line of the clamp. The double-sided tape that comes with the fletchings can then be laid along the side of each line. Then, taking a fletch in a bull-dog clip, it can be laid directly up against the line on top of the tape, giving a consistent alignment of the fletch. If you are using the 1¾in spin-wing vanes there is a special jig produced by Beiter that holds the fletch, allowing you to put the tape directly onto the fletch; the jig then enables you to attach the fletch to the shaft at the same angle every time.

For my X10 550 arrows, I choose between 'Rite Flights' (Quicks), 'K Vanes' or spin wings. If it is

*A fletching jig or Beiter Tri-liner can be used to mark the arrows prior to fletching with spin-wing type fletches.*

calm, I use the 1¾in spin wing or K vanes. If it is windy, I have found that the 'Rite Flights' group better. They are 1¾in but lower profile than the spin wings. The 1⅟₁₆in spin wings also work well in the wind. There is no hard and fast rule when selecting fletchings; you will have to test to see which give you the best results.

Another factor to consider is how far from the nock the fletchings are placed. Some archers use the analogy of a rocket, stating that the fins on a rocket are placed as near to the back as possible, but as you may have noticed a rocket is quite rigid. As an arrow comes out of the bow it is flexes, so are you better off having the fletching nearer the nodal points on the shaft? A difference in tuning can be seen on a different placement of the fletchings, so each archer needs to experiment to find their personal preference.

Once the spin wings have been attached, a thin wrap of tape can be used to hold the fletch in place. I use the spin-wing tape, but first cut it down the centre to make it thinner and I only tape the front of the fletching. If you catch too much of the front of the vane it will open out a little, showing more of the face of the vane. If, however, you tape the back of the fletch because of the steeper angle but catch too much of the back of the fletch it will straighten up. I then put a blob of glue on the back of the vane to keep it in place. A few years ago I was shooting at 70m and it was going well but my fletchings were a little worn so I went home and refletched all my arrows, putting tape on both the front and the back to hold them in place. The next day I went down to shoot and the arrows would not group, with some as far out as the blue. Knowing that the only change I had made was to the fletchings, I had a good look at them and found that the ones leaving the group had fletchings that were straight. I took the tape from the rear of the fletch, checked the angles and adjusted them accordingly. On shooting again, the arrows went back into the grouping pattern of the day before.

## Preparing a New Set of Shafts for Top Performance

One of the reasons that aluminium/carbon shafts are so expensive is that it is difficult to get the carbon layer around the aluminium core to be of an even thickness. There can also be a difference in weight between points in a set. So it is worth spending time checking and adjusting the shafts to get the best out of them.

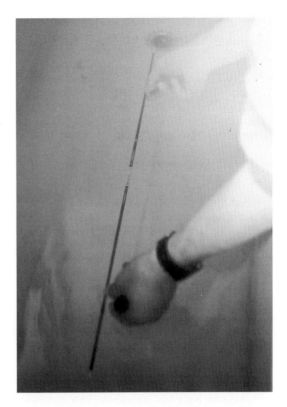

*Once the bubbles have been cleared from the shaft it can be released into the bath.*

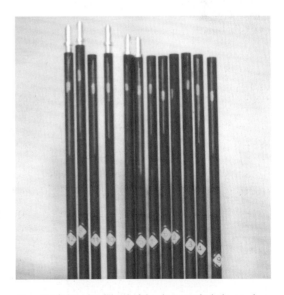

*Once the light side of the shaft has been marked, the numbers can be put onto the shaft for identification when shooting them bare shafted for consistency.*

---

**Matching Arrows' Weights**

Depending on the diameter and type of the shaft it is possible that with the point fitted the arrow will float point down when put into water (a piece of 4in water pipe blocked at one end). You can then float all the arrows; if they all float at the same height they are of the same weight.

---

Once I have cut my X10 550 shafts to the length I require, I determine which is the heavy side of the shaft by putting them in the bath. To do this, I run a bath of tepid water and block each end of the shaft off with pin nock inserts. If the water is too hot the air inside the shaft will expand and blow out the pin nocks. This stops the water getting inside the shaft and, because the pins are cylindrical, will not bias the test. I put a little washing-up liquid into the bath to help lower the surface tension of the water and then hold each shaft just under the surface of the water; ensuring there are no bubbles attached to the shaft, I then let go. With my length of arrow, the shaft will be heavier than water and sink slowly to the bottom of the bath. As it does so, the shaft will rotate so that the heavier side of the shaft will be to the bottom. You may find that the shaft will float, but one side will always end up uppermost. Remove the shaft from the water, noting which way up it finished, and mark the shaft with a pencil at the nock end. Do the same for the rest of the shafts. Once the shafts are dry, you can then use a gold/silver pen to re-mark the arrows over the pencil mark.

Take the points you are going to use and weigh them to ensure that they are in fact the same weight. You can get small electronic scales quite cheaply, or the old-fashioned miniature beam balance scales to check the points. If you find that the weights are different, find the lightest and, using a file, make them all match. Fit the points, trying to use a similar amount of glue on each point. Then fit the nocks with the marked (light) side of the arrow away from the bow. Now number all the arrows so you can identify them.

Take these arrows to the range and shoot them all bare shafted at 30m (using a tuned bow). Carry this out a number of times, taking note of the number of shafts that do not go into the main group. Turn all the nocks so that the light side of the shaft is now against the button and carry out the test again. Decide which shaft position gives you the best main group, then turn the nock slightly on any arrows that still do not still impact on the main group to see if that will 'tune' them into the group. Once you are satisfied with this, you can go to 70m and try again (this needs to be on a calm day or indoors). Once the arrows have been adjusted so that they are in the best group, you can re-mark the shaft to give you the correct nock position. This will give you the best performance from your arrows.

## Summary

This chapter has discussed the basics of arrow selection and how to get the best from your arrows. The level you are at and the level you want to reach will determine how much time you spend on your arrows. The best way of selecting arrows is, before you buy, to try other people's arrows that are similar to the ones you think you need. The charts will only give you an indication of the spine you require.

# Chapter 11

# Making Bowstrings

The bowstring is an integral part of the bow and so the selection of the right material and composition is an important part of making your equipment work well with your shooting style.

Bowstrings can be bought ready made – these will get you shooting quickly and are a good start when you initially put a bow together. You can even get custom strings made for you by various companies, but they will take time to order and will not be as good as the ones you can make for yourself after some practice. When making strings for yourself, you can make each string to the exact length and number of strands that you want to try. Once you become proficient this will only take around half an hour, which means that you can easily have a new string ready for the next day's shooting.

A friend of mine, Jim Buchanan, told me how he and fellow archer Callum Miller used to make fifteen strings for one bow, each 3mm (0.12in) longer than the previous one. They would shoot them all to find out which one gave the best results, then they would make three more strings the same length as the best string from the initial fifteen and pick the best string from those four. Eighteen strings in total to find the best string with the right amount of twists in it for the bracing height. This is what it can take to get the best string to match you and your equipment.

## Types of Material

There several different types of material available, not only to make the string itself but also serving materials to protect the string and to hold the nocking point in place. Each one has its own characteristics and suitability to the archer. Dacron (B50) stretches a little as the arrow is shot from the bow, which ensures that there is not so much shock on the bow, thus helping to protect some bows from damage (particularly bows at the lower end of the market).

Always check with the bow's manufacturer what string material is suitable to use on your bow. Modern performance bowstrings are made of a material that is designed not to stretch as the arrow is shot, thereby imparting more power into the arrow as it leaves the bow. If your bow is designed to shoot the softer Dacron and you shoot one of the harsher materials it will void the warranty and may break the limbs.

The most commonly used of the performance materials is Fastflight; when starting to make strings this is a good choice. There are three main companies that make string materials: Angel, Brownell and BCY Inc. All make good string materials, with each having slightly different properties. As with all archery equipment, it is finding one that will suit you and how you shoot, which can only be done by testing. The strand thicknesses given by each company for each type of material varies and it is not possible to find a direct correlation between thicknesses of strands to make up similar thickness strings between manufacturers. I would use:

- seventeen-strand Fastflight
- nine-strand 450
- nineteen-strand 452 (450 and 452 are the same material but different strand thickness)
- twenty-strand Angel Dyneema
- seventeen-strand D75
- nineteen-strand TS-1.

I use No. 2 Beiter nocking points, which fit snugly on the string. When using new material, I make up the first string with enough strands so that the nocking point has a similar fit. It may not be the correct amount of strands, but it gives me a start point to work from which will be close to the previous material.

Serving materials differ from company to

company and are available in different thicknesses and manufacturing processes. I have used the soft twist with Dacron bowstrings for the club and lower performance bows. For the best performance I like the braided types and am currently using the Halo and Angel servings. As with the string materials, these are made up of different compositions of materials. I look for a material that does not slip once it has been served onto the string. You will find that some combinations between string materials and servings allow some slippage as the bow is shot. This will alter your nocking point and therefore the tuning as you shoot the bow, which is not desirable. Putting the serving on as tightly as possible is not a good way to cure this as it can crush the threads and cut into the strands.

### Strands (Fastflight)

The number of strands in the string will alter the speed of the bow – the more strands in the string, the slower the bow. Altering the number of strands in the string is one of the final parts of tuning to make small differences in how the arrow works. You are limited to how few or many strands you can make the string with. A 30lb bow can shoot a fourteen-strand string quite comfortably, whereas sixteen strands is probably the lower limit for a 40lb bow.

As a rule of thumb:

- <30lb starts at fourteen strands
- 30–35lb start at sixteen strands
- 35–40lb start at seventeen strands
- 40lb< starts at eighteen strands.

## Making an Eighteen-Strand Fastflight String

The string consists of a single strand wound around the end posts of the string jig until the desired amount of strands for the string is reached. A serving material is then placed over the string material to stop the string from touching the limb and wearing through the string material. To make a string you will need a string jig, knife, ruler, pen, wax, string material, serving, serving tool and plenty of room.

Some clubs will have a string jig that you can borrow, or you may be able to borrow one from a club member. If not, you can buy one or, better still, make one. (Plans for a wooden-based jig are at the end of this chapter.)

To start with, set up the jig so that the end posts are in line. This will help to keep the tension in the strands even. When you buy or make a new string it can take a number of shots before the string

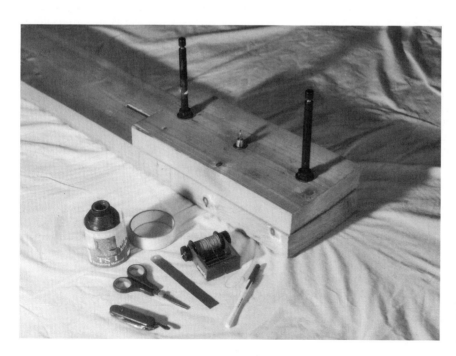

*Jig, string material, ruler, pen, tape knife, serving tool, serving material and scissors.*

*The end of the strand is tied to the inside post.*

settles in and all the strands have the same tension. The closer you can get each strand to the same tension, the quicker the shooting in will be. Take the string that is currently on your bow and slip one end loop around one of the posts. Take all the twists out of the old string and then stretch it out to the post at the opposite end. Pull the jig to tighten the string and lock off the jig. Remove the old string from the jig, open up the jig 1cm more, which will give you a good starting point from which to make your first string. If you do not open up the jig by 1cm, the string will possibly be too short, giving you a high bracing height. Write down the length you have opened the jig, so that if you need to you can modify the length on subsequent strings. Take the Fastflight and tie it to the inside post (start post) at one end, then loop the string around the outside post at that end, then down to the post at the opposite end of the jig.

Wind the string around the jig until there are nine strands on either side of the jig, giving you eighteen in total. There needs to be a reasonable tension on the strands, otherwise when put the servings on with the serving tool, it will give a poor result as the serving strands will not be tight enough. You will be tying the string off to the outside post at the end you started. First, while keeping the tension on the end strand, unlock the post end and rotate it through 90 degrees so that the posts form a small base of a triangle. The posts

should be turned so that when the end of the string is tied off it will be the opposite post to the start post. This will make a crossover of the ends between the two posts.

Once you have turned the posts, jiggle them gently and pull lightly on them. This will help to even out the strand tension. Then tie off the end of the strand. With a ruler, mark the centre position between the two posts; mark the string 40mm (1.6in) either side of the centre mark – when completed, this will become an end loop. Now run a little wax over the area to be served; this will help to stop the serving slipping. Fit the serving material you want to use into the serving tool, setting it slack

---

**Keeping the Tension Equal**

I use an Arten jig and in order to get the tension of each strand the same, I work on the carpet (short pile) – as I get to each end post I pull the jig slightly across the carpet, which gives me a similar tension for each strand. There is a tendency to wind on the string too hard when first making strings, thereby bending the jig and making the string short while also giving a different tension to each strand.

*Once the required amount of strands has been wound onto the jig, the end post can be turned to allow the other end of the strand to be tied on.*

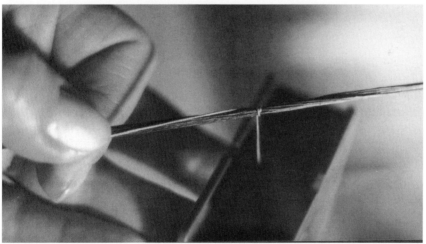

*To start the serving, thread the end (tail) through the strands, then wind the material over the top of the tail.*

to start with. Take out 150mm (5.9in) of serving and weave it into the string at one end of the marked string.

Start the serving off by hand, initially serving over the end that you wove into the string and including the two end strands. Once you have got it started, wind the serving onto the tool, adjusting the tension up a little and serving the end loop to just short of the 80mm (3.12in) required by approximately five turns.

It now needs to be finished off; the finishing knot that is used is the same for all ends of the serving. For the end of the loop, only five turns need to be used and should not be cut. With the end serving finished, cut the two ends of the string from the posts, close to the loop serving, and remove the waste ends from the posts. Turn the end posts again

so that they are once more in line, then adjust the serving so that it is evenly around the post with both ends next to each other and level. Now apply a little wax to this area prior to serving. Then serve three or four figure-of-eights around both ends of the loop, taking care not to go over the served string. The serving can then be pulled tight and the two sides of the string served together.

I keep either side of the string astride the inside post as this stops the string taking twists before it is put onto the bow. I serve for 10cm down the string and then use the finishing knot. For main serving ends, I use twenty turns to finish. This ensures that there is a good 'tail' under the serving and it will not come undone when you are shooting. You can now cut the serving material – this is the first end loop finished.

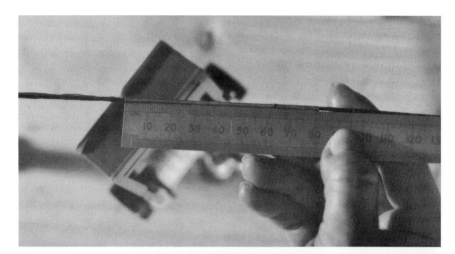

Once the serving is long enough for the loop, the end can be finished and the end of the jig turned in line.

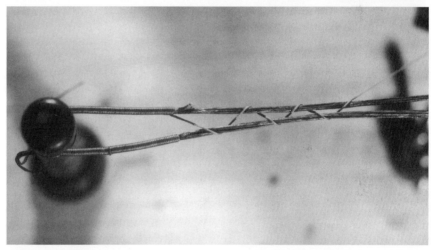

With the jig turned, the loop end can be levelled and the serving wound in a figure of eight around the string. It can then be pushed up tightly against the end loop serving, prior to starting the main serving.

Finishing the serving, a loop is made and the serving wound onto the string inside the loop. The end is then pulled along the serving and the string loop wound over the tail.

Once all the loop has been wound over the end, the tail can be pulled through, finishing the serving.

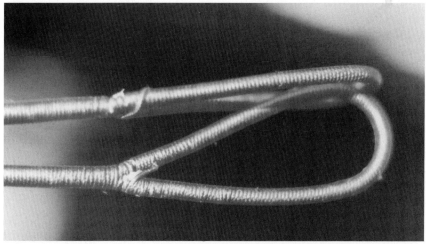

When the loops have been finished they should be the same size, with no over-serving of the loop, giving a flat profile.

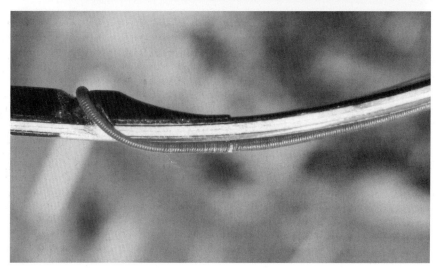

When fitted to the limb, the string lies flat on the limb surface – a slight gap between the loop end and the main serving is acceptable.

To make the second loop, before turning the jig posts, mark the string in the centre of the post. This will give you the centre between posts when the posts are turned. For the second end, mark out 40mm (1.6in) either side of the centre mark. It is better if both loops are the same size as this ensures that the pull on each limb tip is even. Before starting the serving, place an extra strand of Fastflight between the two posts. Because the string crosses over on the other end there will be ten strands under the serving loop. By placing the extra strand between the posts it will also give you ten strands under this loop. The second loop is made in the same way as the first. Prior to tying off the loop with the finishing knot I recommend that you turn the posts to see if both ends will be the same length when you do the figure of eight. A little winding on or off may be required to achieve this.

Once you have completed the second loop, the string can be removed from the jig. You should now have a string that has two loops and servings of the same size. To make the centre serving, the string needs to be put onto the bow. As it is being put onto the bow twists should be put into the string. The minimum amount of twists is around fifteen, trying to get the bracing height that you need. Fewer than this and you will need to make a longer string. The more twists you put into the string the shorter it will be, but as the arrow is shot it will have a somewhat more give/stretch, which will make the shot a little softer.

Another important factor is the way in which the twists are put into the string. Traditionally, for a right-handed archer when viewed from above, with the string attached to the top limb only, the bottom loop should be turned clockwise. The reason given for this is that as the string 'rolls' off your fingers as you release it, the top part of the string will increase in twists and the bottom half decrease, so moving the nocking point up fractionally. Another way to determine the way to twist the string is to look at the lay or twist of each individual strand that makes up the string and then twist the string so that the twist of each individual strand is increased. These two methods can be combined to satisfy both arguments. To do so may mean laying the strands around the string jig in the opposite direction to the string you have made.

Once you have the string on the bow and enough twists in the string to bring the bracing height to the correct level, you can then put on the centre serving. The centre serving is there to locate the nocking point and to protect the string material if the string accidentally hits your arm. If you are using a cotton or dental floss type of nocking point, you can put one continuous serving on the string. Use your bracing height gauge to find where your nocking point should be and mark up approximately 45mm (1.8in) above, then 80mm (3.12in) below the nocking point. If you make the serving much shorter than this it will have a tendency to move when you are shooting, thereby moving your nocking point.

When making strings with an odd number of strands each end will contain an end of the string, but apart from that the method of making the string is the same. If you are going to make Dacron strings you will not need to add the extra 1cm before you start because when the new string is initially put onto the bow it will stretch substantially.

*The string is twisted in the same direction as the twist in the individual strand.*

## Nocking Points

The brass nocking points should be used if required to help you to find your initial nocking point position, but after that they should be replaced because they are heavy and may damage the face of the finger tab. If the nocking points are hard or positioned too close together they can pinch the nock and give you errors in flight and grouping. Waxed dental floss (not tape) makes a reasonably good nocking point. If the nock is a little loose on the serving, the centre can be bulked up with a layer of floss under the nock, and the method of putting one on is similar to making a short serving, with the finish knot being the same. If the nock fits well on the string you will have to use two pieces of dental floss, one above and one below the nock's position, and the knot for that is slightly different. The drawback to this type of nocking point is that it tends to widen up when shooting high volumes of arrows and the nock fit between strings is not so consistent.

I use Beiter nocks and Beiter nocking points because this gives me a perfect nock fit every time, and is the same fit from string to string. Occasionally, these nocking points break and a new one will have to be served in, but once on the string they have much lower maintenance that the dental floss type. There are two types of Beiter nocking point, No. 1 and No. 2. They both come in 1/8in and 3/32in sizes. I prefer the No. 2 threaded type, as once it is on the string I cannot feel it under the tab.

Both types are fitted in a similar way, but it is important to start the serving onto it directly at the edge of the nocking point. This ensures that the string stays flexible at the end of the nocking point. If you serve up to the nocking point, the string looses its flexibility and the centre of the nocking point becomes the most flexible point, causing the nocking point to split. There is an excellent guide to fitting the nocking points on the Beiter website (www.wernerbeiter.com). Once they have been fitted, it is best to push the serving in towards the nocking point by walking the threads with the square edge of a multi-tool or a bracing height gauge. This will ensure that there is not a gap between the threads, which would cause the nocking point to move position as you shoot.

## Waxing the String

Most strings come already waxed, with some more waxed than others. The more wax on the string, the heavier it will be. So once you have tuned the bow, do not put too much extra wax on as it will change the tuning. If there is a lot of wax on the string, wrap a length of serving thread around the string once, then pull it tight and draw it down the length of the string to remove the surplus wax. If you are waxing the string, just use your fingers to rub the wax into the string. The friction of your fingers will help to warm the wax and let it bond to the string better. Do not rub the wax into the string with leather or a similar material, as the string may get too hot, changing its chemical composition and

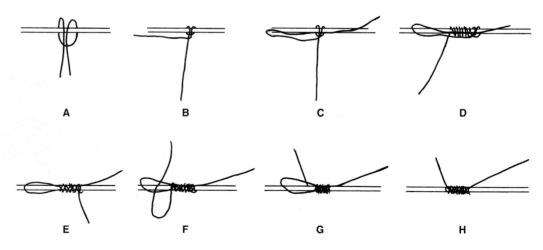

*A to H illustrate the sequence for tying a single nocking point.*

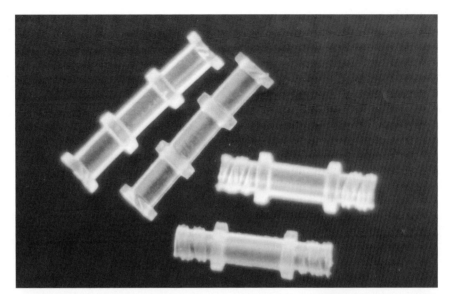

*The two types of Beiter nocking points – reel and threaded (No. 1 and No. 2) – come in two sizes to fit No. 1 and No. 2 nocks.*

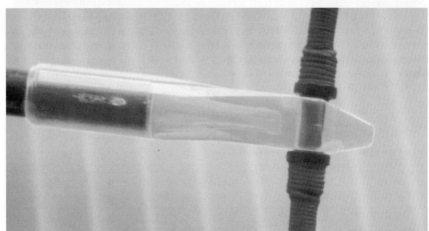

*A No. 2 nock and thread type nocking point. Note that the long side of the nock angle is to the top.*

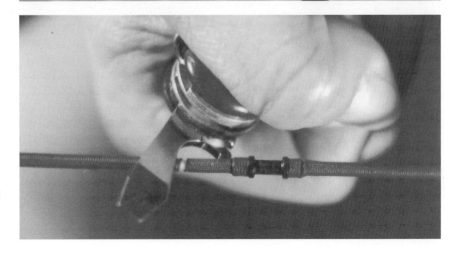

*Once the nocking point has been served in, the serving needs to be walked to the nock to ensure that the nocking point does not move.*

making it brittle and prone to breaking. If, when rubbing the string, it is too hot for your fingers it will be too hot for the string material.

## Making the String Perform

Once you have started making strings you can change each one's manufacture to change its characteristics. The loop ends need to finish before the cut-out in the limb, but varying the size of the loop will change how the bow sounds. If the end loops are too small it will tend to make the bow noisy. What material you use on the end servings will change the speed of the bow slightly. If you use a heavier serving material and make the serving from the loop longer, the bow will be a little slower, making the arrow marginally stiffer. Likewise, with the centre serving, changing its length and material will affect the stiffness of the arrow. The other consideration is how the string feels on the fingers. If the string is thicker and the tab face a little thick, there is less of a positive position in the first joint of the fingers. If I use a thinner serving material, and the thickness of the tab is correct, I can get the same finger position on the string every time.

Varying the amount of twists in the string will also change the performance. This will take time to test. I have my No. 1 string; I may decide to make a string slightly longer, giving more twists for my bracing height. If it is better it becomes my No. 1 string; if not, it goes into the box. I may then make one slightly shorter and if that works better it will become the No. 1 string. The replaced string will then become the No. 2 string, so I always have plenty of spares.

## Summary

I do not think that there is a 'best' string material, just one that is suited to the archer. Some materials will make the shot seem softer and some harder – it will be up to the archer to decide what suits. In my opinion, it is better to make your own strings because more care will go into them, as you are the one looking for the results. Making your own will help to ensure that you have the right string to match you and your equipment. Once you have made your string, put the materials away in a cupboard as the string material can be affected by the light and may change its chemical composition.

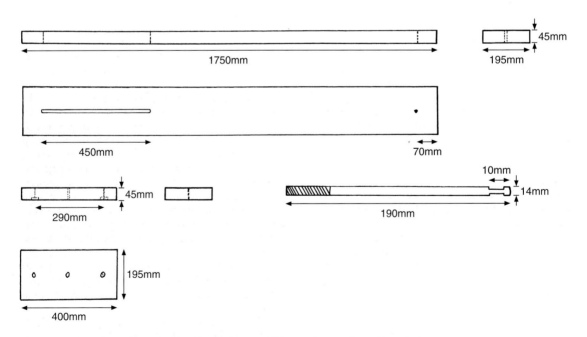

*This simple jig can be made quite easily, although the pins will have to be manufactured by a local engineer.*

Chapter 12

# Better Shooting

This chapter is designed to give you more information on improving your shooting. The shooting itself is the easy part – it is the other factors that are not usually considered which affect your shooting. The following sections deal with the main ways in which you can improve your shooting:

- clearance
- arm and shoulder position
- shooting well in the wind and rain
- shooting with a telescope
- sight marks
- light conditions.

## Clearance

To shoot well, at full draw the string must only be in contact with the fingers and the limb tips and therefore should be clear of the chest. When the string is released and leaves the fingers, it must be clear of the arm until the nock is released from the string. This seems to be quite an obvious part of shooting well, but until the arrow is shot in a way that fulfils these requirements, further work on technique and tuning will be hampered.

### Chest

If the string rests against the chest, the string's natural line from the fingers to the bottom limb will be distorted. This will lead to inconsistencies in grouping and give false results when tuning. Normally, a chest guard is worn to keep the clothing in tight and to stop it catching in the string, but this can disguise how much pressure the string is placing on the chest. If you remove your chest guard and shoot just with a tight T-shirt on you will be able to feel if the string is pressing on your chest. If you do this during training you will start to feel the best body position to enable you to get clearance.

Women, due to their difference in physique, can find getting clearance more of a challenge and may need to alter their body's vertical position to help to give better clearance.

Even when shooting like this, the body's centre of gravity needs to stay between the feet. A sports bra or no bra will also help to streamline the torso, with the chest guard adjusted firmly to keep the chest as flat as possible. Depending on draw length, a shorter bow may give the necessary extra clearance. If it is still not possible to get full clearance, special care should be taken on the pre-draw so that the position of the string against the chest is as consistent as possible.

### Arm Clearance

Once the string is released, it must have a clear path without hitting the arm. If the string touches the arm or bracer before the nock has become detached from the string, it will alter the trajectory of the arrow, making the groups bigger. Many aspiring archers are held back because the string touches the arm as the bow is shot. The bracer is very good at deflecting the string, but in doing so it is very difficult for the archer to ascertain if the string is actually hitting it, as the bracer absorbs most of the feeling. The easiest way to see if the string hits your arm is to shoot bare-armed without a bracer. If the string hits, you will soon know about it! This may seem a bit harsh, so either shoot with a very tight-sleeved thin sweatshirt, or get some tube-grip from the chemist and put it over your arm. As you shoot you will be able to feel if the string is hitting the arm without causing too much bruising. This is also a good method to use if the string hits the arm occasionally due to the odd arrow going out of the group.

To remedy the string contacting the arm, look at the hand position in the grip of the bow. It might be in too deep or the bow shoulder may be too far

*Margarita Galinovskaya (Russia).*

*Natalia Nasaridze (Turkey).*

*Katja Milanovich (Belarus).*

*Arching the back can help to give more clearance; Anna Karaseova (Belarus).*

*The centre of gravity is still maintained; Anna Karaseova (Belarus).*

*The hand position determines the position of the arm. Slight inconsistencies in the hand position can lead to the string hitting the arm occasionally. Michele Frangelli (Italy) shows a good hand position.*

forward. The body position alone may not give you the necessary clearance. It may be that the arrow's set-up in the bow or the bracing height is not correct. If either of these is set incorrectly it may increase the amplitude of the string's path as it is released, which may cause the string to hit the arm. If you do not want to shoot without a bracer, dust some lipstick or talcum powder on the bracer. If the string hits the bracer it will leave a mark in the lipstick/powder and it will be apparent that you are not getting clearance.

## Arm and Shoulder Position

When the bow is drawn to full draw, the angle between the torso and the arms must keep the same relationship.

Although shooting at targets of varying elevations is seen as part of the field discipline, it is also an important part of target archery, although the variations in elevation are not so pronounced. The angle that the bow has to be held at for the arrow to make the distance will vary depending on the power of the bow; the lower the poundage of the limbs, the higher the angle that the bow has to be held at. It is important that the angle between the shoulders, arms and torso is maintained. This is achieved by tilting the hips. This ensures that, at what ever distance that you are shooting, you are practising the same shot. If you keep the torso upright for every distance you shoot, it will have to be the arm to torso angle that changes. This, in turn, means that you are learning to shoot a different shot

for each distance; so on a FITA you are training to learn four different shots.

The effect of this will be more apparent when shooting the three-spot vertical face at 18m. Because you have a face to yourself, it is easy to see the group patterns for each face. Many archers do not like the three-spot vertical, because their group is inconsistent when the three faces are put on top of each other. If the group position is not similar for each face, it is likely that the angle between the arms and torso will be different for each shot. This

*The angle between the torso and the arms must be maintained at all distances; Hiroshi Yamamoto (Japan). (Andrew Callaway)*

*The angle of the arms and the torso should remain the same. (Karen Henderson)*

*The Formaster is a good way to learn to adjust the body. (Karen Henderson)*

*The tilt angle should come from a slight change in the angle of the hips. (Karen Henderson)*

changes which muscles are used to draw the bow, in turn affecting the release and consequently the placing of the group. If the relationship between the arms and torso is kept consistent, the groups will also remain consistent.

A good way of practising changing the angle of the hips is with the bow set up with a reversal sling and cord. Draw the bow back, keeping the cord just under the chin, then practise tilting the hips slightly, keeping the cord in the same position against the chin.

If you change the relationship of your arms and torso you will easily be able to notice the difference. This can also be used outside prior to shooting each distance. Put the sling onto the bow, practise aiming at the distance selected and get the feeling for the correct body position.

## Shooting Well in the Wind and Rain

Shooting well in the wind and rain is more about the psychology of improving your confidence, as your shooting style should remain the same.

Make sure that any clothing intended to keep out the wind and/or the rain is fully tested in training and that you have different combinations to suit the different conditions. If you have warm clothing and footwear in which you know you can shoot unhindered, your confidence will increase as you will not be distracted by being uncomfortable. If your opponents are not as well prepared, they will be busy trying to stay dry or finding that the shoes

they have on are letting in water and therefore they will not be concentrating on their shooting.

The main point about shooting in poor conditions is that you are all shooting in the same conditions. Some archers lose sight of this and think that they are the only ones affected by the weather. I like shooting in poor conditions, because most archers do not, and this gives me even more of an advantage. If you tell them that you like shooting in the rain, not only are you reinforcing your positive attitude to the conditions but you are keeping the advantage, as they will probably start moaning to themselves about how difficult it is. All these factors of preparation and mental approach to the poor conditions increase your advantage before an arrow has even been shot.

*Shooting Well in the Wind*
In my opinion, it is your body's movement in the wind that is a bigger contributing factor to the size of the group than the arrows being blown off course. A few years ago at my club we had to move fields for a season while work was being done to our shooting field. The only field available was on the top of a hill. This meant that we had great views of the countryside, but also received full blast from the weather. At first this seemed disappointing, but we soon got used to shooting in all types of wind conditions. As the field had no facilities we used an 8ft metal container to store all the equipment. On windy days, we would set up the target so that we could shoot from the sheltered side of the container.

*An open field is a good place to learn how to shoot in the wind. (Marykirk)*

When we were standing in the lee of the container in calm conditions shooting our arrows out into the wind we found that the arrows still grouped very well. If we stood in the wind, the groups got significantly bigger. Ergo – the buffeting of the body and equipment by the wind led to bigger arrow groups on the target.

When I shoot, I keep the sight in the central position and aim off; this ensures that if the wind drops I can then aim in the centre of the target. If you move your sight to compensate for wind and the wind drops, where do you aim? The only time I do move the windage is if it is good conditions but a very light wind. If my point of focus is the centre of the gold and my arrows are drifting into the nine, I will tend to adjust the sight slightly to keep my group centred on the ten.

In order to keep my mind positive when there is wind I play 'colour the wind', which involves guessing the 'colour' of the wind. If your point of focus is on the gold and the arrow hits the red – it is a red wind. If it hits the blue – it is a blue wind. If it hits the black – a black wind. With a wind is blowing left to right, if you think it is a blue wind you maintain your point of focus on blue and shoot; if the arrow goes in the gold it is a blue wind. If it goes nine o'clock in the red, it was a red wind. If it goes at three o'clock in the red, it was a black wind. Just adjust the colour of the wind accordingly. As you can see, this is a method of aiming off that keeps things light-hearted, a game within a game. There is no need to be frustrated if you get the colour wrong – just guess again and see if you get it right. In practice, you can shoot your arrows just aiming at the gold; how far they drift will give you the parameters of the wind. Perhaps all your arrows will go in the red and blue while keeping your focus on the gold. This gives you a wind that is varying between blue and red. If you shoot your first arrow at the blue–red divide, you should get a gold. Remember that the width of the gold spans the same distance as two colour bands and that the ten is the same diameter as a single colour band. This means that when is it windy you can still keep the arrows in the ten. The point of focus when aiming off still needs to be a point in the colour you have chosen, as this will keep the groups tighter.

Next, add in contributing information that will help you to decide the colour of the wind. What are the other flags on the field and other targets doing? Can you see the grass moving and are there trees making a noise in the direction from which the wind is coming? Can you hear the wind in the tents behind you? Once you get used to it, you will be almost able to see the wind billowing like clear smoke rolling across the field towards you.

This will help you to decide when to shoot. Try to shoot all the arrows in the same force of wind, in a lighter wind if possible, but you need to pick a colour of wind that is predominant in the time available, in order to make the best use of your time.

A head or tailwind will affect the vertical position of the arrow on the target. A tailwind will lower the group and a headwind will raise it. Although I do not move the windage of the sight to compensate for a shear wind, I will vertically adjust the sight so that I always have a point of focus level or above the centre of the target face.

You need to factor in the time available and make the best of it. If there is a light wind, time is not really an issue, but when the wind is stronger and you are trying to shoot all the arrows in similar conditions to keep the point of focus consistent, the shots must still be shot well and not rushed. I find that within the four minutes there is plenty of time to shoot six arrows, although I do like to have shot three arrows within the first two minutes. For the shorter distances, having only two minutes in which to find favourable conditions, archers are more prone to running out of time. So for the two minutes I have a plan – the first arrow must be shot within the first minute, the second arrow must be shot within the next thirty seconds, which leaves a full thirty seconds to shoot the last arrow. By following this plan I never run out of time and always get a good score. It may seem on occasions that if you had waited until the last forty-five seconds, calm weather might have occurred and you could have got away your three arrows in favourable conditions, but there is a much higher probability that it would have remained windy and you would have run out of time. So have a plan and stick to it.

Bend with the wind. If you try to fight it, you will become tired more quickly and your shooting will become more rigid and stiff. If you are at full draw and the wind blows, sway with it and then sway back, keeping the muscles relaxed and keeping the line as though there was no wind. This will ensure that you maintain good shots.

### Shooting Well in the Rain

All the principles of shooting in the wind hold true for shooting in the rain. The good thing about the rain is that it helps you to see the wind, so that you can judge it better. The rain will make your arrows drop, but by how much will depend on the power of the bow and the type of arrows you shoot; if in doubt, aim a little higher than you initially judge. In light rain, try to keep your bow dry if possible by giving the limbs a wipe-down prior to going onto the line. In heavy rain, I keep the bow in the rain and just try to prevent rain getting into the button.

Whatever the conditions, it is important to keep the bow in a consistent condition. This will help to keep the shot and group consistent. Water on the limbs will slow the bow down, as will water on the arrows. If you keep them both wet, the bow will shoot more consistently between shots. If, when the rain is heavy, you try to dry the bow between ends, the bow's performance will vary over the ends due to the changes in the amount of water on the bow. Before shooting the first arrow of each end, 'ping' the string prior to putting the first arrow in the bow. This will help to remove as much water from the limbs as possible and each shot will then clear the water from the limbs. You might find that the first shot goes a little lower than the subsequent arrows of that end, as not so much water is removed by 'pinging' the string. I therefore usually aim my first arrow a little higher to compensate.

An important aspect of shooting in the rain is to maintain your normal shooting rhythm. You will notice that when it rains some archers rush out onto the line, shoot their arrows quickly and then get back to the tent as quickly as possible. You must maintain your normal routine whatever the weather. This will ensure that you keep shooting well. If you have the right clothing to wear when the weather is inclement, the rain should not bother you much.

The best way to improve your shooting in poor conditions is to practise in them. This needs to be balanced by executing shots in good conditions in order to maintain your style.

## Shooting with a Telescope

Especially when the weather is poor, a telescope will enable you to see where your arrows are hitting the target. If you can see the fall of each shot you can adjust for it arrow by arrow. If you do not use a telescope you can only adjust for it after six arrows; in competition a good group in the black will hold you back. As with everything else, you need to learn to shoot with a 'scope in practice and make sure that it is in a good position. At some competitions you will find that there is not a lot of room on the shooting line so you will need to practice having the 'scope very close to you. I have found that if the 'scope is too high, it can be seen out of the corner of the eye as you are shooting the bow. The brain's natural reaction is to keep the body safe, so it will react to something in the peripheral vision by moving the body away from the object. If you put the 'scope down lower, you will be able to maintain your body position better. There is also a temptation to look through the 'scope too early to see the arrow land; therefore 'scope discipline needs to be learnt. Execute the shot fully. The shot finishes when the arrow is in the target, then you can look through the 'scope to see the position of the arrow.

Use of the 'scope in training needs to be tempered with what you are trying to achieve. If you are shooting for form or training on a certain aspect of the shot, train without the 'scope. When you are in practice mode use the 'scope, as it should become part of the shot routine; you also need to identify the arrows that were shot well. By knowing which arrows landed in the ten you can learn what it feels like to shoot tens. In archery, all you need to be able to do is learn to shoot a ten, then do it over and over again. If you do use a 'scope when you shoot you must use it the same for every distance. If you only use it for long distances and not for short, you will be trying to learn two shot routines. There are enough variables in archery without purposefully introducing more. Using a 'scope all the time ensures that you can see where your arrow landed at whatever distance.

Some 'scopes are reasonably waterproof but still may need a hood or cover placed over the top to stop the rain getting onto the lenses. A 'scope is no use if you are unable to see out of it. The waterproofing on some 'scopes can be improved by putting Vaseline on the body joints. If water does get into the body of the 'scope, you will need to open it up to drive the water out.

You should choose the colour of the fletches and nocks that you use in conjunction with the 'scope to give a combination of colours that you will find the easiest to see and hopefully a combination that is not too common. It is always best to have a spare set of different coloured nocks in your box just in case another archer on the target has the same combination of colours, which is not unusual. You need to be able to see your fall of shot after every shot.

## Sight Marks

A competition can be won just by having accurate sight marks. If you can get your first arrow in the gold at each new distance you can put twenty points on your score for the whole competition. With the first arrow in the gold, your confidence in the fall of shot will be improved. Therefore, attention needs to be paid to getting a good set of sight marks, in not only the vertical but also the horizontal position of the sight for each distance. Write them down twice, always keeping one set in your box. A large proportion of archers get to a competition to find they have left their sight marks at home and then consequently get a poor result.

To start with, ensure that your shooting field is accurately marked out and that, as you check for the different distances, you use the correct size of face for that distance. Using the wrong size can give you an error in the sight mark. I usually set the field up with the four distances for a FITA, then practice shooting one end at each distance, moving up and down the field, to make sure that I get used to moving between distances and giving me the confidence to shoot good groups at each distance change. At some shoots, you will have the opportunity to practise on the field the day before the shoot. You can use this time to check your settings to make sure that the distance settings are the same as the ones from your own field. It is only necessary

to shoot a couple of ends at each distance to confirm the sight's position. Do not get carried away and shoot too many arrows; the day before the shoot is too late to practise.

At the competition, record in your diary the sight setting and the conditions, wind, rain and sun, for every distance. This will enable you to get a more accurate sight mark for the next day on a two-day shoot. The more shoots you go to, the more sight marks you will accrue. Different fields may well give slightly different sight marks, depending on the conditions. With a good selection of sight marks, it will be easier to find similar settings from a previous similar day, giving you a more confident start to each distance.

## Light Conditions

As with shooting in the wind, the light conditions will also alter your sight marks. On a brighter day, they may be a little up and on a dull day, a little down. When shooting in conditions of broken cloud try to shoot all your arrows either in the sun or in the shade. This will help to keep the vertical height of the group more consistent. The changes

*A good combination of hat and glasses will ensure a more consistent light on the eyes throughout the day. Don Rabska coaching at the 1999 pre-Olympic event.*

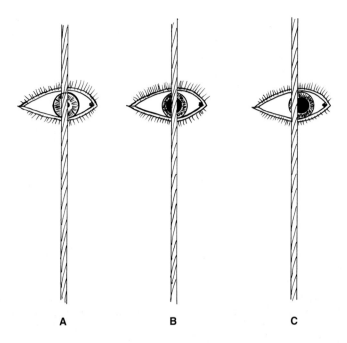

A            B            C

*(A) With the pupil small, the eye and string can only be on one position. (B) and (C) With a large pupil dilation, the alignment of the eye and string is more variable.*

of intensity in light affects the size of the pupil, so to cut down the variation in pupil dilation, a visor or brimmed hat can be worn.

This will keep a more even intensity of light falling on the eye, so the dilation of the pupil will be more consistent. Caution should be employed if wearing sunglasses. If they have very dark lens and cover the eye well the pupil will widen to allow more light in, but in doing so the string picture will be less consistent. With medium or slightly tinted lenses more light falls onto the eye, making the pupil smaller and giving a more consistent string picture.

Shooting indoors while wearing a visor can also help with consistency of the groups, as the light conditions between venues can vary. Some sport centres have sodium lights that give off an orangey light, which affects not only how the target appears, but also the brain's rhythm and can lead to an altered pattern of mental activity. Wearing a visor can cut down on these effects. You will, of course, get the comment 'Is the sun in your eyes?', which is always very witty, but most indoor arenas also have window panels through which the sun can come streaming. Also, depending on the time of the shoot, the light intensity can change dramatically as it gets dark outside. As the light conditions change, so the position of the visor can be changed to keep the light level on the eyes consistent, giving more consistent groups.

# Chapter 13

# Fine-Tuning Your Equipment

Initial tuning puts the bare-shafted arrow level with the fletched group. To carry out successful fine-tuning the bare shaft needs to be moved as close to the fletched group as possible. To start fine-tuning, the furthest out from the group I would want the bare shaft to be is the blue at 30m, on an 80cm face, with the sight aperture in the central position. Any further out than this, I would try to match the arrow spine to the bow better before fine-tuning.

You will need to work with the set-up to prove the best adjustment for all the settings of the bow. In this chapter, I will go over the fine-tuning steps that will help to improve the groups. Tuning is reliant on how consistently you are shooting. The better you shoot, the more easily you will be able to interpret the results;, any tuning will help the groups get smaller. When the group is smaller you will shoot better, which then means you can tune better. Fine-tuning is a continual process which is directly linked to your shooting ability. It involves these steps:

- recheck the bracing height
- fine-tune the button position/tension
- adjust the nocking point
- change the arrow speed
- shoot your distances
- change the string composition
- tiller tuning.

Tuning should be carried out when you are shooting well and in calm conditions or indoors. Shoot at a distance you are comfortable with to enable you to get reliable results when shooting for groups. When shooting with a bare shafts, use at least three to ensure that the bare shafts. are consistently matched. If two go together every end and one goes off, it may indicate an errant arrow. If they all go in the same place it enables you to get a clearer reading of their position more

quickly than if you were only shooting one bare shaft per end. as it will give you the average position. Shoot at a distance of no further than 30m to give you reliable readings. When shooting with the bare shafts, you are comparing the deviation of trajectory between the fletched arrows and the bare shafts, so the longer the distance the more apparent the deviation. Further than 30m, inaccuracies in the bare-shaft flight may give erroneous readings.

As with initial tuning, keep the sight just to the left of the central position so that the bow points towards the target. The left and right of the group should be adjusted using the tension of the spring in the button.

## Recheck the Bracing Height

I start by rechecking the bracing height. Start with a longer string, giving you a low bracing height of 7¾in. Although this may seem too low, it is better to start out well below the range you might need or that suggested by the manufacturer. By starting low, it ensures that as you check the arrow groups at varying heights it is obvious whenas you come to the correct brace height. You may be surprised at how low the right bracing height actually is. Some limbs work well on a low bracing height (for example, Hoyt G3). Shoot at a distance of 18m to start with. Shoot for groups. The best way of checking your group size is to plot it on a paper score/plot sheet.

I would suggest that you shoot at least twenty-four arrows to give an average group size. Alternatively, if you have a Personal Digital Assistant (PDA) you can use 'Target Plot' (*see* Chapter 14), a computer-based arrow plotter. During this process only look at the size of the group, not the position of the group on the target.

After every few well-shot ends at the initial bracing height, put another four twists into the

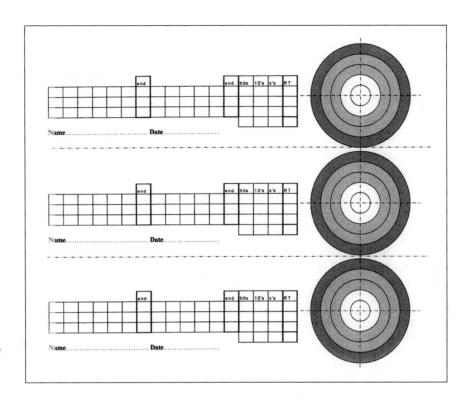

*Sheets like this enable you to score and plot the groups, giving you a good indication of group size and position.*

string, making it shorter. As the bracing height rises you should find that the groups will get better. Continue raising the bracing height until the groups get bigger once again. Once the bracing height has got significantly bigger, let it down again until you get the best groups. You will usually find that as you lower the bracing height the groups will slowly get better, then within eight twists lower the groups will get significantly bigger.

Once you have found the best bracing height, move on to 30m, then make further small adjustments to the bracing height to give you the best results. Once you feel that you have found the best group at this time, fit your normal string back on the bow to that bracing height.

## Fine-Tune the Button Position/Tension

In initial tuning, the button was set so that the point of the arrow shaft can be seen to the left of the 'centred' string and the button tension adjusted so that the bow was pointing at the target with the sight in the central position. This initial setting will be close to the final setting, but the correct position of the

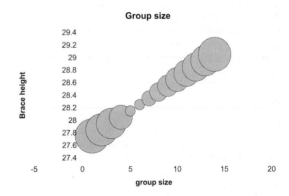

*As the bracing height is adjusted so the size of the group changes. As the brace height increases the group will get rapidly smaller then as it is increased it will increase more gradually.*

button needs to be proved by shooting for groups. This can be carried out over a specific tuning session or checked on a weekly basis at your club night.

Choose a direction in which to move the button – for example, move it out. Move the button out half a turn, shoot some sighter arrows and adjust the button spring pressure as required to keep the arrows in the centre of the target. Then shoot a twenty-four-arrow sequence, plotting the size of the group. You can shoot the bare shafts as a check for tuning to see if there is any height difference in the bare shaft position. The main focus during this exercise is the size of the group. The bare shafts can be used to ensure that the position of the nocking point remains in the right place. Small adjustments to the nocking point may be required to keep the bare shafts level with the group. Once you have shot your twenty-four-arrow sequence, move the button out a further half turn, readjust and shoot the group sequence once again. (Repeat as required.)

When you reach the point that the group size is getting bigger, return the button to the initial setting and carry out the group sequence once again, moving the button in; again, stop when the increase in group size is recognized. Look over all the results and note where the button position was in relation to the best group size. From this point, carry out the test again, this time only moving the button a quarter of a turn, in and out. This enables you to find the best position for the button. To carry this out successfully, you need to go past the best group size to prove that it cannot be bettered. Even if the button ends up set at the initial position, you have proved that this is the best one, which will help to increase confidence in your equipment.

The button tension can now be adjusted to ensure that the arrow-to-bow match is within the bow set-up's tuning range. To do this without adjusting the sight setting, shoot fletched arrows aimed at the centre of the target. Making a note of the button-tension adjuster's position, slacken off the button tension. Keep aiming at the centre of the target – the arrows should now start impacting to the right of the gold. Now increase the button's tension until the pressure of the button passes the initial setting and increases. As it increases further, the fletched arrows' point of impact should move to the left of the gold. If the match of arrow spine is good, the shafts will move from right to left across the gold.

If the arrow group moves to the right as the button tension is decreased, but when it is increased comes back to centre but does not move past the centre however hard you make the button tension, it indicates that the arrow spine is too weak. Conversely, if the arrow impact point does not move to the right as the tension is decreased, but moves to the left as it is increased, it indicates that the arrow

is stiff. If the arrow bow is stiff or weak, adjust your equipment as suggested in Chapter 4.

You should now have the bow set up so that the group is good and the button, when adjusted, moves the group across the target both left and right. If you are not able to adjust the bow enough to change the spine of the arrow, adjust the button pressure so that it is active (the fletched group will move to the right as the button pressure is decreased, but will not move to the left however it is adjusted). To do this, move Move to 60m and shoot your fletched arrows, decreasing the button pressure until the group significantly moves to the right. Then increase the button pressure a small bit at a time. The group will move to the left again; when the group stops moving to the left as you increase the button tension, decrease the pressure slightly until the group just starts to move to the right. This means that the button is active as a little adjustment of the button pressure either way will move the group., Although you may be at the end of the tuning range of the button to the arrow, your groups will be better and more consistent.

## Adjust the Nocking Point

This exercise is similar to the button-pressure exercise. Pick a direction and move the nocking point 1mm at a time by walking the centre serving up, then down, the string. Shoot for groups, recording your results and find the best position of the nocking point by the size of the group. Once you have found the best position for it, shoot your bare shafts and note the position of them in relation to the fletched-shaft group. When you are setting up other strings or bows, adjusting the nocking point and spine so that the bare shaft goes into the same position in relation to the fletched group will enable you to get the tuning closer to optimum more quickly.

## Change the Arrow Speed

Now work with changing the arrow speed. You may find that a slightly stiff or weak arrow will suit how you shoot. Normally, I would do this by changing the amount of strands in the string – just one strand more or less than the string you are using may give a tighter group. When you are doing this you still need to work with the button pressure to ensure that the button remains in the active

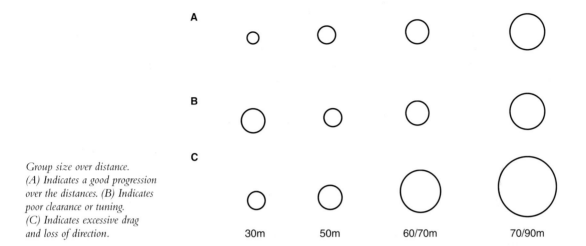

*Group size over distance. (A) Indicates a good progression over the distances. (B) Indicates poor clearance or tuning. (C) Indicates excessive drag and loss of direction.*

range. Even changing the thickness of serving may change the weight of string enough to give you an improved group.

## Shoot Your Distances

Now shoot your competition distances, making sure that the group size is relative throughout the range.

If the group size is disproportionately bigger at the shorter distances, you may have a clearance problem. Make sure that the string is not touching the chest or arm. If it is clear of both these areas, check that the arrow is not touching the button or rest as it leaves the bow. Initially, you can check the fletchings to see if they are catching as there may be a mark left on the fletch, or, if using spin wings, a will crease in a fletch. It is more likely that the shaft of the arrow in front of the fletch position is touching the button/rest.

Although this is easy to see with high-speed photography, it is a little harder to determine without it. The best method is to dust the area of the arrow suspected of touching the bow lightly with talcum powder. It may take a number of shots to

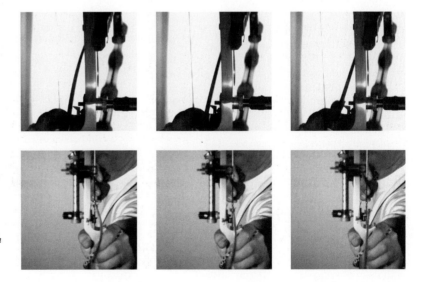

*As the shaft flexes in towards the bow, the shaft and fletches can catch the rest and button as they pass. (Werner Beiter)*

make a mark, although in In some cases the mark on the shaft will be very apparent and can be seen clearly without a dusting. The other way of checking is to put a thin layer of bright lipstick onto the shaft. When the arrow is shot, if the shaft touches the button or rest it will leave a layer of lipstick and the contact point on the arrow should be visible. On some bows where the match of arrow to bow is poor (juniors using long arrows to 'grow into', for example), the arrow may hit the sight bar on the 'T' type sights. This can be remedied by putting a packing piece between the bow and the sight block, moving the 'T' bar out from the trajectory of the bow.

If the group sizes are disproportionately bigger at the longer distances, it is likely that the arrow is losing speed too quickly and so losing direction.

Go back to the arrow charts and make sure that when you have been trying to match the arrow to the bow you have not taken too much weight off the point to make the arrow stiffer. If the point weight is low the arrow will tend to drift, so make sure that the point weight is not below the recommended point weight for the shaft you are using. Inspect the fletches; if the fletches are set at too much of an angle or are too big, they will spin the arrow well but slow it down too much. Change the fletch angle, ensuring that you can still see the face of the fletch so that the arrow spins, but cut the angle down and see if that makes a difference to the group size.

Try smaller fletches. Juniors and women shooting lighter arrows will need to pay particular attention to the fletches to give them the best

performance. Try putting the fletches closer or further away from the nock and shoot for groups. One reason that the groups at the longer distances could be bigger may well be that you just do not practise them enough!

As you shoot the different distances you may notice that you have to change the windage (lateral movement) of the sight. In theory, you should be able to set the sight to shoot at the longest distance and shoot in the gold, then move to the shortest distance, only moving the sight up, and shoot in the gold again without having to adjust the sight's lateral adjustment. In practice, there are two aspects that will determine why you have to make lateral sight adjustments as you change distance. The first factor is tuning – the 'walk-back' method of tuning, which is explained in Appendix 1 – uses the fact that if the arrow is weak or the button pressure is too soft, as you go to greater distances the group will move to the right. It the arrow is stiff or the button pressure is set too high, the group will go to the left. Small adjustments to the button pressure may keep the sight's lateral position more consistent throughout the distances.

The second factor is the string picture. Although you try to keep the same visual relationship with the string to the bow throughout the distances and it seems to be the same, the target in fact changes appearance at each change of distance. This varying face appearance can change the relationship of the string-to-bow appearance slightly, altering the alignment of the bow to the target. This is manifested in the movement of the lateral sight for the different distances. This can be compensated for by recording the difference in windage for each distance or by offsetting the sight bar to cancel out the visual error, so that as the sight moves down it also moves to the side slightly. Remember you are tuning to get the best groups at all distances.

Once you are satisfied that the group size is consistent at all distances, you can then revisit the nocking point test for each distance. I have found that if I set the nocking point so that the bare-shaft arrow impacts below the group at 30m, I would get the best groups and score at the long metric. If I set the string so that the bare-shaft arrow impacted above the group at 30m I would get the best score at the short metric. If I shot the long metric string at 50m I would score around 310 out of 360. If I put the short metric string on the bow to shoot 50m I would score 330 – a significant difference. All I had to do was set up two strings to shoot a FITA.

### Tuning for Longer Distances

A reason other than tuning for larger groups at the longer distances is when the archer tries to watch the arrow's flight. Although at the shorter distances, although the archer should remain concentrating on the point of focus, there is a tendency to watch the flight of the arrow. At the shorter distances the arrow flight can be seen without moving the head too much. As the distance gets greater the arrow follows a higher trajectory to get to the target and there is a tendency for the head to riseraise slightly as the string is released, giving bigger groups at the longer distances.

## Change the String Composition

Once you have the bow shooting well, try different types of string materials and colours. Different strings have different properties and will therefore have a different feel when shot, so try different types of material to see which suit you. The sensitivity of your eyes and the light conditions. . It will affect how you see the string and the string picture. If you use a darker string in poor light conditions (such as indoors), the string picture may become indistinct and it may be a challenge to get a consistent string picture.; a. A white or lighter string indoors therefore may be the answer to more consistent groups. However, using a white string on a sunny day may make the string too bright and seem very wide, so using a darker string outdoors may be preferable.

## Tiller Tuning

In initial tuning, the tiller was set to 4–6mm (0.16–0.23in) positive. With a matched set of limbs, the fingers placed normally on the string, one finger above and two below, and the bow's dynamic and static balance set, 4–6mm is a good place to set the tiller.

With the tiller set correctly, as the bow is drawn back and shot, the riser will stay in the same perpendicular plane and the long rod will stay in the same horizontal plane until the arrow leaves the string. The positive tiller setting compensates for the string being pulled above the centre line. This allows the top limb to work slightly less, so that when the string is released from the fingers, both limbs close at the same rate, so as the arrow is released from the string both limbs hit bottom at the same time. This ensures that the arrow's nock end is propelled from full draw to string release in a flat trajectory.

The two main factors that alter this balance of limb movement are the tiller setting and the balance of the riser above and below the pivot point (*see* Chapter 3). If the limbs are set so that the top limb is stronger than the bottom, as the bow is drawn back the top limb will not travel as far as the bottom limb. As the top limb is stiffer it will pull the top of the riser towards you slightly, as the turning forces around the pivot point are higher at the top than the bottom. As the string is released, there will be an imbalance in the distance that the limbs travel, causing the nock of the arrow to travel in an ogival path. If, however, the tiller balance is correct

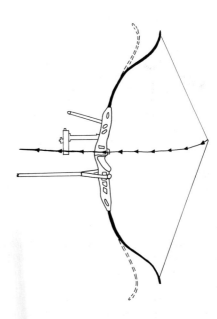

*With the limbs out of balance, the nock follows an ogival path that leads to inconsistencies.*

but the weight of the riser is heavier above the pivot point (top of the riser heavier than the bottom), as the bow is drawn back the riser will stay in the same vertical plane, which is what you want. But, on the release, the top limb will work harder than the bottom limb, as it has more mass to work against, and the nock of the arrow will take an ogival path, and not the horizontal path that you want the arrow to take.

### Other Factors Affecting the Tiller

Although one would hope that the limbs were matched, you may find that some limbs are slightly out of balance. Although you may have a consistent hand position, depending on the size of your hand and the point of pressure within the grip and the size, spacing and pressure of the fingers on the string all affect the tillering of the bow. One factor may cancel out another or exaggerate it. So setting the tiller position to 4–6mm may not always suit the archer.

### Determining the Best Tiller Position

The dynamic balance of the bow is quite easy to determine and should be rechecked first. If the dynamic balance is not correctly set, the tiller can

*The balance of the bow is opposite the pressure point of the bow hand; Lana Needham (GBR).*

be used to compensate for this imbalance to a certain extent, although the bow will be less forgiving. When you are adjusting the tiller you will also be adjusting the power of the bow, as the tiller adjustment bolts move the end of the limb in and out. In order to keep the power of the bow balanced, both the top and bottom adjuster must be adjusted by the same amount to maintain the draw weight. If you know that your arrow spine is a little stiff or weak, the adjustment of the tiller can be done in a manner that helps to match the spine further.

### Visual Tiller Check

To carry out a visual tiller check, you will need to have an observer. Draw the bow back, in as flat a draw as possible, for a number of times. The observer should look from the side and from behind and try to judge if the sight and the long rod stay in the same plane during the draw. If the sight and the long rod rise, it indicates that the top limb is working too hard and the tiller of the top limb should be increased; if they appear to drop, the tiller should be decreased. It is quite hard for the archer to maintain a flat draw so this is a somewhat subjective test. The observer not only has totoo see the rise or fall of the bow, but also ensure that the movement of the sight or the long rod is not due to an uneven draw. This is therefore only a static test. Some coaches claim they can see the limbs closing as the bow is shot, but in my opinion this can only be determined accurately is if the bow is filmed at very high speed then slowed down to determine the movement of the limbs.

### Mechanical Tiller Check

It is possible to check the tiller using a Dial Test Indicator (DTI); again this is a static test. A DTI is bolted onto the riser and adjusted so that when an arrow is placed on the string and the rest, the DTI can be zeroed. The bow is then drawn back and the DTI reading taken again. If the tiller is correct, the DTI will still read zero. If it is a positive reading, the top limb is working too hard; if it is a negative reading, the bottom limb is working too hard and the tiller will have to be adjusted until the reading is the same throughout the draw.

Both these tests are static in nature and will not give you a dynamic result. When the tiller is correct, the limbs will stop their movement relatively quickly and an experienced archer may be able to balance the tiller by feel alone.

### Dynamic Tiller Test

This dynamic tiller test is only possible using the Beiter rest, as it is the only one that has a Vernier scale, which can be used to reproduce specific rest positions. Dynamic tiller takes into account both hand positionpositions and the stabilizer balance of the bow as the results are of the bow being shot.

### Theory

A few years ago I was lucky enough to go to a talk by Mr Ki Sik Lee, head coach in Korea at the time and now head coach in Australia. One of his comments at the talk was that the nocking point height was not overly critical, so if it moved a little up or down it would not affect the groups too much. If the tiller is set correctly, the nock end of the arrow will follow a horizontal trajectory as it leaves the bow, ensuring that the arrow bends only in a lateral plane.

A bare shaft is shot out of a properly tillered bow, with the nocking point set so that the bare shaft impacts level with the fletched arrow, then. Then, the rest position is raised up (raising the arrow in the bow) a set distance and shot again and the results recorded. The rest position is then lowered by the same set distance, shot again and the result recorded. The relationship above and below the original group position should be similar.

*How to Tiller-Tune Dynamically*
A Beiter rest should be fitted to the bow to carry out this tuning. The rest may have to be adapted to get the arrow shaft to the correct initial position. If you use a magnetic rest the arm can be removed so that the Beiter rest can be fitted. Stick on rests will have to be removed.

**Position 1** With the rest arm in the central position, put the arrow into the rest with the centre of the shaft against the centre of the button. This is the initial position. The rest comes with two sizes of arm, one for carbons and one for aluminiums. With the X10 arrowsarrow's the shaft fitted on the carbon rest will probably be in the correct position. If you are using thicker arrows, the top of the rest

blade will have to be cut down so that the arrow will be in the correct position, or the aluminium rest blade may have to be used.

**Position 2** The blade is adjusted to the top end of the rest, bringing the centre of the shaft of the arrow to the top of the button. This raises the angle of the arrow in the bow.

**Position 3** The blade is adjusted to the bottom end of the rest by the same amount as it was raised in position 2, bringing the centre of the shaft of the arrow to the bottom of the button. This lowers the angle of the arrow in the bow.

*Tuning Sequence*
**Step 1** To start tiller-tuning, put the rest to position 1. Shooting at 30m with three bare shafts and three fletched arrows, adjust the nocking point until the bare shafts are exactly level with the fletched group. The best way to do this is to plot the groups to find the average centre of each group. Once you have adjusted the nocking point so that both groups are level, draw a line on the target horizontally across the centre line of this group.

**Step 2** Without adjusting anything else, adjust the rest to position 2. Shoot both the bare shafts and the fletched arrows, aiming at the same point as in step 1. Plot the centre of the groups on the target face and note the position in relation to the centre

*Mechanical tiller check. With the bow at full draw, the reading, in theory, should be the same, but can be easily changed by altering the pressure of the bow hand in the pivot point.*

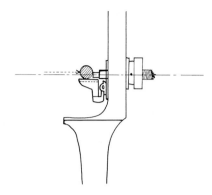

*Position 1. The rest is in the central position; with the arrow in place the shaft should be made to rest against the centre of the button.*

*With the arrow on the rest, cut the amount off the blade that the arrow is above the centre of the button.*

*Position 2. The rest is moved to the top of the track to raise the arrow against the button.*

*Position 3. The rest is lowered by the same amount that it was raised in position 2.*

**Projected plot**

Pos.2.

Pos.1.

Pos.3.

*As the tiller is increased, so the pattern of the three groups changes; 4mm positive gives the most even pattern, indicating balance of the limbs.*

| 0 Tiller | 2mm + | 4mm+ | 6mm+ | 8mm+ | 10mm+ |
| --- | --- | --- | --- | --- | --- |
| (A) | | (B) | | | (C) |

line of the first group. Shoot this a number of times until you have an average position for the bare and fletched groups.

**Step 3** Without adjusting anything else, move the position of the rest to position 3. Shoot for groups again, aiming at the same place as in step 1. Plot the position of these groups and note the position of the groups in relation to the line drawn on the target in step 1.

*Results*
Check the results against the projected plot chart.

If the group is balanced either side of the group shot in step 1 (B),). the tiller is balanced. If the groupings of the three positions are similar to the pattern in (A), the positive tiller should be increased. If the groupings are similar to the pattern in (C), the positive tiller should be decreased. If the group pattern is not the same as in (B), the tiller should be adjusted accordingly.

Once the tiller has been readjusted, *all* of the three steps will have to be carried out fully again. It is best to record the tiller change that you have made, as the change in tiller is directly proportional to the change in the vertical pattern. This means that within three rounds of the test you should be able to get the bow to the correct tiller. To get the best results, care needs to be taken in adjusting the nocking point in step 1.

## Matching Bows

When matching bows to each other initially you can set them by measurement, but to get both bows shooting the same, they need to be tuned dynamically. It is usual to get both bows to shoot the bare shaft to the same position by adjusting them horizontally for power and button tension and position; by, incorporating dynamic tiller tuning you can match the patterns of fletched and bare shafts both horizontally and vertically.

## Tuning the Tab

It is important that the finger tab is not forgotten in tuning. Different types of tab should be tried with different combinations of face materiel material and thickness. The tab needs to be trimmed so that the face protects the fingers but there is no excess to catch the string and give variable results when tuning.

*Material*
Different face materials will suit different archers. I use a combination of a Spigarelli vulcanized face on the front and a cordovan face for the backing. The face needs to stay in place during the shot but some of the backing faces that come with tabs are soft and quite quickly distort, catching the nock as it is released. If you have a leather worker near you, you may be able to obtain a leather scrap to suit your needs. Patent leather can give good results. The charity shops may have leather jackets and boots that can be a good source of material to test. Some of the archery shops have squares of cordovan that can be cut to suit any tab.

*Thickness*
The thickness of the tab face is also a factor. If the face is too thin it will not protect your fingers, which will get sore and distract your shooting. If the face is too thick you will get good protection, but it can lead to inconsistencies in the finger placement on the string as the position of the string in relation to the first joint cannot be felt easily. The face should therefore be thick enough to protect the fingers, but thin enough so that a positive finger placement on the string can be felt. Although you can order a spare face to fit your tab, there can be a variation in thickness depending on what part of the animal it comes from. If possible, it is better to go to the shop and select the material and thickness that you want.

*Trimming the Face*
Once the tab has been shot for a little while, the finger positions will be visible on the rear of the backing face.; a. A little talcum powder on the fingers can be used to highlight their position. Once you can see the finger position, the tab can be trimmed down to remove the excess leather. Cut it down a little at a time; trimming can be carried out more easily if easier is you have an observer to see what the finger placement is like at full draw. The finished tab should fully protect the fingers but needs to have a reasonably close fit around the nock.

If the slot in the tab is too small it will interfere with the nock on release, giving bigger groups. If, on the other hand, the slot is too big there is a good chance of a vertical inconsistency of the fingers on the string, as the larger slot allows the tab and fingers to be placed high or low either side of the nock, again leading to bigger groups.

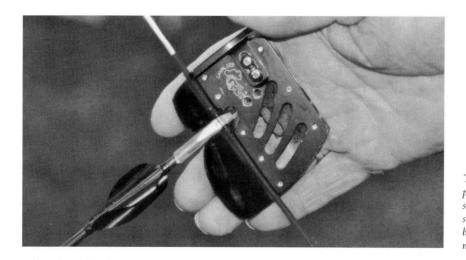

*To ensure that the tab is placed on the string at the same point every time, the slot in the tab should not be much bigger than the nock. (Karen Henderson)*

*Platform Position*

Some tabs have a removable/adjustable platform, which must be adjusted so that it rests against the jawbone but still allows the hand to touch and follow the line of the jaw. If the platform is set too high, the hand losesloosues contact with the side of the face and consistency will suffer.

## Bow Grip

Care needs to be taken when making changes in form to the bow's grip. The vertical centre line of the grip needs to be maintained, because as the bow is drawn back the pressure on the grip needs to be directly behind the bow. If one side of the grip is built up higher than the centre line, as the bow is drawn back the pressure increases on the high spot and the bow is torqued away from the centre line. This can be checked by standing on a chair behind the archer – at full draw the string should still fall through the centre of the limb and long rod. The wider you make the grip, the easier it is to exert pressure on the side of the grip and cause the bow's alignment to move away from centre.

Depending on the grip on the bow and the size of your hand it may well be advantageous to adjust the shape of the grip. With removable grips this is not a problem. If you make a mistake you can always buy another one. If you want to build up a grip, Loctite makes a twin-pack filler that comes in a dual-layered roll. Cut a small piece off and mix the inner and outer part of the roll together. Once mixed, place it on the grip in the appropriate position, then put cling-film over the top and shape to the design you want. When the cling-film is removed, it will give a good finish. Another good filler is Araldite (normal), mixed with talcum powder to give a strong filler that is easy to work.

Some grips are interchangeable with other bows and with a little modification can be made to fit the bow you are shooting. Make sure that the inner part of the grip takes the full weight of the riser as the bow is drawn and the grip is packed so that it cannot twist from side to side. If you do not want to work on your grip yourself, there are great custom grips available from James Loesch (www.bow-grips.com). The company makes grips to suit individual needs and all bow types.

## Summary

Tuning is a balance of shooting well and adjusting the equipment adjusted to give the best results. This balance needs to be reflected in what you do in training. If you are always adjusting the bow, you will not be doing the shooting practice you require, so your shooting style will not progress. Tune the bow, then concentrate on improving your shooting over a couple of months, after which you can tune the bow again, this time better, because your shooting will be more consistent.

Changing technique can take time to improve the groups and adjusting the bow's settings will either make the groups better or worse. Tuning is about proving that the bow's adjustment is in the best position for how you are shooting today. In two months' time it may require some small adjustments.

Chapter 14

# Top Tips

This chapter is a collection of tips and suggestions which are not concerned directly with shooting and equipment but which may help with some aspects of your archery.

- the Beiter Center
- flying
- arrow speed meter
- laser alignment tool
- 'Target Plot'
- release – ladies v gents
- changing your rest.

## The Beiter Center (The Werner & Iris Center)

Although most archers in the world refer to this as the Beiter Center, the 'Werner & Iris Center' is its correct name. In my opinion, this is the premier centre for technical excellence and understanding

archery. I have been fortunate enough to visit the centre a number of times and it has always helped my shooting, not only by the technical help given but to witness the fascinating drive of Mr Beiter, who strives for perfection in all aspects of his work.

Mr Beiter's business is, among others, in medical plastics. Someone who has had a hip replacement is very likely to have had a Beiter 'centralizer' fitted. Part of the plastics in a hearing aid are likely to have been designed and produced by Mr Beiter. It is not only the design aspect that is vital to a Beiter product, but also the quality and suitability of a material for a particular design. In archery, the plastic that the nock is made from is designed to ensure that the nock fit is the same on every shot, no matter how many times it is shot. This gives the archer the consistency that is required to keep shooting tight groups. Even if one nock needs to be replaced through arrow damage, the new nock will perform the same as the others that have been shot 1,000 times. The plastic which the plunger is designed

*The shooting range at the Werner & Iris Center from the 70m line; the televisions overhead mean that coaches and observers can see the fall of the shot and the archer clearly.*

169

from ensures that it does not wear. In the years that I have been shooting I have not worn the tip on my Beiter button. This means that once I have tuned my bow and set the button, no matter how many arrows I shoot the button's position always stays the same. Most other buttons are prone to the tip wearing, which means that as it wears the bow's tuning changes and the position of the plunger has to be constantly monitored.

Fortunately for archers, Mr Beiter's hobby is archery. He has built a 90m indoor range, with a conference area and short range on the upper floor. The lower floor contains the main range, with the 70m metre shooting line being used most often. Expert help is always on hand at the centre.

The facilities can be hired by teams, clubs or individuals by arrangement with the centre. With the extensive range of facilities, a huge amount of improvement in one's equipment set-up and tuning can be completed in a very short time, which makes this very popular with top archers around the world.

The shooting range is set up with a network of televisions and video cameras.

These are set on the targets with the live feed being sent back to the shooting line so that archers and coaches can see the result of each shot. There are additional cameras set up around the shooting line so that an archer can be seen from three angles at once, giving the coach an all-round view. The range is furnished with bicycles and E-Scooters so that arrows can be collected quickly, enabling more

shooting to be carried out.

There is, of course, a full selection of Beiter equipment to work with to see if there is a combination that will suit your shooting style better than your own current set-up. It may just prove that your own set-up is the best for you anyway.

There is an electronic draw-weight measuring machine, for once your draw length has been set. It will then be reset to your bracing height. Once the machine is started, it will draw your bow to your draw length and let it down again, plotting a draw-force curve of both the draw and the let-down, then the results are printed off. These results can be matched against the huge archive of information that has been collated, to ensure that your limbs are working in the correct manner.

If you want your arrows spined and matched for ovality, there is a special computerized spining machine that can spine a set of arrows and check for ovality, then print off the results within five minutes. If you want your arrows spined, you need to ensure that they are numbered prior to being tested. The test will give you the match of the arrows and a renumber sequence to match them from weak to stiff. It will also give you the best matched arrows out of the set to shoot in competitions.

In my opinion, the best part of the facilities is the high-speed cameras, including a digital colour one that is fed straight into the computer system. This makes it possible to study the way the arrow actually leaves the bow and will instantly show if

*Shooting on the Beiter range. The paper above the left two targets enables observers to see the silhouette of the arrow's flight. (Barry Eley)*

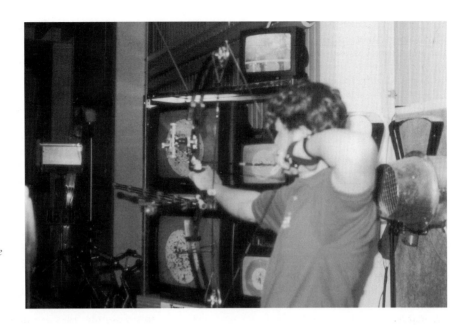

*Chris White on the range with televisions showing the targets and a wind machine on the wall. (Barry Eley)*

the arrow is touching or is very close to the bow as it is shot. The bow and long rod can be filmed to show how much and what movement there is in a different combination of rods. To get the bow, archer and camera in the correct position can take a lot of work, both on behalf of the archer and Mr Beiter. To get the correct picture involves coming up to full draw and then holding the position while the lights and camera position are checked. During

one of my visits there, five hours of reversals produced about fifteen minutes of slow-motion footage. Consequently, if you are thinking of visiting the centre make sure you are fit enough to carry out a lot of reversals, otherwise you will not be able to make the best use of the facilities.

Should you visit the centre, you will have the opportunity to shoot three dozen arrows at 70m for a score. The top twenty scores for both ladies

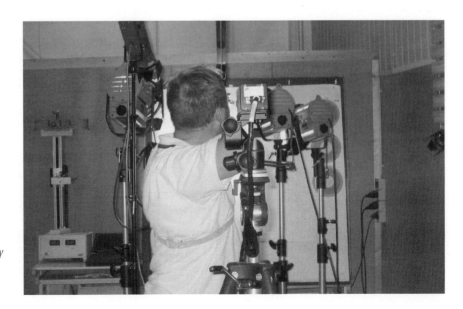

*The author surrounded by spotlights to give enough light for the high-speed video. (Barry Eley)*

and gents are recorded on a board for all to see. If your score is high enough, you will have your name placed on the board at the score you shot. There are many other pieces of equipment that help archers get the best out of their equipment and shooting. Every time I visit, there is something new to help the archer to improve.

# Flying

At some point, you may need to fly with your archery equipment, which can be a little daunting at first. I usually separate flying into two categories: scheduled flights and budget flights.

*Scheduled Flights*
With all flights, first look at the allowed baggage allowance. At the time of writing, the heaviest single item is set at 32kg (70.5lb). The airline will usually stipulate how many items of baggage they will allow. Most allow for two pieces. Flights to the USA usually allow for two pieces with an individual limit of 32kg each, plus hand baggage. When travelling with the British team, I am expected to take two bows, so I have a heavy box (23kg [50.72lb]) when full, but flying to the USA is no problem. Other flights around the world differ, with some allowing only 30kg (66.2lb) or less for two pieces of luggage. Including my box, this only allows 7kg (15.4lb) for my other clothes including shooting cloths.

Work out how many days you will be away for and take only what you need. Underwear can be washed every night as you shower and hung up to dry, as can T-shirts. So taking a length of cord or a travel washing line can help to keep the weight down. The weight of hand luggage can vary, but it will carry an extra set of clothes. I find that a small rucksack is great for getting through airports as it leaves your hands free to deal with tickets and getting through the scanners.

*Budget Airlines*
Budget airlines can be a little trickier. For example, Ryanair, at the time of writing, only allows for 15kg (33lb) in the hold, although if you telephone the airline might get you an extra allowance for sporting goods.

For limited weight allowance I transfer my equipment to my lighter box (currently a Win & Win box). Make sure that you transfer all the equipment needed for shooting. The best way of

doing this is to transfer it all to the light box a few days before you go and do a couple of training sessions with the repacked box. This will make sure that you have all you need. In the Win & Win box I can get both bows and the full set-up for them both with two sets of arrows. I do not use foam in the box, but instead cushion my equipment with shooting clothing. When I have the box packed, I can get it down to 15kg. This leaves the rest of the clothing, plus the 'scope and tripod, to go into hand luggage. Although you are only allowed one piece of hand luggage on Ryanair it can weigh up to 10kg (22lb), but there is a size limit for it. You can also have a bumbag, which can carry all your money, passport, mobile phone and other bits and pieces. You can also carry separately a computer in its bag, or a camera case, and put extras in that. On top of all that, you can also have a coat or jacket, so if you take a jacket with an unzippable liner, this gives you two coats in one and you can put other items in the pockets, like lightweight waterproof trousers and a hat. So even on the budget airlines you can take all that you need to compete.

Remember to check with the airline regarding the different baggage allowances and when packing make sure to put any sharp or metallic objects in the bags that will go in the hold. For women with long hair, make sure that your hairslide is not sharp and pointy, as some airlines will ask you to remove it and leave it with them.

When downsizing your archery box for lightweight travel make sure that all your shooting equipment fits in the one box, as having long rods or arrow tubes separate from the rest of your equipment can lead to them being left behind.

Clothing for travel is better if it is loosely fitting and comfortable. On long flights, I usually take my shoes off and walk around in my socks, so I wear a pair that suitable for that. When selecting clothing for travel make sure that it has little or no metal content and pack your belt and studded boots in the hold baggage to avoid setting off the metal detectors at airports. Keep your passport and ticket on you at all times.

Some airports may be quite lax about weight limits on the way out, but, generally, the returning airports are keener to charge you excess baggage. Make sure that you clearly mark all your baggage with your name and the address to which you are going. If your baggage does not arrive on the same plane as you, the airline will usually deliver it to your hotel or house if you have an address on it.

# Arrow Speed Meter

Although arrow speed meters are available to use at most of the archery retailers, it is a good idea to have one within the club's equipment. There are two types available, both for around £65, at the time of writing. One fits onto the front of the bow, which means that you are less likely to shoot it as it is fixed below the line of arrow flight. The other type is placed on a tripod that you shoot through. Care needs to be taken with the shoot-through type, as there is a tendency to shoot the meter itself if the sight is set in the wrong place, so always ensure that you have someone to help you line up with the open space above it.

The meters are more than a tool to find out how fast your arrow goes. Having a well-tuned arrow is better than having a poorly tuned fast arrow. The meter is useful when changing equipment, as it shows how the different combinations affect the speed of the arrow. Different tab faces may also affect the speed of the arrow. As you change the thickness of the string by changing the strand sizes, you can see how this affects the dynamics of the bow.

With new limbs, you can test whether they are shooting the arrow at the same speed or greater than the old limbs. It is quite easy to get caught out by speed changes due to advances in limb technology. Just because your last set of 40lb limbs shot the ACE 620 well does not necessarily mean that the new limbs marked at the same weight will shoot the arrow at the same speed. Testing with an arrow speed meter will enable you to find a match for your arrows quicker.

Arrow speed meters can also be used to check the consistency of the shot. If the speed shown on the meter is the same with every shot, it indicates that the shot is more consistent. Variances in arrow speed indicate inconsistencies with the release. At the longer distances this will manifest itself as changes in the height of the group. When using a speed meter, the archer can be made aware of which arrows were shot well, by looking at the consistency of the speed.

The speed meter that bolts onto the front of the bow is ideal for novices and juniors, as it fits onto the long rod and is out of the way of the shot wherever the bow is pointed. Although light, it does affect the balance of the bow slightly, so if you are looking to test without making any changes to the bow's weight the shoot-through version will be better.

# Laser Alignment Tool

The laser alignment tool bolts onto the bow where the sight block is normally fitted and is adjusted to the centre of the riser on a thread. The bow's true

*An arrow speed meter allows the speed of the arrow to be checked for consistency.*

*The tool is bolted to the bow in place of the sight block.*

173

centre and limb alignment still need to be set up and checked to ensure that the riser is straight. This tool makes setting the initial position of the arrow in the bow a lot quicker and cuts out the human error in the game of 'Where do we think the arrow lies?' It also enables inexperienced archers to see the visible alignment of the bow with less ambiguity. For bigger clubs, when there are archers needing the bows set up on a regular basis, it allows the club coaches to set up the bows quicker and more reliably.

## 'Target Plot'

This is an excellent program that works in conjunction with a PDA and your computer. The program has been developed in Australia by Mariane Rieckmann (info@targetplot.com.au) and is being improved all the time. 'Target Plot', as the name suggests, enables you to plot the position of all your arrows and the order in which you shot them. It enables you to keep a diary of what the conditions were like, the equipment you were using, the distances you were shooting in metric and imperial and how you were feeling. It will display the target face you are shooting at and the score zones that you want. Once back home after the session, you can download the results onto your computer.

Used in its most basic way, 'Target Plot' will record the results of the arrows that you shoot, but you can do far more with it than that. There is a facility on the display to show the centre of the group. This enables you to adjust your sight minutely between ends to ensure that the centre of the groups falls in the centre of the target, thus giving you a higher score. When tuning the bow, if you plot the fletched arrows and the bare shaft arrows alternately, as though shooting three arrow ends – three fletched then three bare shafts – and keeping to that order as you shoot them, the main display of results will show the centre of both groups. This will show you the average centre position of both the fletched and bare-shafted groups, enabling you to adjust the bow accurately so that you get the exact position of both groups.

Once the results have been downloaded onto your computer, it is then possible to re-centre each group to give you the highest score for the group size. This enables you to see the highest possible score if the group was shot centred on the target. This tool is very useful when testing equipment, for example, nocks. Set up the target and shoot for groups with one type of nock, plotting the results but keeping the sight in the same position. Change nocks and shoot again. Traditionally, the type of nock which shot the highest score would be chosen. However, using 'Target Plot', when the groups are adjusted to centre by the computer it will show by score which type of nock shot the tightest

*'Target Plot' enables you to plot the groups as you shoot.*

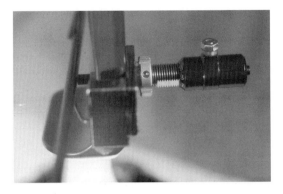

*When changing from the Yamaha rest to the Spigarelli, the button's barrel position should remain the same.*

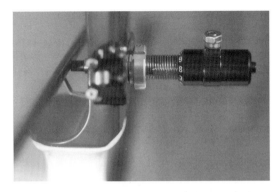

*This ensures that the plunger distance with either rest is the same, maintaining the tune of the bow.*

*With the pitch of the tread being approximately 1mm, the distance of the plunger out from the bow has only to be measured to the nearest millimetre, in this case 9mm.*

*With 9mm showing against the ruler, the button barrel position determines the final adjustment.*

groups. This tool can be used when testing any aspect of any piece of equipment, from shoes to long rods.

Another excellent facility on the computer is 'project to distance'. Two aspects of this can be of immense help. Firstly, if you have limited distances that you can shoot, particularly in the winter, you can shoot at a shorter distance and the computer will project that short distance group to the longer distance, to give you an idea of how your shooting is progressing. Secondly, it can be used to predict the scores and show group sizes through the distances. You can then compare them with actual groups and scores. If you shoot a score of 330 at 30m, it will predict the score at all the other distances that you shoot. It will also predict the shorter distances from a score plotted at longer distances. If the actual results are not as the predicted

results, you can then check the shooting style and equipment to try to find out what is causing these discrepancies. This is just an overview of some of the potential of 'Target Plot' to enhance your shooting.

## Release – Ladies v Gents

Part of the selection of bow weight is relevant to the release of the fingers from the string. The higher the bow weight, the faster the string is pulled from the fingers as the archer starts to relax his fingers on the string. Some archers will attempt to shoot a high poundage to get a cleaner release. If the weight of the bow is above the level that an archer can control, the fingers will hold the string too tightly and, in conjunction with the overloaded muscles, he will not be able to shoot consistently. This may also lead to injury.

The lighter the weight of the bow, the longer the string remains in the area of the fingers and the longer the arrow remains in the bow, therefore ladies and juniors shooting lighter weight bows need to have a better, more consistent release to compensate for the lower poundage. This is one of the reasons why it is important, if you want to compete, to select the highest bow weight that you can control. You must shoot the bow, not the other way around. The answer to a better release is to practise the release, not to increase the weight of the bow. It is interesting to note that, at quite a few of the international events, the women tend to get the higher scores during the head-to-heads with the men and on the whole their technique is better.

## Changing Your Rest

Many archers are concerned that if they change from a simple stick-on type of rest to a magnetic rest that fits under the button, the button may change position, altering the tuning. Changing the rest without altering the tuning is very easy. The position of the button's plunger is determined by the position of the button barrel.

If the button's barrel position is the same at the start and the finish of the procedure, the tuning will remain the same. Initially, measure how far the plunger sticks out from the riser and note the position of the barrel in the bow.

If need be, the button barrel can be marked to help realign the barrel as the new rest is fitted. The Beiter button has a 'flat' on the barrel and the nut on the pressure adjuster, both of which can be used for an alignment check. Fit the new rest so that the button is a similar distance out from the riser, but, more importantly, the button barrel is in the same position as when the original rest was fitted. This will ensure that the button position is the same at the end of the procedure as it was at the beginning, keeping your tuning consistent.

# Appendix

# Tuning References

## The Walk-Back Test

This tuning method involves shooting fletched arrows at a target at increasingly longer distances. You will therefore only be able to do this when you have the range to yourself. To carry out a walk-back test, pin a small square of paper 50mm (2in) square towards the top of the target. At a distance of 6m (19.7ft), making sure that the sight is adjusted so that the arrow will hit the paper, shoot one arrow at the paper and move back 1m (3.3ft). Without moving the sight, shoot at the paper again. Move back another metre and so on, until you run out of arrows or they get close to the bottom of the target. As you move away from the target the arrows will form a line down the target – the shape of the pattern of the arrows will determine the adjustments to the bow.

Personally, I have found this method of tuning to be inconsistent. Generally, I get a straight line straight down the target whatever the adjustment of the button position and pressure. I do use part of this method of tuning at distances between 30m and 70m, by shooting fletched arrows at both distances and only moving the sight up and down and making small adjustments to the button pressure (*see* Chapter 13). However, some archers find this method of tuning to be satisfactory.

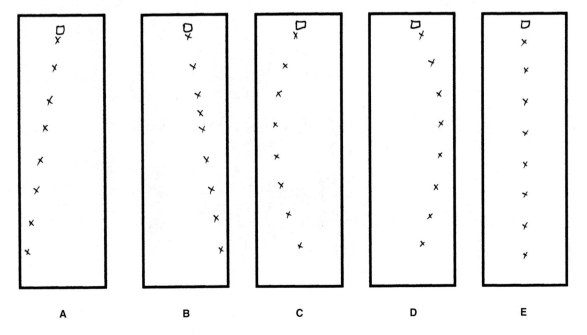

(A) Button too far out. (B) Button too far in. (C) Plunger pressure too high. (D) Plunger pressure too low. (E) Button and plunger adjusted correctly.

## Paper Tuning

Paper tuning is mainly used for compounds, but some aspects of it can be used with the recurve. To carry out paper tuning you will need to make a frame or a stand that will hold the paper firmly, as you will need to shoot through it.

You can only get good results from paper tuning if you use paper that has no grain to it; newspaper is no good as it has a grain and so will tear in one direction better than the other. Greaseproof paper or thin lining wallpaper are quite good for this purpose. The zigzag paper used with some printers is excellent as it is also perforated, so making it easy to move up to get a new piece in front of the archer.

Once you have the stand and paper set up, it needs to be aligned with the boss so that when you shoot through the paper the arrow will hit the boss. The idea of paper tuning is to shoot your arrows through the paper and then inspect the holes to see how the arrow tore a hole as it passed through.

As you have already seen from some of the images of the arrow leaving a recurve bow, the arrow moves horizontally as it leaves the bow. This can give false readings in the horizontal plain. I use paper tuning if the weather is bad and I am not able to bare-shaft tune, but I only use it for setting the nocking point. Therefore, I will only adjust the bow to get a flat, horizontal tear in the paper.

For compounds you would carry out the adjustments so that you get a bullet hole (the point and the fletch through the same point), but this must be carried out at varying distances to ensure that the trajectory is consistent and the bullet hole is the same. This shows you the behaviour of how the arrow is flying as it leaves the bow. It can be shot at whatever distance you want, but up to 30m will probably be sufficient.

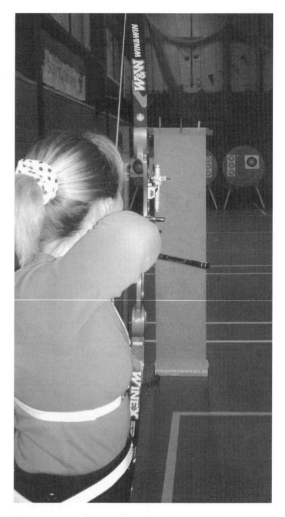

*Using greaseproof paper allows the archer to take the results away with him. Recurve archers use it to help adjust the nocking point height.*

| A | B | C | D |

*(A) Nocking point too high. (B) Point of the arrow too far left. (C) Combination of (A) and (B). (D) Arrows passing directly through the paper – adjustments are correct.*

# References and Suggested Reading

## Books/Publications

Dr Harry Adler, *NLP* (Biddles Ltd)

Ray Axford, *Archery Anatomy* (Souvenir Press, 1995)

Lanny Bassham, *With Winning in Mind* (XPress Publications, 1988)

Anita Bean, *Sports Nutrition* (A & C Black, 1995)

Douglas Brooks, *Your Personal Trainer* (Human Kinetics, 1999)

Tony Buzan, *Make the Most of Your Mind* (Colt Books Ltd, 1988)

Rita Carter, *Mapping the Mind* (Weidenfeld & Nicolson, 1998)

Easton Archery, arrow tuning and maintenance guide (www.easton.com)

W. Timothy Gallwey, *The Inner Game of Golf* (Pan Books, 1981)

Richard L. Gregory. *The Oxford Companion to the Mind* (Oxford University Press, 1987)

Lew Hardy, Graham Jones and Daniel Gould, *Understanding Psychological Preparation for Sport* (John Wiley & Sons, 1996)

John Kremer and Deirdre Scully, *Psychology in Sport* (Taylor & Francis, 1994)

Rick McKinney, *The Simple Art of Winning* (Leo Planning Inc, 1996)

The National Sports Medicine Institute (UK), *Cook and Train Without the Strain* (NSMI, 1996)

Terry Orlic, *In Pursuit of Excellence* (Leisure Press, 1990)

Terry Orlic, *Embracing Your Potential* (Human Kinetics, 1998)

Thomas Whitney & Vishnu Karmaker, *Advanced Archer* (Centre Vision, 1992)

## Videos

Jay Barrs, *The Mental Game* (1994)

Jay Barrs, *Tuning and Execution* (1994)

*1992: Olympic Archery*

*2000: Olympic Archery*

# Glossary

**Arrow** The projectile shot by the bow. It can be made of aluminium, carbon or a combination of both.

**Arrow shaft** The tube of the arrow, not including the point, nock or fletchings.

**Back of the bow** The part of the bow that faces the target.

**Backstop netting** Placed behind the targets, usually in indoor ranges, so that any arrows passing the target are stopped by the net and not the wall.

**Beeswax** Traditional wax for putting on the string. Some newer string materials require a synthetic wax, but the manufacturer should indicate this.

**Beiter** A specialist manufacturer of high-quality archery ancillaries.

**Beiter Center** Properly, the Werner and Iris Center. A 90m shooting hall in Dauchingham, Germany. In the author's opinion, the best technical facility in the world for archery. It can be booked for individuals and teams.

**Blunts** Fitted to the front of the arrow to give a flat surface to the front of the shaft. Traditionally used in hunting of small game, so that the skin was not pierced. They are now used more for training.

**Boss** The block of material pinned to the target face that is used to stop the arrows. Traditionally made from compressed straw rolled into a disk. There are now foam bosses of various construction available.

**Bow stand** The bow is placed on this to keep it off the ground so that it is not damaged; it can be fitted with a spike outdoors to help it stay upright in the wind.

**Bow press** This is used in conjunction with compound bows, which are either portable or fixed and are used to change and adjust the cables/strings on the compound bow. Utmost care must be taken when using this equipment, especially with the portable type, due to the high pressure of the set-up.

*Backstop netting. The net is strung behind the targets to protect the wall and help save the arrows from damage. (Barry Eley)*

*Beiter Center. The Beiter Center shooting and technical range.*

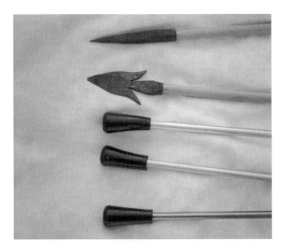

*Blunts. Three blunt arrow heads with a bodkin and hunting point above.*

**Bow scale** This device is fitted to the string and is used to pull the bow to the archer's draw length. It measures actual draw force at full draw.

**Bracing height** This is the distance between the bow and the string, measured from the string to the button.

**Bracing height gauge** A 'T' shaped ruler that clips to the string and will indicate the bracing height and the nocking point placement on the string.

**Bracer/Armguard** Placed on the forearm which is holding the bow, to protect the arm from the string when released.

*Bow stand. The stand keeps the bow off the ground. (Andrew Callaway)*

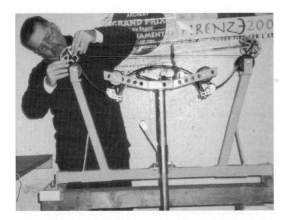

*Bow press. A club-owned press to enable the compound archers in the club to be able to adjust their bows safely and easily enabling them to get maximum performance from their bows.*

*Bracer/Armguard. The arm is protected from the string as the arrow is shot.*

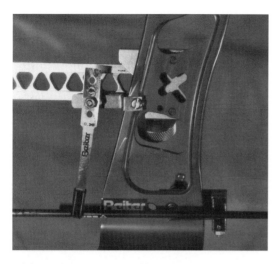

*Clicker. A clicker extension enables slightly longer arrows to be used and still keep the clicker blade upright.*

*Clout. There needs to be plenty of space for clout shooting. (James Cutts)*

**Cam/wheel** The pulley on the outer end of a compound bow, which the string fits around. There are many different types, with different profiles available.

**Chest guard** Fitted to the bow arm side of the chest, to keep clothing and body out of the way of the string at full draw.

**Clicker** Used only on recurve bows, this is a spring steel blade placed over the arrow. As the bow is 'drawn' back the arrow slides under the clicker. When the point of the arrow passes the blade it is released and 'clicks' against the bow. This ensures that the arrow is drawn back to exactly the same length every time, thus imparting the same power into the arrow every time.

**Clicker extension** A device which is frequently used by Juniors, as the arrows tend to be left long to allow for growth. An extension is fitted to the back of the bow so that a clicker can be used.

**Clout** A competition shot at a flag, stuck into the ground up to 180m depending on bow type, gender and age. The round is shot in six ends of six arrows. A pre-prepared measuring tape is placed on the pole of the flag, and pulled around the flag, the arrows being picked up and scored depending on which zone they land in, that is 5, 4, 3, 2 or 1. A 'Clout' occurs when the arrow lands in the 5 score zone. This can be shot as an Imperial or metric round.

**Compound bow** This is a multi-string, pulley-bow. It has a pulley (cam) at the end of each limb giving a mechanical advantage, allowing the archer to shoot a bow that for a given poundage, holds a proportion of its full weight at full draw (approx 25%) depending on the manufacturers specifications).

**Compound – Limited and Unlimited** These are the two classes of compound. Limited compounds are shot with similar rules to those for recurve bows – finger release and one sighting aid without a lens. Unlimited compounds are allowed to use optical sights, a rear peep sight and a mechanical release.

**Crest** This is the marking on an arrow which identifies it to its owner. Today arrows are usually marked with initials and numbers. Historically, different colour rings on the shaft near the fletchings identified the owner of the arrow during a count of dead bodies on the battlefield.

**D-loop** Fitted to compound bows only. It can be fitted to the string around the nock. The release aid is then attached to it, so that as the bow is drawn back, the pressure is applied directly behind the arrow.

*Crest. Arrows need to be marked with a form of identification to enable you to identify your arrows and the difference between them. Decals can be bought from the retailers.*

*Elbow sling. A Formaster or elbow sling that allows you to exercise and train the correct muscles to shoot. (Karen Henderson)*

**Damper/Doinker** Can be fitted to the end of the long rod, and/or twins to help absorb vibration. Consideration needs to be taken when using these as they can also damp out good vibrations.

**Draw** The term used to pull the bowstring back to the face, with the arm holding the bow straight out.

**Easton** Manufacturer of archery products. Most notable are their world record-beating arrows, as well as long-rods and twins.

**Elbow sling** A training aid consisting of a double strap sling that is fitted onto the drawing arm elbow, then attached with either a cord or elastic to the nocking point area of the bow string. This device ensures that the archer draws the bow using the correct muscles.

**End** This is the collective noun used to indicate the number of arrows shot at one visit to the shooting line. At indoor events three arrows make up one end and outdoors six arrows make up one end.

**Extension (Stabiliser)** This is used between the bow and the V-bar to move the stabiliser weight forward on the bow.

**Fast** Derivative of 'Hold fast' now used to indicate that no arrows are to be shot, as there is a danger on the field, and that to continue might cause danger to others.

**Field shooting** A competition that takes place over a course of targets at varying distances and angles. Is meant to replicate hunting. Courses can vary from simple to extreme.

*Field shooting. Kirstin Lewis (right, South Africa) shooting on the Isle of Skye.*

**Finger sling** A loop of cord, usually fitted around the index finger and thumb of the bow hand. It allows a relaxed hand on the shot, but keeps the bow in the hand.

**Fletchings** The vanes on the rear of the arrow shaft which help to stabilise and spin the arrow in-flight. Traditionally made from feathers, these are now made from synthetic materials.

**Fletching glue** Specific glue used to hold the fletchings to the arrow shaft. With the advent of modern materials, specific glues may well be required for each different fletch type.

**Fletching jig** A simple mechanical device used to place the fletchings equidistant and at the appropriate angle on the arrow shaft.

**Fletching Tape** Strips of double-sided sticky tape used to hold spin wing type fletchings to the arrow shaft. These are usually supplied with the fletches.

**Flight** A competition to shoot an arrow the furthest distance possible. True flight competitions feature specially constructed bows and arrows. In Britain, the bows shot are the same as those shot in target competitions, and are classed by bow weight. The bows should not have been modified from the normal target set-up.

**Full-Draw** When the bow arm is fully extended and the string is back to the face.

**Grip** Usually detachable and the point at which the bow hand contacts with the bow.

**Hunting bow** A bow that is designed for hunting and is usually shorter and more powerful than a target bow. This is because when hunting you

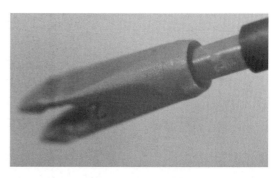

*In-out nock. The nock is designed to fit inside the shaft and around the outer edge.*

would expect to shoot only one shot. These bows can be used for field shooting but will be of a more comparable poundage to a target bow.

**In-out nock** A Beiter nock that fits both inside and outside the shaft, affording greater protection.

**Kisser** Usually made of plastic and tied onto the string above the nocking point, so that when the bow is drawn back the 'kisser' touches between the lips, giving a reference point.

**Kudo** Japanese archery. 'Ku' meaning – bow. 'Do' meaning 'the way of'. Therefore, Kudo means 'The way of the bow.'

**Limb** The part of the bow which flexes when you draw the string back. The upper limb being the top and the lower limb the bottom. These are usually laminated, with the type of material used in

*Fletching jig. Arrow set in fletching jig; the Beiter nock has a nock adaptor to keep the arrow central in the jig.*

*Peep sight. The peep sight is just in front of the sighting eye; Morgan Lundin (Sweden).*

the laminate determining the speed of the bow for a given poundage, and the price you pay for it.

**Limb Gauge** A Beiter product that is fitted to the limbs adjacent to the riser. It is used to help align the limbs and arrow to the bow.

**Limb saver** A rubber mushroom shaped device that can be fitted to the limbs to help damp out vibration when the bow is shot.

**Longbow** The bow that was used to great effect against the French at Agincourt, traditionally made from yew, although it was made from many types of wood. Bickerstaff still make fine examples of these bows.

**Long rod** The long main stabiliser fitted to the front of the bow for balance, and to help prevent 'yaw' when the bow is shot.

**Nock** The slot addition to the end of the arrow that attaches the arrow to the string. Nocks are usually made of plastic, and can be either glued or slotted onto the arrow depending on their type and style of manufacture.

**Nocking point** The particular point on the string where the arrow attaches. Nocking points can be made of plastic (Beiter nocking point) and served onto the string, or can be made of cotton or waxed dental floss.

**One piece bow** A bow that is made in one piece, riser and limbs. This is as opposed to a take-down bow, which comes in three pieces.

**Over nock** A nock that fits over the outside of the arrow shaft.

**Peak-weight** A compound bow uses a pulley-system, which means that at full draw only a percentage of the full bow weight is held. Peak weight is the highest poundage that is felt on the string as it is drawn.

**Peep sight** This is a small aperture fitted to the string of a compound bow, and is used as a rear sight.

**Pile/point** It is fitted to the front end of the arrow which adds weight to the front of the arrow to bring the centre of gravity forward, thus making the arrow fly correctly. It can be made of one piece, or made up of parts. The Insert fits into the shaft, and the point screws into the insert.

**Pin nock** Made by Easton, this is a twin-ended pin that fits into the back of the arrow, one part fitted down the back of the shaft, and a special nock fitted onto the other end of the pin.

**Popinjay** A competition that involves shooting at targets at the top of a tall pole. Special precautions need to be taken, as 'what goes up must

*Popinjay. (A) The targets are fixed at the top of a mast. (Muriel Kirkwood)*

*Popinjay. (B) The archer shoots to hit the target. (Muriel Kirkwood)*

come down!' Due to the dangers involved, not many popinjays are shot in Britain. However, it is a popular shoot in Belgium, where they have a good number of suitable venues.

**Poundage** When the poundage of the bow is referred to, it can mean one of two things:
(1) The limbs are marked in pounds, and will indicate the length of the bow for the marked poundage.
(2) Usually measured to the pivot point. The length of the riser changes the poundage, the shorter the riser the shorter the bow the higher the poundage. My limbs are marked as 44lb's @28".
On the fingers means that it is the poundage held 'At full draw.' This will usually be different from the marked poundage, as the length of the draw will dictate the poundage. Care should therefore be taken when buying limbs.

**Puller** Usually a rubber sheet or grip that fits into the palm of the hand, used when pulling arrows out of the target. It enables you to achieve a better grip on the arrow, which means that you use less effort to pull the arrow, leaving you more strength for shooting. It also protects the hand from carbon splinters that can occasionally come from the arrow shaft.

**Quiver** This is used to hold the arrows.

**Recurve bow** Also called 'Olympic style'. This has a single string which attaches to the end of the limbs. The 'recurve' refers to the type of limb. The limb is made in such a way that when it is stringless it curves away from the archer, so that when it is strung it gives more power than when the limb is of flat construction. The further you pull back the string, the higher the poundage.

**Release-Aid** This device can only be used in conjunction with a 'Compound Bow'. It is a mechanical trigger designed to release the string.

**Riser** The main part of the bow to which the limbs, sight, stabilisers, etc., are all attached.

**Round** The term which refers to a competition. These will either be Imperial or metric, measured in yards or metres. International competitions will be measured in metres, British rounds will be measured in yards.

**Samick** A Korean archery manufacturer, making a good range of bows and equipment.

**Scope** The term can be used for the optic front sight used on a compound, or a telescope used to spot the arrows when shooting at longer distances.

**Serving** A thread material that is wound around the string, usually at the ends and centre, to protect the string from wear.

*Release-Aid. The release aid is held in the right hand that triggers the release of the string. (Andrew Callaway)*

**Serving tool** A hand-held tool used to put the serving material onto the string at the correct and even tension.

**Sling – Wrist/Bow** Fitted to the bow-hand, so allowing it to be relaxed during the shot, but keeping the bow attached to the hand.

**Stabilisers** Generic term for the rods and weights fitted to the bow for balance, and to steady the bow during the shot.

**Stance** This term refers to how an archer stands on the line and also incorporates the position in which the feet are placed over the shooting line, and the position and posture of the whole body.

*Serving tool. This enables you to place the serving material onto the string at a regulated, even tension. (Beiter)*

**Sight** The device fitted to the bow to enable the archer to aim the bow at the target. Recurve archers can only use a non-optical sight fitted to the bow. Compound bows (unlimited) can have a rear sight (peep sight) and are allowed to use an optical lens.

**Sight block** The part of the sight that is directly screwed onto the bow. It is left in place when the bow is packed away.

**Sight pin** The threaded bar and aperture that the archer looks through in order to aim the bow. There are many different shapes and sizes, the main rule being that the length of the sight cannot be longer than the diameter of the aperture.

**Shooting line** This is the line that the archer shoots from. All archers must stand with one foot either side of this line, ensuring that no-one is in front of any other archer.

**Stand** This is what the boss is placed on. Outdoors the boss and stand must always be tied down, as otherwise the boss can be blown over by the wind, which could break all the arrows in the target.

**String** The sting is usually made up of a single length of material, which is looped around two pins of a string making jig set at an appropriate length. Strings are measured by their length and the number of strands which make up the string. Materials vary with modern bows using materials which are resistant to stretch. If you have an older one-piece bow, or a starter bow, you may have to use 'DACRON', as this material has

*TFC. The Torque Flight Compensator fits between the V-bar and the twins. (Andrew Callaway)*

stretch built into it. When a bow is shot with this type of string there is 'give' in the string so that the bow does not break. Always check with the manufacturer to ensure that you are using the correct material.

**String jig** This device can be used to make your own strings. It is adjustable so that you can make strings of different lengths. These can be either shop bought or home made.

**Stringer** Used to bend the limbs safely to allow you to string the bow. If this is not used, either the archer can be injured if the bow slips or the bow itself can be damaged, as the bow has to be 'strung' without twisting the limbs and riser.

**Tab** This is held in the shooting hand and protects the fingers from the string on release.

**Tab-face** Refers to the material used in the tab that comes directly in contact with the string. It is generally made up of a number of layers of thin leather, but other man-made materials can be used.

**Tab spacer** Fits between the index and middle finger of the drawing hand, holding the tab in position.

**Take-down bow** Refers to a bow where the limbs are removed from the riser when it is packed away, as opposed to a one-piece.

**Target pins** Holds the target face to the boss. They are usually made from plastic so that if they are hit, the arrow will not be damaged.

**TFC** Torque Flight Compensator. It can be used in the stabiliser set up to help damp out vibrations and change the dynamic of the bow.

**Tiller** This is the measured distance from the string to the point where the limbs meet the riser; therefore, there is both a top tiller measurement and a bottom tiller measurement. If the measurements are the same, the bow is set to 'zero tiller'. Most bows are set with the top measurement larger than the bottom measurement, a setting known as a 'positive tiller'.

**Twins** The matched pair of short stabilising rods fitted between the long rod and the riser on the V-bar. They help prevent torque when the bow is shot.

**V-Bar** This device holds the 'twin stabilisers' in place. There are many different makes, each with their own geometry, which is generally flat or angled. A flat V-bar holds the twins in the same plane as the long-rod, while adjustable ones allow you to change the twins' angles.

**Win & Win** A major South Korean manufacturer of quality archery products.

# Useful Addresses

**Quicks the Archery Specialists**
18–22 Stakes Hill Road
Waterlooville
Hampshire
PO7 7JF

Tel: 023 9225 4114
Fax: 023 9225 1519

**BowSports Archery Centre**
Calibre Park
Laches Close
Four Ashes
Wolverhampton
WV10 7DZ

Tel: 0870 241 21 21
Fax: 01902 791821

**Wales Archery Specialists**
Crick Manor
Crick
Newport
Gwent
NP26 5XU

Tel: 01291 420321

**Centre Shot Archery Supplies**
50 Fruitlands
Malvern Wells
Worcestershire
WR14 4XA

Tel: 01684 579109

**Perris Archery**
Fennes Estate
Fennes Road
Bocking
Braintree
Essex
CM7 5PL

Tel: 01376 331017
Fax: 01376 331018

**Arrowhead UK**
8 Mount Pleasant
Moretonhampstead
Devon
TQ13 8NY

Tel: 01647 441212

**KG Archery**
King Stand Farm Archery Centre
Mansfield Road
Rufford
Newark
Notts
NG22 9DU

Tel: 01623 824877

**Merlin Archery Centre**
Bull In The Hollow Farm
Leicester Road
Loughborough
Leicestershire
LE12 4DD

Tel: 01509 233555

# Index

# DVD also available

# ARCHERY IN ACTION
## Bow set-up, tuning and shooting
SIMON S NEEDHAM

## Contents

• Setting up the bow • Selecting arrow length • Ready for tuning • Shooting techniques

DVD region: 0   Approx. running time: 77 mins   ISBN 978 1 84797 007 7
For further information, visit
**www.crowood.com**